CAROL SHIELDS AND THE EXTRA-ORDINARY

Carol Shields and the Extra-Ordinary

Edited by

MARTA DVOŘÁK AND MANINA JONES

McGill-Queen's University Press
Montreal & Kingston • London • Ithaca

ISBN 978-0-7735-3220-5

Legal deposit first quarter 2007
Bibliothèque nationale du Québec

Printed in Canada on acid-free paper

This book has been published with the help of a grant from the
Canadian Federation for the Humanities and Social Sciences, through
the Aid to Scholarly Publications Programme, using funds provided by
the Social Sciences and Humanities Research Council of Canada.

McGill-Queen's University Press acknowledges the support of the
Canada Council for the Arts for our publishing program. We also
acknowledge the financial support of the Government of Canada
through the Book Publishing Industry Development Program (BPIDP)
for our publishing activities.

Library and Archives Canada Cataloguing in Publication

Carol Shields and the extra-ordinary / edited by Marta Dvořák and
Manina Jones.

Includes bibliographical references.

ISBN 978-0-7735-3220-5

1. Shields, Carol, 1935-2003 – Criticism and interpretation. I. Dvořák,
Marta II. Jones, Manina

PS8587.H46Z63 2007   C813'.54   C2006-904926-2

Illustrations in Chapters 2 and 6 are published by permission of Donald
Shields, for the Carol Shields' Literary Trust.

Typeset by Jay Tee Graphics Ltd. in Adobe Garamond 11/13

Contents

Acknowledgments   vii
Contributors   ix

Out of the Ordinary: Introduction   3
MARTA DVOŘÁK AND MANINA JONES

1 A View from the Edge of the Edge   17
CAROL SHIELDS

PART ONE   ESSAYING/ASSAYING GENRE: BIOGRAPHY, ARCHIVE,
SHORT STORY, NOVEL

2 Voice and Re-vision: The Carol Shields Archival Fonds   33
CATHERINE HOBBS

3 (Es)Saying It Her Way: Carol Shields as Essayist   59
CHRISTL VERDUYN

4 "Dolls, Dolls, Dolls, Dolls": Into the (Extra)ordinary World of Girls and
Women   80
CHRISTINE LORRE

5 Carol Shields's *The Republic of Love*, or How to Ravish a Genre   97
TAÏNA TUHKUNEN

6 Larry's A/Mazing Spaces   115
CORAL ANN HOWELLS

PART TWO   MARGINS OF OTHERNESS: REFLECTION,
SUBJECTIVITY, EMBODIMENT

7 A Knowable Country: Embodied Omniscience in Carol Shields's *The Republic of Love* and *Larry's Party*   139
LORNA IRVINE

8 Pioneering Interlaced Spaces: Shifting Perspectives and Self-Representation in *Larry's Party*   157
PATRICIA-LÉA PAILLOT

9 Scenes from a (Boston) Marriage: The Prosaics of Collaboration and Correspondence in *A Celibate Season*   172
MANINA JONES

10 "Artefact Out of Absence": Reflection and Convergence in the Fiction of Carol Shields   191
ELLEN LEVY

11 Eros in the Eye of the Mirror: The Rewriting of Myths in Carol Shields's "Mirrors"   205
HÉLIANE VENTURA

PART THREE   EXTRA-ORDINARY PERFORMANCES: PRODUCTION AND RECEPTION

12 Disappearance and "the Vision Multiplied": Writing as Performance   223
MARTA DVOŘÁK

13 Large Ceremonies: The Literary Celebrity of Carol Shields   238
LORRAINE YORK

14 Mischiefs, Misfits, and Miracles   256
ARITHA VAN HERK

Index   271

Acknowledgments

The editors of this volume would like to thank the authors and the following institutions and individuals for their contributions to the ongoing dialogue that produced this volume: the Social Sciences and Humanities Research Council of Canada, the Canadian Federation for the Humanities and Social Sciences Aid to Scholarly Publications programme, the University of Western Ontario, the Sorbonne Nouvelle, the Centre d'Études Canadiennes de Paris III–Sorbonne Nouvelle, the anonymous readers for McGill-Queen's University Press, Nathalie Cooke, Jonathan Crago, Cécile Fouache, Faye Hammill, Michelle Hartley, Coral Ann Howells, Elizabeth Hulse, Michèle Kaltemback, Afra Kavanagh, Jean-Michel Lacroix, Joan McGilvray, Marcienne Rocard, Marilyn Rose, Lee Thompson, Aritha van Herk, Kristen Warder, and John Zucchi. We are especially indebted to Carol and Donald Shields.

Contributors

MARTA DVOŘÁK is professor of Canadian and Commonwealth Literatures at the Sorbonne Nouvelle.

CATHERINE HOBBS is literary manuscript librarian, Canadian Literature Research Service, Library and Archives Canada.

CORAL ANN HOWELLS is professor of English and Canadian literature at the University of Reading.

LORNA IRVINE is professor of English and women's studies at George Mason University.

MANINA JONES is associate professor of English at the University of Western Ontario.

ELLEN LEVY is *maître de conférences* at the Université de Toulouse–Le Mirail.

CHRISTINE LORRE is *maître de conférences* at the Sorbonne Nouvelle.

PATRICIA PAILLOT is *maître de conférences* at IUFM d'Aquitaine.

TAÏNA TUHKUNEN is *maître de conférences* in the department of English at the Université de Nantes.

ARITHA VAN HERK is a writer and professor of English at the University of Calgary.

HÉLIANE VENTURA is professor of English at the Université d'Orléans.

CHRISTL VERDUYN is professor of English and Canadian Studies at Mount Allison University.

LORRAINE YORK is professor of English at McMaster University.

CAROL SHIELDS AND THE EXTRA-ORDINARY

Out of the Ordinary: Introduction

MARTA DVOŘÁK AND MANINA JONES

We believe we are at home in the immediate circle of beings. Beings are familiar, reliable, ordinary. Nevertheless, the lighting is pervaded by a constant concealment in the double form of refusal and dissembling. At bottom, the ordinary is not ordinary; it is extra-ordinary.

Martin Heidegger, "The Origin of the Work of Art"

In March 2003, literary scholars, students, and creative writers gathered in Paris for a colloquium entitled "Carol Shields and the Extra-Ordinary," a forum designed to open up an international critical dialogue on the career of Carol Shields. Shields, a prolific writer whose work includes novels, short stories, poetry, plays, criticism, biography, and essays, is by all measures an extraordinary, internationally recognized literary figure: her uncommon talent has been acknowledged by a Pulitzer Prize, a National Book Critics Circle Award, an Orange Prize for Fiction, a Governor General's Literary Award, a Canadian Authors Association Award, the Charles Taylor Prize for literary non-fiction, and a companionship in the Order of Canada. And yet, as Lorraine York demonstrates in her essay on Shields's literary celebrity in this volume, even the author's negotiations with her own unquestionable fame and her role as an exceptional woman of letters register at the very least an ambivalence about the categories of the ordinary and the extra-ordinary themselves. What the attendees of the Paris conference wanted to talk about, it turned out, for all their fruitful differences in theoretical approach and analytical method, was just how deeply implicated in one another the categories of the ordinary and the extra-ordinary are in Shields's work. Hence, though perhaps the most straightforward definition of "extraordinary" involves a sense of the exceptional, the unusual, the *singular*, the essays collected here explore dualities, multiplicity, and otherness, the ways Shields's work shows the extra-ordinary as emerging out of the ordinary, issuing from the very matrix of everyday life, and illuminating the complexities, the indeterminacies, the contradictions, the *value* at the heart of the ordinary.

The participants in the colloquium wanted, in a number of ways, to claim the ordinary and extra-ordinary as *critical* categories; the essays in *Carol Shields and the Extra-Ordinary* demonstrate that an assessment of the valences of these terms is fundamental to an understanding of the philosophical import of Shields's writing, of her complex play with literary genre and narrative technique, and of the social critique implicit in the gentle, satirical impulse of much of her work. From her earliest collection of poetry in the 1970s and especially since the spectacular success of *The Stone Diaries*' minute tracing of the life of one domestic subject, Shields's diligent and often comic anatomization of the mundane, homely world has prompted both amusement and irritation from critics. Indeed, reviewers of her fiction have demonstrated a remarkable tendency to frame their praise and censure of her work in similar terms. Her writing has been, as Eleanor Wachtel observes, "greeted quietly or subtly patronized," "perhaps because of [its] primarily domestic circumference."[1]

Shields herself commented that her first four novels were "generally described, sometimes pejoratively, as being naturalistic,"[2] an observation confirmed by Barbara Amiel's estimation of her work as "smaller than life."[3] At the same time, Shields has been dubbed an "alchemist of the everyday,"[4] acclaimed for her minute exploration of "middle class, middle-aged and middle of the road" characters who lead "relatively uneventful live[s],"[5] and widely lauded as what *Quill and Quire* reviewer Andrea Curtis calls "that master of the ordinary, bard of the boring."[6] By the publication of *Dressing Up for the Carnival* in 2000, her success and notoriety as an author whose narratives are fuelled by what Shields herself called "the natural gas of the quotidian"[7] were such that she could parody this vogue of the commonplace as if it were a pop culture craze, in a story called "Soup du Jour." "Everyone is coming out these days," it begins, "for the pleasures of ordinary existence. Sunsets. Dandelions. Fencing in the backyard and staying home. 'The quotidian is where it's at,' Herb Rhinelander wrote last week in his nationwide syndicated column. 'People are getting their highs on the level rollercoaster of everydayness, dipping their daily bread in the soup of common delight and simple sensation.'[8] As Shields's parody of her own reception reveals, aggrandizing and belittling attitudes toward the everyday seem somehow connected, but the critical implications of her emphatic attention to the "extra" *within* the ordinary remain largely unexplored.[9] Understanding that surplus value, the interpretive and narrative *consequence* of that which is almost by definition inconsequential – or, as Ellen Levy so insightfully puts it in her essay, understanding how "daily soup, if properly mixed, becomes an opus" – is the goal of this volume.

In his eccentric little book *101 Experiments in the Philosophy of Everyday Life*, Roger-Pol Droit slyly suggests to his reader that "you would be advised not to neglect the subtle links that exist between infinitesimal caress and ineffable ecstasy. They certainly constitute one of the frontiers of European history."[10] Surely the pleasure of reading Shields's work involves its ability to connect the infinitesimal and the ineffable, its joining of the moment and the momentous, and its implication that history itself is implicit in instances of profound intimacy. Shields may be seen as a writer extending what theorists such as Mikhail Bakhtin have identified as prosaic wisdom or prosaic intelligence. As Gary Saul Morson and Caryl Emerson put it, "At their best, prosaic thinkers do not deny that great events can be important. Rather, they are inclined to ask whether other, much more important events have been overlooked simply because they are not striking."[11] At what point – and how – does an attentiveness to and reflexivity about prosaic details of everyday life translate into transformative, transcendent moments of illumination? Might Shields's writing represent a genuine, if modest, revision of literary realism in which the ordinary is subject to contemplation, and not just celebration, as some reviews uncritically suggest? What might her re-estimation of the value of domesticity suggest about gendered subjectivity, and what are its implications for women writers? Does Shields's work propose a philosophy of ordinary life that relates to the thought of such theorists of the everyday as Bakhtin, Arthur Danto, Michel de Certeau, Henri Lefebvre, and Sami-Ali? Such questions were a starting point for the extended critical exchange that began in Paris in 2003. The essays included in this volume are the outcome of that discussion; they represent a wide range of international scholarship, for the contributors are specialists in Canadian literature from France, Great Britain, Finland, the United States, and Canada. They address the powerful and often innovative narrative and discursive strategies central to Shields's aesthetics, the ways in which her work so frequently situates itself not just on the border between the ordinary and the extra-ordinary but also on the edges of fiction and non-fiction, of production and reception, of perspective, voice, mode, and genre.

The recurrent disruption of the ordinary by the extra-ordinary in Shields's work stems from the undeniably carnivalesque mode subtending many of her narrative patterns. These distortions conflate with the torsions of an epistemological and metaphysical reflection, quietly privileging the dynamics of epiphany. Shields's recourse to numinous moments as a structuring principle is rooted in certain subsidiary tendencies of modernism that postmodern currents have chosen to prolong, even on other sides of the globe. Salman Rushdie, after all, remarked in *Imaginary Homelands* that "fragmentation made trivial things seem like symbols," and that the mundane thereby acquired "numinous qualities."[12] Our discussions of Shields's incursions into the extra-ordinary therefore also take into account their relation to such metaphysical dimensions, as perhaps most memorably evoked in Heidegger's often-cited ontological investigations in *The Origin of the Work of Art* (excerpted in the epigraph to this introduction).

Carol Shields and the Extra-Ordinary opens with "A View from the Edge of the Edge," a previously unpublished piece by Shields herself, who had dearly wished to participate in the conference held at the Sorbonne, but whose ill health prevented her attendance. Instead, she affectionately offered as her contribution this thought-provoking contemplation of her extra-ordinary position of (as Heidegger puts it) being "at home in the immediate circle of beings," while at the same time always positioning herself (as Shields puts it) "on the edge of the edge" of that circle. Her meditation appropriately sets the stage for the international character of the essays collected in this volume: prompted by a question posed by a journalist in London, England, and delivered in 1997 at Harvard University in the United States, this essay cum autobiographical account ponders both Canadian literature's and Shields's own "edgy" roles in the "seething, smoking, chaotic, multicultural middle which is, in fact, our reality" as Canadians. Shields evaluates her roles as a woman writer, a Canadian, and a middle-class woman from a "relatively happy home," in order to reassess conventional understandings of those "ordinary" categories.

The first cluster of essays in this volume, titled "Essaying/Assaying Genre: Biography, Archive, Short Story, Novel," focuses on questions around Shields's "edgy" approach to genre. It begins with an essay by Catherine Hobbs, literary manuscript librarian for the Canadian Literature Research Service at Library and Archives Canada. "Voice and Revision: The Carol Shields Archival Fonds" offers the narrative of an archivist's encounters with the Shields fonds.[13] Accompanied by fourteen illustrations, photographs, and manuscript reproductions from the Canadian national collections, this account creates for readers the effect of being immersed in the archives as they are being discussed. Hobbs offers a tantalizing view of the wealth of archival materials on Shields, reading them through the filter of certain fictional topics, including naming, food and entertaining, letter-writing, and documents of everyday experience. In effect, Hobbs reads Shields's fiction through her fonds and her fonds through her fiction; both, inevitably, bear the traces of her biography.

This revealing reciprocal analysis, then, also incorporates an exploration of the relationship between biography, archives, and fiction, taking into account Shields's notorious self-consciousness about the equivocality of biography and autobiography, her interest in life's ephemera, and her deployment of documentation in her fiction. By her own account, Shields was, from very early in her career careful to preserve the documentary records of her life; her diligent acts of "self-preservation" through documents speak eloquently (though sometimes elusively) not just, as Hobbs shows, to her understanding of the complex dynamics of text, story, and biography but also, as Lorraine York explores elsewhere in this volume, to Shields's negotiations with and contributions to popular concepts of "literary celebrity" in Canada. Both archivist and fiction writer are concerned with the intricately complicated task of interpreting the document's "flexible and partial relationships to lived reality." Hobbs's essay thus constitutes a necessarily reflexive, ironic examination of the role of the archivist in representing her subject, one that anticipates the emphasis on the complex and problematic nature of the biographical genre in other essays in this volume.

In her contribution "(Es)Saying It Her Way: Carol Shields as Essayist," Christl Verduyn takes up Shields's considerable, but under-acknowledged and under-theorized accomplishments as an essayist. Like Hobbs, Verduyn testifies to unplumbed archival riches, including a number of unpublished essays that await editorial and scholarly attention. Equally important, she explores issues of generic experimentation raised by Shields's work in a revealing discussion of the author's "essaying" practices in her book *Jane Austen* (which Shields called "an essay with a biographical spine") and pieces drawn from various essay collections, each of which demonstrates Shields's "belief in the centrality of story or narrative to life and to its artistic representation." Beginning with her own brief but seminal "essay" on the history and form of the genre itself, Verduyn concludes that the essay is, in essence, an anti-genre, making accessible opportunities for innovation and transcendence and raising questions about how knowledge is generated from experience, rather from pre-ordained doctrine. In effect, then, the essay is by definition an "extra-ordinary" genre, in the sense that the word designates that "not according to rule" (OED). Verduyn explores the slippage in Shields's work between the short story and the essay and the essay and philosophical speculation. Because of its flexibility, the essay form, she suggests, has been an especially good "fit" for women writers in Canada, a suggestion with which Shields would surely have agreed, given her role in prompting women to write about the intimate, defining moments in their personal histories for the best-selling *Dropped Threads* anthologies she co-edited in 2001 and 2003.

Christine Lorre's essay on the short story "Dolls, Dolls, Dolls, Dolls," from Shields's first short story collection, *Various Miracles*, shows how Shields explores the border between the ordinary and the extra-ordinary by resorting to a hybrid genre: "Dolls, Dolls, Dolls, Dolls," Lorre argues, could be read equally as an essay and as a short story.[14] In a close textual reading grounded in solid cultural contextualization, she investigates the ways in which Shields represents the doll as a domestic artifact related to feminine subjectivity and pivotal to our understanding of women's life narratives. A commonplace item in the lives of girls and women that also has deep significance, the doll functions as the site of the projection of imagination and human feelings, as a marker of biographical time, as a conduit for human relations, as a signifier of myths of origins. The doll, in other words, shapes the time and space in which personal – and especially feminine – identity is formed. Lorre discusses this short story as an experiment that anticipates the concerns of later works in the ways it crosses genres and narrative dimensions, reading its structures as the elaboration of Shields's sense of the double dimensions of everyday life: like dolls themselves, "Dolls, Dolls, Dolls, Dolls" is both ordinary (straightforwardly factual, material) and extraordinary (invested with unsuspected meaning and power).

On another front, Taïna Tuhkunen identifies Shields's novel *The Republic of Love* as "one of the most extraordinary essays at voicing one, wish to live in peaceful, yet not necessarily placid, coexistence with one's fellow creatures, even in our bleak and boastful modern times." Tuhkunen considers *The Republic of Love* as both a serious philosophical essay on love and a "novelistic exposé of one of the least beloved subjects of artistic expression – that of an ordinary happy life." In her essay she puts into play some of the formal flexibility Verduyn identifies, in her playful personal exploration of *The Republic of Love*. Tuhkunen responds sympathetically, for example, to Shields's frigid Winnipeg setting from her own location in snowy Finland. She takes her readers through a series of insights gained by carefully tracking and documenting the dynamics of reading Shields's challenges to the conventions of amatory writing. In such gestures, Tuhkunen also anticipates Aritha van Herk's writerly excursion in the concluding essay in this volume. "How does [Shields] manage to weave in mystery, secrecy, and intercontinental mermaid mobility into … the fixed and frozen day-by-day existence of ordinary people?" Tuhkunen asks. In other words, how does Shields rescue the language of love from the realm of banality and cliché, from habituation, from, indeed, its *generic* status? In order to renew the rhetoric of love, Tuhkunen demonstrates, Shields generically renews the love story itself, restoring some of its lost charm by multiplying its potential meanings, implying the impossibility of any reassuringly fixed or stable definition of that worn-out, but vital and enchanting, term, "love."

Coral Ann Howells's essay examines Shields's challenges to the biographical genre in *Larry's Party*, bringing Henri Lefebvre's theories about the production of space to bear on the novel's biographical narrative. Shields's work, Howells argues, plays across two concepts of space suggested by Lefebvre: lived material and symbolic space; a/mazing situations in Larry's life are located on the borders between the two. In *Larry's Party*, Howells demonstrates, Shields challenges and redefines the chronological basis of biography, offering a spatial figuring of Larry's life story, rather than a temporal one. In her digressive narrative's refusal of models of linear progression, Shields opens up ways of representing the accidental and surprising. Howells focuses on three epiphanic moments or "sideways slippages" from the ordinary into the extraordinary – sites where Shields mediates between the everyday world of fact and the subjective world of the creative imagination, opening up the realistic fictional frame to move beyond ordinary vision to a world where sacred mysteries are hidden paradoxically within the structure of the quotidian.

Larry's Party and *The Republic of Love* provide a bridge into part two of this collection, which addresses "Margins of Otherness: Reflection, Subjectivity, Embodiment." In "A Knowable Country: Bodily Omniscience in Carol Shields's *The Republic of Love* and *Larry's Party*," Lorna Irvine inaugurates an extended discussion of the representation of subjectivity in Shields's work in her examination of how Shields locates characters both in terms of literal geographies and in terms of geographies of the *body*: "Everyday acts," as de Certeau memorably observes, create "the world on the scale of our bodies."[15] To understand this gesture, Irvine theorizes the most pedestrian of tropes, adapting the metaphor of walking from de Certeau's *The Practice of Everyday Life* and Rebecca Solnit's *Wanderlust: A History of Walking*. Irvine is thus able to contemplate the way embodied characterization and omniscient narration orient themselves within particularized space and time. Each story, she avers, is "localized, its angle of vision inverted, seen, as it were, from below, beside, among. At these moments, the story moves at the speed of one or other of the characters, issuing from inside the body; the reader is put in the position of looking out of the character's eyes." Irvine subtly deploys narrative theory to map the complexities of the two novels, including their simultaneous presentation of multiple, often conflicting, points of view and their destabilization of the narratee. Shields's narrative technique is thus revealed as a delicate device of psychological characterization but, even more strikingly, as a representation in the very way she observes her fictional world of a philosophical stance on life's contradictory quality and a consequent valuing of community.

Patricia-Léa Paillot, meanwhile, in her essay "Pioneering Interlaced Spaces: Shifting Perspectives and Self-Representation in *Larry's Party*," is also interested in angles of vision and the transformation of ordinary perception. While Howells's earlier essay attends to the spatialization of the biographical narrative in *Larry's Party*, Paillot extends this interest to the spatialized construction *of identity itself*, a feature of the novel that makes the supposedly mediocre Larry an exceptional "pioneer of his own interlaced spaces." Guided by the work of Georges Bataille, particularly his notion of the "labyrinthine construction of being," and using Jorge Luis Borges's story "The Garden of Forking Paths" as a literary analogy, Paillot reads *Larry's Party* as a "reversible" novel that shifts at will from ordinary story to extra-ordinary quest narrative and revises the concept of a definite and limited identity through its multiplication of perspectives, its multifaceted self, its prismatic narrative. In its construction of meaning, the novel negotiates "a paradoxical twofold movement of validation and invalidation where the seemingly wrong directions become the true substance of meaning," and identity is a product of wrong turns, accidental excursions, digressions, and impasses. Importantly, Paillot also indicates the ways in which the maze functions not just as subjective space but as intersubjective – and even intergendered – space in *Larry's Party*.

Manina Jones's essay "Scenes from a (Boston) Marriage: The Prosaics of Collaboration and Correspondence in *A Celibate Season*" develops

Paillot's interest in "doubled structures" as well as her conceptualization of intersubjective and intergendered space. This essay traces parallels between Shields's collaboration (largely conducted through letters) with co-author Blanche Howard and the "corresponding" marital relationship of the protagonists in the epistolary novel *A Celibate Season*. Shields and Howard's novel is a work, Jones argues, that locates its narration on the boundaries of both characters' and authors' point of view. In her detailed analysis of the novel, Jones mobilizes the Bakhtinian notion of "prosaics," "a form of thinking that presumes the importance of the everyday, the ordinary, the prosaic,"[16] in order show how *A Celibate Season* dramatizes the politics of intimate domesticity as it operates at the very centre of what is conventionally considered the extraordinary realm of national politics and history: as a pun suggested by *A Celibate Season* implies, the "extraordinary" workings of politics on the Canadian parliamentary stage are, it turns out, themselves Housework, constituted as they are by the politics of less spectacular but no less important housework, the nitty-gritty details of ordinary domestic arrangements. Jones elaborates Bakhtinian prosaics to develop the idea of what she calls "prosaic desire," a concept that registers the "otherness" that paradoxically generates intimacy, which Jones sees as operative within both marital and collaborative partnerships. The reversible trope of collaboration as marriage and marriage as collaboration, she suggests, is a way of understanding intersubjective relationships in *A Celibate Season*, one that refuses idealized notions of wholeness and harmony, in favour of preserving unassimilable difference.

In her wide-ranging essay "'Artefact Out of Absence': Reflection and Convergence in the Fiction of Carol Shields," Ellen Levy offers an engaging examination of structures and motifs of doubleness across Shields's corpus of fiction, from *Small Ceremonies* to *Unless*. Interestingly, Levy takes up the question of Shields's fictional couples as part of this project. Levy's concern with representations of husband-wife pairings focuses on their potential as a vehicle for exploring "margins of otherness"; Shields's couples "know that not only are other lives essentially mysterious, but that the core of one's own may be equally out of reach," writes Levy.[17] Self-definition is achieved in her fiction, Levy suggests, through complex multiplications of perspective. Levy's identification of various levels of doubling in this essay leads to an illuminating meditation on the author's use of interstitial spaces, her modes of indirection and metaphor. She muses provocatively on such elements as Shields's delicate choreography of table scenes, setting them in parallel with the mirror

motif and the construction of the intimate relationship in the interplay
of identity and distance. Levy's musings on the short story "Absence,"
from *Dressing Up for the Carnival*, particularly her identification of its
representation of "a metalinguistic crisis of representation" and her conclusion that "the absence of a word can be an invitation to self-definition
rather than an irretrievable loss," lay the ground for Marta Dvořák's discussion of that story in the third cluster of essays in this volume.

Héliane Ventura also elaborates on questions of mirroring, doubling,
and reflection in her investigation of the workings of specularity and
subjectivity in "Eros in the Eye of the Mirror: The Rewriting of Myths
in Carol Shields's 'Mirrors.'" Ventura's enthralling analysis is interested
in how "Mirrors," another story from *Dressing Up for the Carnival*,
reconfigures tropes and figures from classical mythology. She shows how
Shields develops her own brand of reflexive erotic discourse based on the
notion of an exchange with the other. Or as Ventura puts it, Shields
makes "the divine stranger surface in each of the lovers she depicts."
Ventura's discussion is particularly sensitive to Shields's rewriting of the
myth of Narcissus, an extraordinary transformation because it shifts
from the original's vain, self-seeking material version of love to a transcendent, philosophical, and Platonic conception of Eros in which each
partner in the couple intersubjectively mirrors the other. Ventura demonstrates how, in the story of "Mirrors," when the couple temporarily
abjures mirrors, reflection makes itself all the more felt through its representations in language. In "Mirrors" Shields thus does not simply provide us with an *Ars Amatoria* (a task Taïna Tuhkunen suggests is also
part of her project in *The Republic of Love*); she provides readers with an
Ars Poetica, a lesson in aesthetics.

The final section of *Carol Shields and the Extra-Ordinary*, "Extra-
Ordinary Performances: Production and Reception," includes three
essays that engage, in quite diverse ways, questions of performance. This
section begins with Marta Dvořák, whose essay "Disappearance and 'the
Vision Multiplied': Writing as Performance" makes clear a point
implicit in many of the essays presented here: Shields must be considered in an international context. Dvořák places her work in the context
of contemporary European experimental writing from Virginia Woolf
to Georges Perec. She reads Shields's short story "Absence," from *Dressing Up for the Carnival*, a narrative written without the letter "i" (as a
result, so the story goes, of a broken key on the author's typewriter) alongside Georges Perec's *La Disparition* (1969), the longest lipogram in the
history of French literature. Dvořák's essay explores the writer's craft as

a combination of workmanship and play, shedding important light on Shields's recurrent recourse to self-imposed formal constraints and self-conscious performances of writerly virtuosity in her work. Dvořák, further, elucidates Shields's postmodern stance and its relation to the language theories of Bertrand Russell, Frege, and Wittgenstein. Dvořák demonstrates how, in keeping with these theories, Shields' writing slips from subjectivity and perception into the mythopoeic, marvellous, or extraordinary, suspending the referential functions of language and arriving at epiphanic disclosures.

Lorraine York's essay "Large Ceremonies: The Literary Celebrity of Carol Shields" offers a fascinating account of the author's negotiations with – and performance of – her own fame. Almost certainly the only critical account that mentions Carol Shields and Jennifer Lopez in the same paragraph, it does so to reveal the ways in which Shields's celebrity is marked by a certain anxiousness about the boundaries between the ordinary and the extraordinary and the ways in which domestic, private concerns are frequently grafted onto contemporary celebrity discourse, creating a rhetoric of hybridity. Through her discussion of pre– and post–Pulitzer prize portrayals of Shields in the media, York examines Canadian literary celebrity's arbitration of cultural value and stardom's management of ideological contradictions and debates, including those involving gender, professionalism, and distinctions between high and low art. She also eloquently addresses the slippage between biography and fiction, a theme that weaves its way through this collection and speaks directly to Hobbs's assertions about Shields's self-consciousness regarding the ways in which her own biography is constructed in public sites. This essay considers Shields's own reflections on celebrity, not only in interviews but also in the fictional narrative of the novel *Swann*. It takes into account her skill as a "rhetorical tactician, a balancer of discourses," just as much in her performance of her public persona as in her fiction. It documents, finally, Shields's informed and generous mobilization of her own literary "star power" in Canadian literary culture.

To conclude the volume, Aritha van Herk's ficto-critical foray, "Mischiefs, Misfits, and Miracles," is a tribute to Shields's illumination of unpredictable patterns of human experience in her writing. In this piece, van Herk combines the art of the fiction writer with the craft of the critic, deconstructing certain trademarks of Shields's writerly practices and deploying them as creative building blocks. Indeed, while York calls attention to the ways in which Shields touched creative writers in personal ways and cleared the ground for certain kinds of literary celebrity and sensibility, van Herk's essay (and the creative writing workshops she led at the Sorbonne conference, followed by a public presentation by participants), actually performs the ways in which Shields's writing provides inspiration and opens up imaginative territory for writers of fiction. Van Herk's contribution to this volume is part essay, part homage, part eulogy, part critical theory, part fictional narrative; it also certainly constitutes a dramatic performance in itself. Spinning off on Roland Barthes's premise that a text carries traces of its reader, van Herk tells us that "Carol Shields invents her own reader, proposes a reader who must be able to play with coincidences and carnival, a reader who will be particular with the accidental glories of blister lilies and clothespins, hyphens and radishes." Van Herk thus offers up the fictional Shields reader Grit Savon, whose animated reading of "lines" of laundry imagery in a wide range of Shields's novels and short fiction airs the mysteries, rituals, intimacies, comforts, and sadness that form the fabric of domesticity in Shields's writing. Van Herk concludes, with Shields, that "in the details of domesticity the extraordinary resides." Laundry here becomes a figure through which van Herk demonstrates that in Shields's work, "the outrageous exists in moments hyperbolized by their very miniaturism, their intimacy." Through the character of Grit Savon, van Herk is also able to read *between* the lines of Shields's writing, creating an eccentric fictional character who explores the gaps in Shields's narratives, acting, in effect, as an accessory to Shields's own fiction-making.

    Taken together, then, the essays in this volume contribute, in a range of styles and from a wide variety of personal and theoretical perspectives, to an argument about the power of Shields's writing to represent the ways in which the commonplace and the extra-ordinary reflect, or collaborate with, or verge on, or become the matrix for, or disrupt, or create, or a/maze one another.

NOTES

1 Wachtel, "Introduction," 2.
2 Shields "Arriving Late," 246.
3 Cited in "The Shields Diaries."
4 Yanofsky, Rev. of *Dressing Up for the Carnival*, 14.
5 Bell, "Carol Sheilds," 4.
6 Curtis, Rev. of *Dressing Up for the Carnival*, 68.
7 Shields, "Arriving Late," 247.

8 Shields, *Dressing Up for the Carnival*, 155.
9 Adriana Trozzi's *Carol Shields' Magic Wand: Turning the Ordinary into the Extraordinary* is an exception that, however, bears only a superficial resemblance to the project of this volume. Trozzi conducts a broad survey of Shields's career as a fiction writer (a chapter on each major solely authored book, from *Small Ceremonies* to *Dressing Up for the Carnival*), offering critical surveys of the extraordinary effects in each work. She largely extends the celebratory mode of many of Shields's reviewers, praising the author's ability to render dull existence "unique and brilliant" and her skill at conferring human contradictions and ambiguities on characters, thus making them more realistic. Trozzi's main critical modes for understanding Shields's "magical" ability to render the ordinary in fascinating ways involve an acknowledgment of point of view, emphasis on Shields's description of small details, and identification of themes or "topics" of particular interest.
10 Droit, *101 Experiments*, 204.
11 Morson and Emerson, *Mikhail Bakhtin*, 36.
12 Rushdie, "Imaginary Homelands," 12.
13 "Fonds" is an archival term that describes a collection of materials which originate from the same source. In modern archival practice, the fonds is generally the highest level of cataloguing. It usually describes the whole of the papers of an individual.
14 Indeed, given its multi-part structure and its emphasis on ritual, this is a story that might well be read as a short-story cycle within the short story itself.
15 De Certeau, *Practice of Everyday Life*, 256.
16 Morson and Emerson, *Mikhail Bakhtin*, 15.
17 Indeed, Levy describes the relationship of the artist couple in the short story "Windows" (from *Dressing Up for the Carnival*) as a collaboration.

WORKS CITED

Bell, Karen. "Carol Shields: All These Years Later, Still Digging." *Performing Arts & Entertainment in Canada*, 31, no. 3: (1998) 4–6.
Curtis, Andrea. Rev. of *Larry's Party*. *Quill and Quire* 63, no. 9 (Sept. 1997): 68.
de Certeau, Michel. *The Practice of Everyday Life*. Berkeley: University of California Press, 1984.
Droit, Roget-Pol. *101 Experiments in the Philosophy of Everyday Life*. Trans. Stephen Romer. London: Faber, 2002.
Heidegger, Martin. "The Origin of the Work of Art." In *Basic Writings: From Being and Time (1927) to The Task of Thinking (1964)*, ed. and trans. David Farrell Krell, 143–203. London, Routledge, 1993.

Morson, Gary Saul, and Caryl Emerson. *Mikhail Bakhtin: Creation of a Prosaics.* Stanford: Stanford University Press, 1990.

Rushdie, Salman. "Imaginary Homelands." In *Imaginary Homelands: Essays and Criticism 1981–1991*, 9–21. London: Granta, 1991.

Shields, Carol. "Arriving Late: Starting Over." In *How Stories Mean*, ed. John Metcalf and Tim Struthers, 244–51. Erin, ON: Porcupine's Quill, 1993.

– *Dressing Up for the Carnival.* London: Fourth Estate, 2000.

"The Shields Diaries." *Chatelaine* 69, no. 4 (1996), 110–15.

Trozzi, Adriana. *Carol Shields' Magic Wand: Turning the Ordinary into the Extraordinary.* Rome: Bulzoni, 2001.

Wachtel, Eleanor. "Introduction." *Room of One's Own* 13, no. 1/2 (1989), 2–4.

Yanofsky, Joel. Rev. of *Dressing Up for the Carnival.* Quill & Quire 66, no. 2 (2000), 14–15.

I

A View from the Edge of the Edge

CAROL SHIELDS

When I was in London on a book promotion trip a couple of years ago I was asked one question repeatedly and by every British journalist I talked to: why is so much writing, suddenly, coming out of Canada? And, a secondary question, almost apologetically offered, why so much writing by women? I was not, I'm afraid, very well prepared for these questions, and though I love to invent theories, I was wary of concocting one on the spot. It seems every time I do deliver a fast-food hypothesis I'm confronted the very next day by an example that explodes my conclusion.

And the last thing anyone wants is to get *stuck* with a theory, since these casually tossed-off speculations have a way, like mosquitoes in a sleeping bag, of getting into your bio, so that years later you're charged by a late-night radio interviewer in Calgary – for example – with having said something or other you can't even remember thinking, never mind pronouncing upon. And so, mindful of these painful past embarrassments, I feel brave enough to offer today only a few random thoughts about how Canadian writing looks to me at this moment, that is on 10 February 1997, and why.

On the whole, Canadian writing – and this won't surprise anyone in this room – is in a state of exuberant good health. Why is this, you ask, and why now? There are some who believe that the perceived lack of national identity, of cultural cohesiveness, is a vacuum crying to be filled, and that the sudden burst of new writing clusters around the impulse to identify, define, and make solid what in the past has been random and unnameable. If this is true, I am sure it is unconscious, since I can't imagine a writer sitting down at her word processor and thinking: now I am going to contribute to the nexus of Canadian identity.

There are others who suggest that the Canadian literary body is so new and so loose and uncodified that writers are relatively free and unshackled to pursue their literary track. You'll remember what Robertson Davies said, how we in Canada are the attic of North America and that there's plenty of room in that dark and empty attic to shout.

I am a little reluctant to admit that we may still be colonialist enough in our posture to measure that literary health by the international stamp of approval. And so we at home did not miss the fact last fall that there were two Canadians on the Booker short list. And that of the eight most important books, fiction and non-fiction, chosen by the *New York Times* in December, two of them were by Canadian women, Mavis Gallant and Alice Munro. I was delighted with this recognition of our two major writers, but even more pleased that at home we took the *New York Times* news fairly calmly, a sign that these kinds of triumphs have become (almost) taken for granted. In addition, our recent Governor General's Award and Giller short lists have indicated the richest year ever in strong and innovative fiction, and – here I go again – at least a dozen of these novels are finding international publishers. There is a feel-good air of optimism flowing all the way from major Canadian publishers to beginning writers in the hundreds of writing workshops that dot the land.

The British journalists I encountered, so ready to stump me with sticky questions, were really speaking, I think, out of a concern, even a nostalgia, for the fading English novel of tradition and their simultaneous enthusiasm for the wave of fiction coming out of the post-colonial world. India, Australia, New Zealand, the West Indies, Africa, and Canada. The children have grown up, and are producing their fresh, lively, self-confident, sometimes audacious novels, beamed as they are from parts of the world that had been for so long silent, humble, dependent and distrustful of their own surfaces. This new writing, not *very* new when you get down to dates – Patrick White, V.S. Naipaul, our own Alice Munro – was coming from cultures not, perhaps, perfectly understood by the British reading public, coming, in fact, from the exotic margins of the planet, the far edge, and it is this sense of edge that I want to talk about today.

Years ago, in an introduction to a book of short fiction, the American writer Hortense Calisher talked about the short story being mainly a new-world form. Reports from the frontier, she called them, a lovely and accurate phrase that caught my attention. Perhaps, I remember thinking, this is what all of literature is: a dispatch from the frontier, news from the edge. Even given that the edges and centres of society are forever shifting, it does seem to me that the view from the edge offers a privileged perspective. Also freedom from cynicism if not from anger. Also a kind of real or willed innocence which is what I believe every writer must keep alive in order to write.

As it happens, I'm somewhat acquainted with what it feels like to be on the edge. I live in Winnipeg, a large city, but certainly not the literary centre of Canada. Though I was born in the centre of the United States, it was clear that Midwesterners were, culturally, at the edge – only remember that famous *New Yorker* magazine map of the nation. And also at the edge, in a sense, were members of the middle class – and this is a nice irony, the middle being nowhere near the centre.

I stood at the edge, too, by virtue of gender. Where I grew up in Oak Park, Illinois, I attended, first, Nathaniel Hawthorne Public School, and when I was a little older, Ralph Waldo Emerson Public School. I knew who these bearded, bespectacled, frock-coated gentlemen were; their portraits hung in a place of honour in our schools. They were writers. They were men. They were dead.

It seemed impossible that I could grow up to become a writer, and yet I began, quite early, to write: stories, often with a supernatural theme and a trick ending. I also wrote little poems about spring, and later, as I mastered the mechanics of meter, *sonnets* about spring. (Spring clearly served as a metaphor of some kind, or else provided a safe cover beneath which I could speak of other less admissible passions.) All of what I wrote was derivative in the extreme and yet all enthusiastically applauded by my teachers and parents. "Satin-slippered April," one of these sonnets began. "You glide through time and lubricate spring days." I was a child of a leafy green suburb, of a relatively happy family, which in romantic literary terms is to place me at life's margin. And I had no idea what my real subject would be or what sort of audience I might address. And of course I didn't know that I would grow up, fall in love with a Canadian, and at the age of 22, immigrate to a country at the northern *edge* of the continent, a country I knew next to nothing about.

I was also a reader, and, in fact, I've never been able to separate my reading and my writing life. As you know, there is a time in our early reading lives when we read anything, when we are unsupervised, when we are bonded to the books we read. When we are innocent of any kind of critical standard, so innocent and avid and open that we don't even bother to seek out special books, but read instead those books that happen to lie within easy reach, the family books, the in-house books. These books have a way of entering our bodies more simply and completely than library books, for example, which are chosen, or school texts that are imposed.

It's a literary cliché, largely aristocratic, largely male, that writers in their young years are "given the run of their father's library." You imagine oak panelling, a fire, sets of leather-bound volumes, Shakespeare, of course, but also the Greek dramatists, the Latin poets, the Fathers of the Church, Dickens, Scott, an almost exclusively masculine offering with little visible connection between book and reader.

My parents' library was a corner of the sunroom, a four-shelf bookcase stained to look like red maple which had been "thrown in" with the purchase of the 1947 edition of the *World Book Encyclopaedia.* There was also room on those shelves for a set of *Journeys through Bookland* and two volumes of poetry, the works of James Whitcomb Riley, who I thought was a great poet before I went to university and found he wasn't, and *A Heap o' Livin'* by Edgar A. Guest. The rest of the shelf space, only a few inches, was filled with my parents' childhood books.

My father was represented by half a dozen Horatio Alger titles, *Luck and Pluck, Ragged Dick, Try and Trust,* and so on, which I read, loved and never thought to condemn for didacticism, for didn't I attend a didactic Methodist Sunday School and sit in a didactically charged classroom at school and listen to my well-meaning didactic parents. This was the natural way of the world, half of humanity bent on improving the other half.

My mother grew up on an Illinois farm, attended Normal School, and, as a young woman came to Chicago to teach school. She and three other "girls" roomed for a year on the third floor of the Hemingway house in Oak Park. Ernest was away in Paris writing *The Sun Also Rises,* although my mother didn't know this, of course; she only knew that his parents spoke of him coldly. "Is he an artist?" my mother once asked. "He is a time waster," Dr Hemingway replied. In fact, my mother never read Hemingway; he was not, despite her thrilling connection, a part of her tradition.

Her tradition (and mine, by default, at least for a time) ran to such books as *Girl of the Limberlost, Helen's Babies,* and, curiously, two *Canadian* books, which were, I suppose, portents of the future: *Beautiful Joe* and *Anne of Green Gables.* (This Canadian-ness failed to register, I'm afraid; effortlessly I transported Anne Shirley's Prince Edward Island to the Illinois landscape I knew, just as generations of Japanese have carried Anne off to the East.) My mother, I'm sure, found in *Anne of Green Gables* what millions of others have discovered: a bold consciousness attuned to nature, a female model of courage, goodness, candour, and possessed of an emotional capacity that triumphs and converts. Unlike Tom Sawyer who capitulates to society, Anne transforms her community with her exuberant vision. She enters the story disentitled and emerges as a beloved daughter with admiring friends and a future ahead of her, and she has done it all without help: captured the heart of Gilbert Blythe, sealed her happiness, and reshuffled the values of society by a primary act of reimagination.

And then there is *Beautiful Joe,* Marshall Saunders's enormously popular – though it's hard to see why today – 1893 faux-autobiography of a mongrel dog. Like Anne Shirley, the ironically named Beautiful Joe is not conventionally beautiful, and like Anne, his name is both his shame and his glory. Also like Anne, he is cruelly treated, but, through virtue and courage he finds love, and he tells all this through a voice that is characterized by the most delicate, undoglike tints of feeling – though as a child I never questioned his right to a voice nor to his insights.

Nor did I worry about the sentimentality in my mother's books. Sentimentality, like coincidence, seemed to be one of the strands of American existence; it could be detected every week, after all, in the last two minutes of *Amos and Andy*; it was a part of the human personality.

Anne Shirley, you remember, adored literature: "The Lady of the Lake," Thomson's *Seasons,* and something called "The Dog at His Master's Grave" from the Third Reader, all this making an eclectic sampling, typical of the randomness of early reading lists. What Anne demanded of poetry, she said, was that it give her a "crinkly feeling" up and down her back – I too was devoted to that crinkly feeling, and think, today, how different this is from Emily Dickinson's insistence that a poem must take the top of her head off. Perhaps this, then, is the difference between American and Canadian sensibility: decapitation, the big bang, versus mere vertebral crinkling.

Nellie McClung, the Canadian social activist and writer – you see how we Canadians feel obliged to stop and identify our literary figures – recounts in *her* autobiography how she burst into tears reading a piece titled "The Faithful Dog" in the Second Reader, and how her response was reinforced by a teacher who pronounced: "Here is a pupil who has both feeling and imagination, she will get a lot out of life." And we all know she did.

There was no Willa Cather on my mother's shelf, no Virginia Woolf, no George Eliot, no Jane Austen. My mother, even without dipping into these books, would have thought these writers too heavy, too intimidating for someone of her background. Always a reader, she read her way around the popular *edges* of literature. As a child I was, like my mother, approaching literature very much as an outsider, and I was intimidated by that dark dense sort of book described as a classic, though a kindly high school teacher, speaking of *Silas Marner,* demystified the term by telling us it referred to books that people have liked rather a lot for a long time. Later, though, I found that some of these so-called classics – Hemingway, to a certain extent Conrad – refused to open up to me because they projected a world in which I did not hold citizenship, the world of men, action, power, ideas, politics and war. Somewhat wider read than my mother, I too felt myself at the edge.

This question of edge, though, is problematic, for we have to ask ourselves how the centre is defined – and there are many centres. There is the centre, we think of as the core literature or canon of the Western world, of our North American culture, of the women's tradition, but we see more and more that that core is subject to rapid meltdown or at the very least revision. Then there is the divide between the dominant culture and the marginal culture. The early settlers and the later settlers. High culture and popular culture. And there are geographic or political entities which, for historical reasons, remained detached, isolated, or else colonized, and where a national literature is slow to flourish or else develops into a sort of sacred amber pellet imprisoned in what is believed to be the national ethos.

A Hungarian friend tells me that at the time he left Hungary in the late fifties – and I'm sure this has changed today – the national literature was so small, and at the same time, so widely disseminated, that anyone who possessed a high school education was, ipso facto, familiar with the entire range of Hungarian prose, drama, and poetry.

Part of me yearns for that degree of cultural saturation, a whole tradition compacted like a gemstone. Only imagine meeting strangers – on the street corner, in a bus or cafe or any private home – and finding that every cultural moment is secured, *and* refracted and enlarged, by common references, quotations, allusions, nuances, a body, in fact, of shared belief.

Another part of me would resent deeply the unity of this order. To be defined by a culture as tight and total as this is surely to be confined, and to be handed at the cradle the height, width and depth of a national literature, and all the conduits of connections therein, all the orthodoxies of genre, and gender, the petrification of canon, the cross-network of influences – *to know it all* would be to confess one's self part of a moribund culture. And then, to go one step further – cementing literature belly-to-belly to the national destiny so that every variation is suspect, is threatening, is minor or anomalous or marginal or subversive or condemned to that variant stream we call sometimes with reverence, other times with a rolling of the eyeballs – experimental. In other words, to make the centre so unassailable that the edges are hushed into silence.

I'm more at ease with the rich variables of a randomly evoked, organically spilling, unselfconscious, disorderly, unruly, uncharted and unchartable pouring out of voice. These various surreal juxtapositions of life and literature, of time, and place, of reader and writer seem to me to erase or blur national labels while, ironically, sharpening the particularities of the texts: figure against ground, ground illuminating figure, and contributing to my skepticism on the shape and force of a national literature. How fluid is it? Who gets to name it? Who gets to enter?

And Canadians, these days, are directing serious attention to that very seething, smoking, chaotic, multicultural muddle which is, in fact, our reality. This is risky; one almost wants to whisper – un-Canadian.

Many of these works aren't in the canon, which must now be redressed or demolished; some aren't even in print. They are in an almost literal sense reports from the frontier, and the frontier has been shifting in recent years – in terms of geography, demography, gender, and certainly literary form. There are some curious lags: we have been for some time an urbanized society, but our literature has not, until recent years, noticed this fact, perhaps because most writers are one generation from the farm, from the frontier itself. Similarly, immigrant writers – Rohinton Mistry comes to mind – continue to write about their old countries rather than the Canada they immigrated to. It is difficult in today's Canada to locate the mainstream, the centre. It seems we are almost all at the edge, and that edge embraces aboriginal writing, gay writing, immigrant writing and women's writing.

It may be, the noisy and varied writing coming out of Canada today that makes it difficult to compare that literature with that of the United States, but I don't think such a comparison has *ever* been easy. It has been suggested that Canadian writing, reflecting the immigration patterns of the country, is more community centred while American writing focuses on the individual, the *who are we*, rather than the *who am I*, but this is extremely difficult to prove. Canadian writing is more sombre, it's said, more modest, more self-deprecating, more moderate in its ambitions, but again, novel for novel, this is not easily demonstrated. What we can say with certainty is that Canadian literature is smaller than American literature and younger. There are nineteenth-century novels, to be sure, but not many and no great novels. We can, speaking roughly and without stepping on too many toes, take the year 1960 as the real beginning of our literature. That was the year – just to peg it for you – when there were five novels published in Canada. Five!

Today's refocusing or defocusing of Canadian literature may be a reaction to our experience in the sixties, the time of our centenary, and the years that followed, a period of explosive patriotism, partly genuine, partly pumped-up boosterism, when we were persuaded to rush our literary impulses into a unified statement of national identity. We had a railway, an airline, a new flag, a modified anthem – why not a literature too.

Many Canadians think now with embarrassment of this period, but most believe it was a necessary process. Extravagant claims were made for rather mediocre old texts – and for me the novels of Frederick Philip Grove are out on the marginal edge of the edge – and far too many new novels, volumes of poetry and plays were brought forward and celebrated simply because they contained – and this was and continues to be a catch phrase – Canadian content. Because we needed a critical language to talk about the new Canadian writing, theories were hastily concocted and eagerly taken up. These cobbled-together theories became hobbling tyrants. The idea of the garrison mentality, for instance, which poor Northrop Frye mentioned only once and only in passing, became a verity, until it was, finally, demolished when revisionists began to pay attention to what our nineteenth-century writers had really said about nature and society.

None of this is surprising, perhaps, in a post-colonial country where writers had long been persuaded that life, real life, happened elsewhere. Susanna Moodie set her rather lugubrious novels in England, and in an England that had long since vanished. Hugh MacLennan was driven to despair trying to interest American publishers in his Canada based novels. As recently as the 1930s and '40s, Morley Callaghan published some of his novels in double editions: a Toronto setting for those books sold in Canada, a Chicago setting for those sold south of the border. Gabrielle Roy writes in her autobiography that as a young Franco-Manitoban writer she grew conscious of what she calls a worm in the apple, the feeling that she was so doubly at the edge that she belonged nowhere.

And what can we say about a country whose bookstores still, today, divide their offerings into Literature and – a very small shelf usually – Canadiana; that's where our novels appear side by side with manuals about how to master whitewater canoeing.

Nations are fortunate indeed if they possess texts – *Huckleberry Finn* comes to mind – whose spirit is universally shared – well, almost – and understood even by those who have never read it and never will. *David Copperfield* is, for Britain, a similar cultural key; touch that key and you stir directly into available culture. We may not yet have in Canada such a universally shared cultural reference, though the name Hagar Shipley from Margaret Laurence's *The Stone Angel* goes a long way in that direction.

When Margaret Laurence said to Canadian writers, "If you can nail down one piece of this strange country, then you have an obligation to do it," she almost certainly was gesturing at that well-known irony: that radical regionalism often produces universal response. People are bonded and nourished by a common literature, but only if it has flowered naturally, unprodded by politicians and flag wavers and the prescriptive notions of the Academy.

In 1957, the year I crossed the border with my young husband, all our belongings, including an ironing board, packed into our six-cylinder Ford – 1957 was the year of the founding of the Canada Council – it was decided by a number of concerned citizens and with the blessing of Parliament and with the help of a substantial and timely private endowment, that Canada, this country on the edge, could afford its own culture.

We had at that time only a handful of novelists. Our literature, in fact, was probably a good deal smaller than that of Hungary, and there were probably only a few names – Leacock, Callaghan – who were part of the public currency. Pierre Berton had just begun his explorations; Juliette sang from the radio, and the Happy Gang did their gig every day right after the *Farm Report*.

After 1957, perhaps because of the thrust of the Canada Council or perhaps because it was time, regional theatres and symphonies sprang to life across the country. Art galleries mounted Canadian shows. Plays were produced that were written by Canadian playwrights; this had scarcely ever happened before. And librarians from Newfoundland to Vancouver Island began pasting those little red maple leafs on the spines of Canadian books, although I have to say that writers, even today, are uncertain about whether they applaud this distinction or not; certainly I can't imagine Americans attaching the stars and bars to *their* books.

It wasn't until the middle 1960s that I read my first Canadian novel, which happened to be Marian Engel's *The Honeyman Festival*. Of course I'd seen Leonard Cohen and Irving Layton doing their shtick on television, so I knew there was some literary activity going on. The next novel I read was Margaret Laurence's *The Stone Angel*, and one year after that I found myself registering for a graduate degree in Canadian literature at the University of Ottawa and beginning preliminary research on the Canadian pioneer Susanna Moodie.

Both Marian Engel and Margaret Laurence were young mothers when they wrote their wonderful books, and they were assisted in their work by grants from the Canada Council which enabled them to "buy" time. I don't believe for a minute that we can produce writers by throwing money at them, but the Canada Council has, from the beginning, established a climate of respect for the arts and those who practise them. Writers could be nourished both directly and indirectly, given financial support and awarded social permission to create novels that were wrenched out of the lives of Canadians. It was a gamble and it took time – though a surprisingly short time – and what we have today – our own literature – is as indebted to the Canada Council, as well as provincial arts councils, as it is to Canada's position "on the edge."

But why so many Canadian women? Part of me resents this question, since no one would ever think to ask, "Why are there so many male writers?" Another part of me, though, the more honest part, is deeply curious about this presumed phenomenon. Of course, statistics on Canadian writing don't prove the woman question out; there are, in fact, far more novels published by men than by women, far more men reviewing those novels, and more literary prizes handed out over the years to men than to women. Since the Governor General's Award for Fiction began in 1936, there have been forty men who have been winners and only seventeen women. The names of Robertson Davies, Timothy Findley, Guy Vanderhaeghe, and Michael Ondaatje ring loud across the land. Yet the myth, or truth, persists: that Canadian literature is dominated by women.

It could – let me put this forward anyway – be a coincidence that our four or five most effective, engaging, and gifted writers just happen to be women. It could be one of those statistical anomalies like the pockets of brain cancer or longevity that occur in specific localities of the world.

Or it could be that women are not necessarily writing better novels, but novels about the kinds of things readers are anxious to know about.

Or it could be that serious women novelists are in the ascendancy around the world. The novel, after all, is the one literary form whose birth took place at a time when women were, for the first time, being educated in large numbers. And women, denied the novel of action, the novel of ideas, fell heir to the novel that reflected the daily life of ordinary people. This kind of novel was once shuttled off into a corner called domestic fiction, until it was realized, and not that many years ago, that everyone, men as well as women, possess a domestic life.

Or the current interest in women's fiction could be – and I think this is more likely – because some 70 per cent of those who read novels are women – so the booksellers tell us – and that these women want to hear other women's voices. Perhaps they've always wanted these voices, but we needed Simone de Beauvoir and Betty Friedan to come along and tell us we were smarter than we thought, and then Kate Millet told us – I think it was in 1970 – that we didn't have to take Henry Miller seriously any longer, and what a relief that was! Women spread the word, helping each other along, and there really is – ask publishers – a network among reading women.: "You've just got to read this book," they say, and often it is a book by a woman writer.

Virginia Woolf (like one of the characters in one of my novels, I have a Woolfian bias) – Virginia invoked in me an impulse to be serious. And then Margaret Laurence said to me, through her writing, "serious, yes, but watch out for earnestness." Mavis Gallant shows how it is possible to be intelligent on the page without being pedantic. Margaret Atwood, who is, I suppose Canada's first international star, is just plain brave – she'll tackle any orthodoxy and almost always with wit. Alice Munro describes in one of her stories what real work is. It's not just housework or looking after the husband and children; my real work, the narrator says, is "wooing distant parts of myself." These distant parts, these concealed layers of existence, shame or ecstasy or whatever, are what every writer works to get to the heart of.

Part of the appeal of women writers may be the intimacy of voice. I often think how women writers sitting at their desks are speaking not to the ages or to humankind, but to individual readers, as though those readers were in the same room, and what they are speaking of is the texture of their own lives. Women writers often seem willing to engage with vulnerability, including themselves in that vulnerability. As a woman

who has elected a writing life, I am interested in writing away the invisi-
bility of women's lives, looking at writing as an act of redemption. In
order to do this, I need the companionship, the example, of other women
who are writing.

The writer Kennedy Fraser, in an essay on Virginia Woolf, confesses
that she once suffered a time in her life which was so painful that reading
about the lives of other women writers was the only thing that comforted her. She claims she was slightly ashamed of this, pretending to her
friends that she was reading the novels and the poetry of these women,
but in fact it was their lives that supported her. "I needed," she says, "all
that murmured chorus, this continuum of true-life stories, to pull me
through. They were like mothers and sisters to me, these literary women,
many of them already dead; more than my own family, they seemed to
stretch out a hand." I have seen this passage from Kennedy Fraser's essay
quoted a dozen times, and can only guess that it summons up the
reader-writer relationship that so many of us know and are indebted to.

It may be, too, that women's writing today is more aware of itself,
more inclusive, less oppressed by male patronizing or erasure, less in
danger of its substance falling *off* the edge. Dr Helen Buss of the University of Calgary has questioned the missing mother in our literature, and
Canadian poet and scholar Di Brandt has asked why angry women are
absent from our pages. At one time women characters in fiction were
expected to be resourceful and cheerful. To confront real life was to
become a whining victim. As recently as 1988 one of our finest writers,
Bonnie Burnard, was taken to task by *Globe and Mail* critic William
French. Her book *Women of Influence* was unacceptable to Mr French:
"The melancholy tone is unrelenting," he wrote, "and we want to escape
the emotionally frigid world she portrays with such power ... Burnard
has undeniable talent, and the women's problems she explores in these
stories undeniably exist, but I hope in her next collection, she can make
me laugh, at least once."

No wonder women's books became a refuge for women readers.
There they found themselves; there they could *be* themselves. There they
felt the distance shrink between what was privately felt and universally
known. Women, I think, were hungry for their own honesty, and both
readers and writers were relieved to know that the disparagement they
had suffered at the edge was undeserved. You can tell, a male critic once
wrote of a beautifully cryptic Alice Munro story, just where Ms Munro
knocks off for a cup of tea.

I do worry that we run the risk of two separate literatures, just as today we have boys' films and girls' films, or so my daughters classify them. Now, though, as never before, it seems important that men and women understand each other's experience. That experience, those selves, are abundantly available through the agency of fiction.

It was Muriel Spark who broke the spell for me, finally, in a novel called *Loitering with Intent* with this stirring sentence: "How wonderful it feels to be an artist and a woman in the twentieth century." I'd known all along it was true, but to see it bravely centred on the page made it real, and this utterance encourages me to frame a paraphrase and bring it home: how wonderful to be a woman living and writing in Canada in the year 1997.

NOTE

This is a previously unpublished Harvard address, delivered on 10 February 1997 (second accession of the Carol Shields fonds, B.46 f.8, Library and Archives Canada). Published with the kind permission of the author.

PART ONE

Essaying/Assaying Genre:

Biography, Archive, Short Story, Novel

2

Voice and Re-vision:
The Carol Shields Archival Fonds

CATHERINE HOBBS

Archives are a flow of documents created in time that have been removed from the locale of creation. Looking in the archival files, we see notebooks, manuscripts, letters, and photographs that we can choose to narrate in various ways. Yet this is not a composed narrative: one can start at any point to see a series of dialogues between correspondents or the jottings and notes that are fragments of the author's dialogue and directives to herself, this is because the onlooker chooses to focus on a certain aspect around which details swirl. Underlying the physicality of archives is the physical act of writing. The archival fonds exists at the intersections of what was written and what was never written, and what is preserved and what has not survived. The order of an archival fonds is determined by the archivist in the aftermath of the donor completing her activities; this ordering is the first act of interpretation. Though we can look at the mass of documentation together in one place, the writer does not know at the time of creation that x is the first of a series of stories or that y really is a new novel. A certain amount of faith and experience concerning the act of writing is involved as the writer lives through time.

I was introduced in 1999 to the second accession of the Carol Shields fonds, which, at the time, was a series of stuffed and unsorted boxes. I organized and described the documents, which mainly represent the very productive and astonishing period of Shields's life between 1994 and apartments,   three houses, and yet he has trouble remembering   what   their

life had been made   of. They   were   married,   it always   seemed   to him, back in

the time   of the old poetry, 1958,   when   the world   rhymed   and chimed   and the

ceilings were   higher or, even   if they weren't, the possibility   of their height

was   felt.

        Unless Martin Gill takes early retirement,   as he is being urged to do

by his Head of Department,   Dr. Elaine Arnett-Scott,   he will be given first

year compostion   to teach.

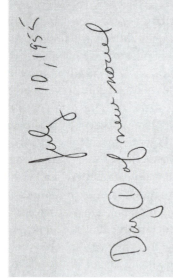

Early draft of *Larry's Party* (later chapter 15) marked "Day 1 of new novel"
(CSf II b.34 f.1)

1998. This was the time when she won the Pulitzer, was awarded the
Orange Prize and the National Book Critics Award, was chancellor of
the University of Winnipeg and teacher at the University of Manitoba,

mentored writers through the Humber School, worked on the Writers Development Trust and the Canada Council, was given honorary degrees by many Canadian universities, travelled widely, and achieved publication in twenty-six languages. It was plain that the notes, manuscripts, and correspondence in the fonds were a marvellous resource for tracing the multitude of roles which Shields has enacted: playwright, poet, novelist, collaborator, mother, chancellor, teacher, and mentor, to name a few. As is usually the case when archival material is interpreted, many ghostlike senses of Shields formed in my mind: Shields the writer, exceptional in her care for individuals in her work and family life; a passionate and faithful letter-writer; and a writer reflecting on her role as a Canadian woman writer on the world stage. She has had extraordinarily close contact with her agent and editors, and even her translators have received the same careful attentions. Looked at now, with its sudden weight, the seemingly explosive buildup of Shields's career is reflected in the physical mass of the fonds: some twenty-three metres of archival records that she generated up to 1998.

Carol Shields began to view her archival material as important early in her career, having attended a writers' conference at the University of Calgary in the 1970s. In a speech delivered at the National Library titled "The Subjunctive Self," she said of depositing her archival fonds, "This is part of the problem, I suppose, of consecrating one's efforts to eternal conservation: the embarrassment of revealing all those false starts, incorrigible precocity, wild tangents, implausible scenes, batty notions, untamed prose, eccentric spelling, and ill conceived attempts that, for all kinds of reasons failed to come to life."[1]

Not only does the Carol Shields archival fonds document the development of her work and the events and connections in her life, but it plays off, expands, explores, and circles back to many of the preoccupations that surface in her fiction. We can see various themes of Shields's fiction bubble up from diverse points of inspiration and become fully developed; included among these themes are a focus on the details of daily life, naming, food and entertaining, letter-writing, and women's roles. However, beyond the interwovenness of the archives in the ideas that interest Shields, I see hints that her allusions to biography and to archival material in her fiction, when brought to bear in interpreting her archives, confound a straightforward interpretation of her archives. This, then, is both an introduction to the archives as seen through a number of Shields's fictional themes and a reflection on the irony of her archival fonds itself.

```
                    Chapter 1

        Morning.  January.  So early it was still
   dark.  The kitchen curtains were pulled closed
   and the overhead lights were on.  Maude, in a
   quilted robe just reaching the floor, navigated
   the familiar bacon and egg swamp, hands opening
   cupboards, finding cups and saucers.  Plates
   winked from a patterned cloth.  A silver spoon
   sat precious in jam.  She moved slowly.
        Upstairs Charlie, her husband, stomped
   his morning two-step, shave and wash to a ragged
   whistle.  Then silence.  He would be knotting his
   tie in front of the walnut framed mirror,
   a small thin knot that belonged to another generat-
   ion.  He would glance at his shoulders, inspecting
   his jacket for lint, always dressing the lawyer's
   role although he never pretended to love it.
        When he came downstairs they had orange
   juice, eggs and toast.  Maude poured two cups
   of coffee and pushed one toward Charlie.  Black
   coffee, hot and familiar.  Looking up from her
   cup she caught Charlie's eyes on her.  The knot
   of concern.  Something reached her through that
   glance, some twist of feeling between pain and loss.
```

First draft of "The Vortex" (CSf 1 b.23 f.1)

DETAILS OF DAILY LIFE

One of the first features making Shields a tremendously interesting archival subject is her interest in minutiae, in details, and in everyday life. She is well-known for layering domestic and everyday detail into her fiction, and this tendency was apparent when she first attempted to write a novel. In the drafts for her unpublished first novel, "The Vortex," the first paragraph rings with phrases that appear, years later, to be familiar Shields style in their attention to the domestic arena. In this first scene, we are introduced to "Maude, in a quilted robe" and told that "plates

How did she do it? How do other writers do it, writers
like Updike, Pritchett, Alice Munro. Ann Beatty. I tried began
to read critically, and must confess that this kind of reading
damaged, probably forever, the old simple pleasure of getting
into a good book. What I began to find was a tremendous attention
to details. The details were often, I thought at first irrelevant.
What did it matter if one character had a mole on her left
breast, that she was prone to allergies, that she was fond of
gold fish, that she favored silk blouses, that her mother had once
had a goiter removed, that her sister lived in Minneaspolis, that

Index card for "Speech on Being a Writer" ca. 1980 (CSf1 b.63 f.1)

winked from the patterned cloth" and [a] "silver spoon sat precious in jam."[2]

In a script for an autobiographical film written in the late 1980s around the time of the publication of *Various Miracles*, Shields describes how she came across the ideas for these stories in her everyday activities:

This afternoon I overhear a man on the bus recounting how the frost got to his tomato plants last night. "I should of picked 'em green" he says cheerfully. "It's my own damn fault." His resignation, his acquiescence interests me, and then I overhear something even more interesting: two young men – could they be divinity students? – are discussing the Bible, in particular Lot's wife and why it was she was turned into a pillar of salt. "Why not stone?" one of them asks. "Why not a burning bush?" says the other. A day or two later I am working on a short story about a group of men who are discussing the metamorphosis of Lot's wife into a pillar of salt. In my story, these are middleaged men, substantial, articulate, professional, and they're not sitting on a crowded university bus pounding along Pembina Highway, but around a dinner table at the Manitoba Club, situated in downtown Winnipeg, next to the Fort Garry Hotel.[3]

In this account one glimpses Shields gleaning details for fiction from her own everyday experience and using these as the seeds for fiction.

In a speech that seems to have been prepared when Shields was a writer-in-residence around 1980, she describes her approach at that time to how details surround character and the self-consciousness about detail that emerged as she read the work of other writers. This is one of Shields's famous lists, to be sure:

I began to read *critically*, and I must confess that this kind of reading damaged, probably forever, the old simple pleasure of getting into a good book. What I began to
find was a tremendous attention to details. The details were often, I thought at first –
irrelevant. What did it matter if one character had a mole on her left breast, and she
was prone to allergies, that she was fond of gold fish, that she favored silk blouses,
that her mother had once had a goiter removed, that her sister lived in Minneapolis
[*sic*], that she went to the chiropractor on Tuesdays, that she sometimes caught cold;
and, sometimes, especially in subways, cursed under her breath; that she had dreams,
birthdays, dandruff, untidy dresser drawers, illusions of grandeur and greatness,
moods of depression which seemed to come from nowhere; what did all this have to
do with the story? I asked myself.
    Everything.[4]

Later in the speech Shields says, "picture a room, a kitchen. A woman is
pouring tea. Does it matter what color the teapot is [?] Hemingway
might have said no; it is irrelevant. Many writers, myself included,
would say yes. The color of the teapot not only helps form an image but
it is one of the *one million* facts about this woman which are going to
contribute to her solidity."[5] If these one million facts contribute to her
solidity, according to Shields, they are linked to the understanding that
the particularities of life are important to us each day as individuals and
that such details ground characters as "real" to the reader.
    In the same autobiographical film mentioned above Shields describes
her workspace at the time of the writing of the *Various Miracles* stories,
stressing the importance of particular objects and surroundings on her
own ability to write: "Early in my writing life I was persuaded that certain requirements had to be met in order to make a congenial environment, a '*place*' where I could work. A quiet room of my own, of course; a
room that did not double as the sewing room or the TV room. Familiar
objects: a certain ceramic container for my paperclips. A dictionary –
not any dictionary, but a large, thready, black-covered Funk and
Wagnall's. A particular typewriter."[6] With these details, Shields's readers
are reminded of the letter opener and pencil jar that later surround the
elderly novelist in the story "Edith-Esther" or the sorry rhyming dictionary of Mary Swann or the separate quilting room so necessary to
Brenda Bowman in *A Fairly Conventional Woman*. The mention of
these details folds us back into Shields's fiction, in which such details are
relied-upon elements used to ground characters and evoke their domestic settings. They show us that she not only gathers from the minutiae of
life to stock her fiction because she relies on domestic detail to support

her life, but that everyday experience and the exploration of everyday experience in fiction may be something of a continuum.

NAMING

Shields is a writer with a remarkable capacity to convey precise socio-economic status, background, and character in a name. The fonds gives numerous examples in which to trace the changes of characters' names: Sarah Maloney of *Swann* was first Sarah Malcolm and then Sarah Riley; Frederick Cruzzi was first Frederick Nellis; Mrs Turner of "Mrs. Turner Cutting the Grass" was once Mrs Herbert, Mrs Ferney and then Mrs O'Farrell; and Elinore Gamble Harris became Daisy Goodwill Flett. In a story sent to the *New Yorker* and titled "Woe" (which is, in fact, an early version of the "Childhood" chapter of *The Stone Diaries*); Barker Flett is named Barker Purdy. We can see in the manuscripts that Martin Gill (the husband's name in *Small Ceremonies*) appears as the main character in the first draft of *Larry's Party:* of course he was later named Larry Weller.[7] In the story "Edith-Esther" the main character was first Holly and then Hildgarde and Lillian, the final choice of the name Edith-Esther sounding decidedly more dated and solid.[8] Each of these name changes shows careful refinement of the echoes and social connotations that the choices imply. Shields's manuscripts are rife with such changes, which demonstrate the care and attention she gave to creating her character labels.

In a few instances in the 1980s, Shields also wrote poetry, which she submitted for publication under male pseudonyms: for the Canadian magazine *Border Crossings* and a Manitoba television contest, she used the pseudonym Ian McAllister, and for another piece for a *Chatelaine* fiction contest she chose the sweetly ironic name Ian Strange. This use of pseudonyms may be important if only to underline her understanding of the currency of naming.

Like many writers, Shields worked through series of titles for her published works in collaboration with her British and North American publishers. This correspondence in the fonds tell us of these choices and refinements: that *The Stone Diaries* was provisionally titled "The Monument" and that several other titles were also in the running for the work, including "The Stone Curtain" and "The Stone Circle." Christopher Potter of Fourth Estate even suggested "Suitable Moments."[9] In the contract for what was later *The Republic of Love*, the provisional title was "Bodies of Water," which has significantly more stress on the mermaid

```
                        Chapter 1: Unless


    Unless your life is going well you don't think of giving a party.

Unless you can look in the mirror and see a benign and generous and healthy

human being, you shrink from acts of hospitality. Which is why Martin Gill

has not given a party in some time. Not for years, in fact. Not since his

second wife, Debbie, left him four years ago. Left him with a closetful of

rough denim outerwear, a bathroom cluttered with hightech hairbrushes and

a row of empty shampoo bottles.

    Otherwise she left him carefully, tactfully, psychologically . There

was a long resoning note, handwritten, folded, sealed inside a business -

sized envelope and placed on his pillow. Tenderly, he assumed. "Darling

Martin" it began. "All this will be easier for you if you think of life as a

book each of us must write alone, and how, within that book there are many

chapters. I think we both know that our chapter, your and mine, has

contained pages of ecstasy, of mutual growth--"

    On and on it went. He found the prose hard to follow, as though it had

been written during a bout of drunkenness, but that was impossible since

Debbie never touched anything stronger than spring water. "Your spiritual

footnotes, dear dear Martin, have illuminated mine, and I like to think that

our combined epigraph has sent shooting stars, sexually as well as

intellectually, across the synapse of our stitched together leaves, igniting

our--"

    Heartbroken, he had smiled over her penultimate paragraph. Dear

bossy, pedagogical Deb. "Now is the time, sweet Martin, to get going on a

blank sheet of foolscap and write your way toward understanding and

forgiveness."
```

First draft of *Larry's Party* (CSf II b.34 f.1)

theme in the work than the final title. To Mindy Werner of Viking Penguin, Shields describes her reaction to a particular title and gives a sense of the free play behind her title choices, saying, "I still prefer *The Republic of Love* which at least sounds crisp. But I'm hoping another idea will

Holly's biographer has been phoning lately wanting to know what she thinks about God. "You seem," he said delicately, "not, hmmm, to have addressed or referenced any particularized deity in your novels."

"Well, I--"

"Or indicated which side of the belief debate you are on."

"I don't believe in God," Holly told him plainly as she could, He sounded disappointed. Holly imagined him holding a pencil straight up on its point, "Are you sure?"

Holly said yes, she was sure.

"Well," her biographer said after a moment, "Don't you believe in anything?"

"You mean like astrology or tea leaves?"

"I mean," he said, "just something. Anything."

Holly caught the scent of desperation, and certainly she understood that a definitive authorized biography must show the whole person, his or her sexuality, creative energy, and spiritual depths and so forth; otherwise the enterprize was just a sequence of events.

"Nothing," Holly said, plucking dead blossoms of her geranium as she spoke. The conversation was making her nervous and also sad. She knew her life was proving a disappointment, "So you believe in nothing," her biographer repeated dully; how he would be tapping his pencil up and down on its eraser end.

She rubbed the geranium petals between her fingers, releasing that heavenly scent, spice and ashes and healthy rot, neither male

"Edith Esther" draft with handwritten revisions (CSf II b.40 f.33)

drop into my head – or yours."[10] Names and titles that convey so much to the reader by their "ring" are chosen by Shields with great care, these appear as effortless, sincere, and everyday phrases.

DETAILS OF WOMEN'S EXPERIENCES

In particular, Shields has been noted by critics for her interest and exploration of the details of women's lives. The importance to her of women's

Travel diary of Inez Warner from a trip to Great Britain, 6 May–12 June 1969
(CSf 11 b.54 f.4)

self-representation and their individual vision of daily life and happenings is foregrounded in the fact that she kept the travel diaries of both her mother, Inez Warner, and her aunt Edna that appear in the fonds. It is their voices that are so contiguous with Shields's narrative when she explores the perspectives of older women.

"Hedgerows line the road & separates [sic] fields which are irregular in shape."[11] This is a quotation from Shields's mother's travel diary, written during a tour of Great Britain in 1969. In the diary, Inez Warner details the itinerary by which the Warners went from Canterbury Cathedral to Penzance, Bath to Scotland, guided by their tour-guide driver, who surfaces in the diary in such remarks as "Eric tells us where to 'ponder' when we stop mid-morning."[12]

"Bridal wreath or spirea – Alec called May blossoms, lined the highway and hedged the fields in the Cottswolds."[13] The repeated mention of hedges in the diary allows one to think that Inez Warner's diary was the source of more than one idea later built into *Larry's Party*. This diary relates most concretely to the diary that the character Dorrie carries on her honeymoon in *Larry's Party*: "Dorrie copied this information into a little travel diary she pulled from her purse ... Larry found his wife's note-taking touching and also surprising. Where had that diary come from? Its cover was red leather. The narrow ruled pages were edged in gold."[14] Inez Warner's actual diary resembles this fictional diary quite closely. Another suggestive detail shown in the inside cover of this diary is that Shields's mother, Inez Warner, lived in Sarasota, Florida, where Daisy Goodwill Flett ended her days.

In the diary, Carol Shields's mother noted down various points on her trip related to the greats of English literature and the royal family and various cathedrals and pubs along the way (none of these are directly cited in *Larry's Party*, but they seem to have supplied the grist for the type of experiences that Dorrie and Larry have). One of the most curious features of the diary is a series of explanations found at the back of the volume relating to English food, dining, hotels, and money. These sections are filled with such useful tips as "Only Americans cut food & lay down knife & eat with right hand"[15] and "No English muffins in all of Great Britain. Bob asked one place & they told him they can't sell them after Easter."[16] A similar interest in food and the minute details of travel is recorded in Aunt Edna's diary concerning her trip to Mexico in 1924: "Pete and Minnie left R.I. at 10 & we met them in camp at Grinnell Io[wa] at 6 o'clock. We all did justice to what was left of the fried chicken and other goodies that Ethel had packed for us also to Lydia's big angel food cake."[17] The precise tone of these accounts is readily attributable to a particular age group of women: those of Shields's mother's generation and those who appear in *The Stone Diaries* and *Thirteen Hands*. One can so easily hear their voices as those of Daisy and the bridge players' generation, with the same expectations, pride, and interest in food preparation.[18]

FOOD AND ENTERTAINING

Of course, one is struck with how many times people's (in particular, women's) relation to food is mentioned in the work of Carol Shields. Entertaining and the preparation of food become central organizational structures in her stories as they do in social life. In the original first scene of *Thirteen Hands*, which was later cut from the play, four women meet on a train and start to talk, to tell their stories to the other three strangers; as Shields said of this scene, each woman is "trapped in a pocket of life, but each bravely takes courage from the life that's been given her,

```
kitchen  sink  overnight.   Hot  water.   It's really  very  odd,  but  in  the

morning    there   it is, the  label,  just  floating   free, all  on  its  own ! What

I find  truly  amazing   is that  the  label  doesn't  disintegrate.    I mean,

it's only  paper  after  all, but  my  husband   believes  that  this  is because

they  use  very  high  quality  paper,  at  least  on  the  better  vintages.

Well,  he  dries  the  labels  out  thoroughly,    arranging    them   on  a paper

towel   and  sort  of blotting   up  the  moisture,    sometimes      I help him  with

that  part.   Then  he  glues  them   into  this  big  album   we  have.   (a long

pause)   He  feels  that  this  way   we'll  have  a  record  of the  many

pleasant    evenings   we've   spent.   Throughout    our  life sort-of-thing.


THE   TRAIN   STOPS   WITH   A  LURCH,   THEN   AFTER   A  MOMENT    STARTS    UP

AGAIN.



         Sleeper


(after  a pause)   Well,  since  you've  broken   the  ice, I don't see any
reason   not to introduce   myself.   I'm a little  sleepy  today,  I was   up so
late last night  baking  a cake.   Now  I suppose   that  sounds  funny,
baking   a cake  at night,  but  it was  meant   to be  a surprise.   I bake  a lot
of cakes.   This  was  a Frosty  the  Snowman    cake.  Take  two  nine-inch
pans,  oil well  and  line  with  circles  cut  out  of waxed   paper.   Also  take
a six-inch  round  pan  and  repeat.   Preheat  oven,  350  degrees.   Cream
shortening   and  sugar  in large  bowl,   and  then  add  six eggs,  beating
after  each.   Next  add  dry  ingredients   a little  at a time,  alternating
with  one  cup plus  three  tablespoons    sour  milk  of butter  milk.   Stir  in
vanilla  and  divide  batter  into  your  three  prepared   baking  pans  and
```

Original first scene of *Thirteen Hands* (CSf 1 b.76 f.1)

doing what women have always done, which is to make the best of things."[19] This scene ends with one woman reading an obituary mentioning the Martha Circle, and there is also a long recipe for a "Frosty the Snowman cake" which begins, "Take two nine-inch pans, oil well and line with circles cut out of waxed paper. Also take a six-inch round pan and repeat." The script describes a confection complete with gumdrop eyes, a flowing cinnamon icing scarf and mitts, and a hat made out of a cut-up chocolate bar.[20]

Much of what sets the scene for the unexpected birth of Daisy Goodwill Flett is the Malvern pudding that her mother, Mercy Stone Goodwill, is preparing from a cookbook. In fact, in an e-mail to her daughter

```
From: Shields, Carol
To: Giardini, Anne
Subject: happy anniversary
Date: December 9, 1996 14:24PM


Dear Anne,

Good grief. There are nine at the table!  Oh lordy, thank heaven for
accountants.  And, yes I see I've made some car mistakes.  But I do have
the 96 Olympics right, don't I?--that was last summer, and that's the
date
of the chapter.  But my confidence is shaken.  It's back to work at
once.

Blanche, who looked it up in the Joy of Cooking,  has informed me that
you
can't get botulism with rhubarb, and so I have had to change to green
beans, which I felt was a loss (tho a friend of mine thinks beans are
funnier--but is this supposed to be funny?)
much love and happy anniversary--
mmmmmm
```

E-mail to Anne Giardini, 9 December 1996 (CSf II b.12 f.1)

Anne years after the book's publication, Shields remembers the actual cookbook held by the Shields family that inspired this fictional pudding: "I've just had a note from a UK food writer who is responding to a food column in the Telegraph who was wondering what recipe Mercy Goodwill was making in the opening chapter of *The Stone Diaries*. I got the recipe for the Malvern pudding out of a cookbook that I later sent to you. I believe the date is around 1880."[21]

Choosing fictional food involves a series of refinements. As we can see in the last lines of another e-mail to her daughter Anne, the fatal food that kills the mother-in-law in *Larry's Party* is changed in the successive revisions from rhubarb to jarred beans, since rhubarb is found out not to be poisonous; this, as Shields relates, is a fact that Blanche Howard discovered by looking in *The Joy of Cooking*. This attention to cooking and dining is one of the overriding ties to the lives of women, but it is somewhat inverted when Shields writes *Larry's Party*, the narrative in which the male character hosts a dinner party. In the manuscripts for *Larry's Party*, Shields makes an effort to strike the right note by successive refinements of Larry's dinner menu: a menu that at first featured "Chicken in mustard sauce" and "peanut brittle ice cream" went on to offer "leg of lamb" and "Austrian chocolate torte." In the final refinements, terms such as "squash" were elaborated to "butternut squash."[22]

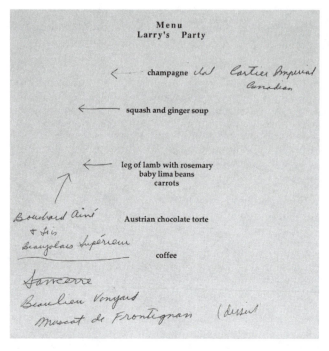

Version of the dinner menu in *Larry's Party* (CSf II b.37 f.2)

Also, in the various drafts of the hand-drawn map[23] and seating plan[24] for *Larry's Party*, one sees the careful planned exactness of these details, which provide a slice of realism and a kinship to the rituals that organize each of our lives. The great attention Shields paid to refining these details is not surprising when we know her work, but it again suggests a recognition of the currency of such terms and traditions to her community of readers.

LETTER-WRITING

In a preface to *A Celibate Season*, Blanche Howard tells the reader that Shields delighted in receiving mail, a fact that is given strong evidence in the thirty-six boxes of correspondence in her archival fonds.[25] Shields maintained many of her friendships through letters. She was also kind in responding to numerous letters from fans. In addition to this passion for letter-writing, Shields had an interest in what compels letter-writers to write. For the CBC program *Crosswords*, Bill Richardson offered a Shieldsian task to several writers, asking them to write a fictional sketch

Photograph of an unnamed beauty school for "A News Roundup ... Class of 1927" (for *Crosswords* with Bill Richardson on CBC Radio; CSf1 b.51 f.59)

using a photograph of the graduates of a beauty school. In a letter of response to Richardson, Shields writes: "I've always been fascinated with the 'round robin' letters women organize, and indeed I've been part of several. (There was always a dead link, someone who held onto the letters for months) Do men have anything similar?"[26] In the final paragraph of her letter, Shields says, "The photo is a treasure. Full of cultural and emotional resonance. Did you notice how innocent their earlobes are of earrings? And oh, those kiss curls!" Her comments resound with her love of letter-writing and her eye for the details of women's lives.

When we consider her love of letters, it is not very much of a surprise that Shields turned to writing an epistolary novel with Blanche Howard on the model, as Shields reveals, of Fanny Burney's *Evelina*.[27] In her first letter, dated 13 September 1983, Blanche Howard mentions their project and a number of other details that make their way into the writing of the book: "Anyway, I loved having a visit with you, and am thinking about our great project. I'm sure it was you who urged me to read Between Friends, by Gillian Hanscombe wasn't it? In any case, I'm just starting it, and as you no doubt know it is in the same format as we've discussed, letters between two friends." A little later on in this letter, which Howard is writing from her Vancouver home, she says: "The party Saturday night was very successful, I think. 65 people in this house is a mite crowded, but no-one seemed to mind, and my caterers did a superb job. I was, needless to say, quite weary afterwards but am recovered now and on my way to Ottawa tomorrow."[28]

In a second letter, Howard has just mailed off the first chapter to Shields and remarks, "I can't tell you how much more fun it is to write for someone else's eyes than just to write for the faceless mass who may or may not read it. I kept thinking, will Carol like this? and she'll laugh at that and so on." Further on in the letter Howard mentions, "I'm sorry if I was this long over it, but have been back to Ottawa twice since I saw you and am due to go again in a week or so. The Vanier thing is getting really awful, but I feel I can't leave at this point."[29] (Howard was working on the board of the Vanier Institute of the Family at the time.)

Shields's and Howard's actual letters document the process (the meetings, the trips to Ottawa, and the Vancouver party) that lies behind the writing of *A Celibate Season*, a novel that combines many of these same topics and events stitched together by letter-writing. These letters between Howard and Shields mirror the fictional letters of the novel and become the workings out of which the letters and events in the epistolary novel are born. For example, clippings and letters to the editor that Blanche sends to Carol regarding the strike in British Columbia become essential background to a novel in which the character Chas is sending clippings and discussing a strike in British Columbia, his housekeeper's involvement in the issue, and letters to the editor. These clippings, letters to the editor, locations, trips, and dinner parties in the correspondence with Howard are all mirrored in the book itself – a playful borrowing from the circumstances surrounding the writing of the novel.

DOCUMENTS OF EVERYDAY EXPERIENCE

Understanding Shields's focus on the everyday, the archivists who have arranged her material have kept a significant amount of ephemera and other momentos of everyday experience in her archival fonds, mainly because her fiction and her life convey a blending and a non-privileging of one aspect of life over another. Momentos from life such as a photograph of Shields cutting the cord at her grandson's birth recall and play off the "squirming foolishness of birth" described at the end of the first chapter of *The Stone Diaries*, for example.

Illustrations that appear in Shields's novels, such as the maps and party plans for *Larry's Party*, also exist as ephemera that she has created

```
                        Carol    Shields
            701--237  Wellington    Crescent
            Winnipeg,   Manitoba,    R3M   0A1
                   (204)   284   9907


7 March  1993


Dear  Christopher,


Snowing   today,  and  the  wind  howling.


Here  are  the  photos  I have.  Hope  they  arrive  safely.  I am  most  interested  in
your  idea of computer    fattening,  and  can't  wait  to see  how  it turns  out.  Let
me  know  if you want  to rumple  the  photograph    of the  Women's    Rhythm   and
Movement    Club.  I think  most  photographers    would  know  how  to "age"  a
photo.  You  will see  in the  picture  of 583  The  Driveway   a man  washing   a
1957  car.  This  is actually  my  own  father  washing   our car  in Oak  Park,
Illinois, but the  caption  need  not,  I suppose,  mention   the  person,  only the
address  (an Ottawa   address  that  doesn't  exist, by the  way--though     I once
lived  at 582  The  Driveway).   If you need  to mention   a name,  you  might  use
Mr. Mannerly  who  would  have  washed    the  Fletts'  car.  (My  father  isn't  living
any  longer,  and  so can't possibly   object.)  Aside  from  saying  I'd like both  the
photo  and  the  drawing   of Fraidy  if possible,  I can't  offer  much   comment
about  how  many   pictures  to use, how  many   per page,  etc.  I trust  you
absolutely  in this manner.   You  may  have  some   completely   different  ideas
and  photos.  I notice  there  aren't  many   of children  and  grandchildren.     These  I
can  certainly  supply  if you like from  my  own  albums.


A few  other  things:  I'd like the  dedication   to this book  to read:  For  my
sister  Babs.


I'd also like--hope   this isn't too much   to ask--for   a little  note  of
appreciation   to read  something    like:  "A  number   of people  have  read  the
manuscript   for this  book  and  offered  encouragement     and  suggestions.    Carol
```

Fax to Christopher Potter of Fourth Estate (CSf 1 b.6 f.25)

for her own characters. One of the most involved examples of this creation of documentation for her characters is when Shields and her publishers and agent wrote back and forth arranging for the photographs
and other illustrations that appear in *The Stone Diaries*. These illustrations were compiled when the book was nearing completion from flea-
market photographs, vintage postcards, and personal family snapshots.
As Shields explains in a letter to Christopher Potter of Fourth Estate:
"Let me know if you want to rumple the photograph of the Women's
Rhythm and Movement Club. I think most photographers would know
how to 'age' a photo. You will see in the picture of 583 The Driveway a
man washing a 1957 car. This is actually my own father washing our car
in Oak Park, Illinois, but the caption need not, I suppose, mention the
person, only the address (an Ottawa address that doesn't exist, by the
way – though I once lived at 582 The Driveway)." And Shields says

Photographs of Don Shields as a baby and one
of Shields's daughters, used in *The Stone Diaries*
(CSf 1 b.45 f.2)

later, "I notice there aren't many of children and grandchildren. These I can certainly supply if you like from my own albums."[30]

Shields and Potter went so far as to fatten the original picture of Mercy Goodwill. Potter writes: "I'm afraid that the fattened Mercy won't photocopy light enough, but I think I can make her work, by loosening her stays and fattening her arms but leaving her head as so."[31] Shields does add photographs of her own children to the mix, and the photograph of Harold H. Hoad as a baby is identifiable on the back of the archival original as Shields's husband, "Donald Hugh Shields almost a year old in 1935." These real-life photographs further the ironic melding that Shields implies between reality and fiction, and these examples explore our relationship to the documentary evidence of life. In fact, a later owner of the Shields house at 582 The Driveway once wrote to Shields to ask her about the photograph of the house, a strong example of the way readers seems to be compelled to seek the fictional "truth" evidenced by this documentation.

Creating documents for characters' lives within the books by using photographs from Shields's own life causes the reader's vision to waiver back and forth between what is so-called fiction and what is so-called reality, extending the border of the fictional world. Looking at the Shields archival documents themselves in light of this melding gives a new sense of the use of archives and the concept of proof: these photographs "prove" both the life of the author and the lives of Shields's characters, again causing our vision to blur about how we normally think documentation functions. This blurring and uncertainty of documentation is even more evident when we look at how archives and the study of biography are described in Shields's fiction.

BIOGRAPHY AND ARCHIVES

A biographer of both Moodie and Austen, Shields in her fiction has explored the sense that the documents of an individual's life will not deliver any real, full-fledged understanding of the subject of research. This theme occurs fairly early on in her published works. In *Small Ceremonies* the main character, biographer Judith Gill says of the relationship between biography and archives: "So much of a man's life is lived inside his own head, that it is impossible to encompass a personality. There is never enough material. Sometimes I read in the newspaper that some university or library has bought hundreds and hundreds of boxes of letters and papers connected with some famous deceased person, and

I know every time that it's never going to be enough. It's hopeless, so why even try?"[32]

If one comes at Shields's work from an archival perspective as I do, one is struck by how often documentation features in her work. Think of the diary of Dorrie Weller in *Larry's Party*; the aborted and plagiarized first novel of Judith Gill in *Small Ceremonies*, based on the notebooks of someone else (and then plagiarized by another writer); the letters by Brother Adam in *The Box Garden*; the manuscript swept into disarray by a gust of wind, with its missing page 46, in the story "Various Miracles"; the maps, menu, and seating plan in *Larry's Party*; the fictional letters that sometimes omit details in *A Celibate Season;* and the "autobiographical" photographs in *The Stone Diaries*. Of course, with its focus on correspondence, its missing notebook, and the documents found under the floorboards, the novel *Swann* most clearly contradicts the notion that the documents from a writer's life form themselves neatly into an explanation of her motives and influences as they are found by an impartial researcher.[33]

As Shields told her audience in a talk given in Paris,

> The idea for *Swann* occurred to me in the mid-seventies when I was writing my thesis on the 19th century Canadian pioneer writer Susanna Moodie. Mrs. Moodie wrote two books about life in her adopted country ... she also wrote a number of dreadful, but highly successful novels, full of melodrama, romance and Christian sentiment. Working on my thesis, I was obliged to actually read these novels, and I found them difficult to locate. They were the popular literature of their day, and thus most of them had been destroyed. There were no copies in the university library and none at the National Library of Canada. Finally, I discovered copies at the University of Western Ontario, and these books were sent to me through an inter-library loan system. I read and returned these books, and then, just before submitting my thesis, I tried to borrow them one more time. A short note arrived from the University of Western Ontario saying: "All the books of Moodie have disappeared."[34]

Shields explains that it was the loss of the Moodie books and a radio interview she heard about a young economist cornering the world market on Mexican jumping beans which eventually became the impetus for Swann. The irony of this mishap and the fatalistic tone of the message were stored away by Shields until she began to write the novel.[35]

Swann is the work that most clearly highlights the precarious and unreliable nature of the documentary record because it features biographers, scholars, a local museum curator, and a publisher, all drawn to "rewrite" the story of a minor rural poet whose papers were thrown out with fish guts and later reconstructed partially from memory. However, in other works by Carol Shields, archival documentation also has this ironic, unresolved, or partial relationship to a character's "reality." As she wrote in the story "Death of an Artist," published in *Dressing Up for the Carnival*, "No one knew him, really knew him. The history of his choleric, odd, furiously unproductive, and thoroughly unsatisfying life is most clearly set out in his diaries, eight plump volumes, but difficult to decipher because of the red crayon he affected, and the cheap lined schoolboy paper. These 'undiaries,' as he himself once called them, are best read in reverse, that is, you should begin with the final entry and work backwards."[36] This is an essentially anti-archival impulse, or at least an impulse to confound the archivist: that the tangibly fragile, affected, and somewhat juvenile diaries of this writer are constructed with the viewer and posterity very much in mind, that they are difficult to decipher, and that they make the most sense in reverse. In this case, these archival materials seem suspect because they are wilfully created to confound and because inevitably they must be interpreted in the absence of their creator.[37]

The biographer Judith Gill in *Small Ceremonies* says, "They know me at the Public Archives. I've spent hours and hours in these shiny corridors working on my biographical research, exploring filing cabinets, pulling out envelopes, and going through the contents, sometimes finding what I need, but just as often not. And always I am astonished at the sheer volume of trivia being watched over."[38] Thus archives are also seen as trivia, the coddled leftovers and detritus of life. As we know from *Swann*, archives are "fishy," to say the least.

Shields's characterization of archives in these ways indicates a skepticism or at least injects a healthy element of doubt into the endeavour of interpreting archival material. Indications such as these in her work show us that the same wry, smiling humour we are familiar with in much of her fiction may also lie behind a reading of her archival fonds. These doubts about archives in Shields's fiction show us that the interpretation of documents depends on the path and the bent of the interpreter as it did for the scholars of Mary Swann's destroyed bag of fishy "archives." As Shields's fiction has demonstrated so well in works such as *The Stone Diaries*, internal life is a product of individual moments – the cast-offs are left behind, the clues impartial and partial, and the richness of the reality that created them larger than comprehension. In other words, the leftovers may tell us precious little to illuminate life's reality.

Loose note titled "Biography," found amidst manuscript for *Swann* (CSf 1 b.74 f.3)

This flexible and unreliable documentation is also complicated by the unreliability of writing about people, which Shields has elaborated on elsewhere. In one speech as a writer-in-residence, she discusses the difficulty of putting a whole person into fiction. She says, "Often I meet people who say, isn't so-and-so a character rightout [*sic*] of Dickens, why don't you put him in your book, Carol [?] But I know perfectly [*sic*] well that fiction, selective animal that it is, will never be able to swallow in its totality this wonderfully eccentric and colorful personality ... Inevitably there would *have* to be some touching up ... In the end I'd have what most writers settle for, an amalgam, part observation, part imagination."[39] The inability of language to convey people and the inadequacy of documentation are related concerns for biographers, particularly those who appear in Shields's fiction.

In a note made to herself titled "Biography," which is found amidst the early manuscript material for *Swann*, Shields writes of a character (here called Coles) and describes a biographer's interest in a son who was abandoned by an alcoholic father. The note reads in part, "The romantic image of the ostracized parent is too fragile to bear the assault of such a question, and what's left is the appalling gap between a successful life and a failed life, or between what's perceived and what's unknown."[40] A gap exists, then, between a life and its biographical interpretation, as it does between a life and its archival documentation.

In a story that foregrounds the biographer's overlay onto the reality of the writer's life, Edith-Esther is a Shields character who resents being quoted or held to what she said long ago. As is explained in the story, "She understood how careful you had to be with biographers; death by biography – it was a registered disease. Thousands had suffered from it, butchery by entrapment in the isolated moment. The select moment with its carbon lining. Biographers were forever catching you out and reminding you of what you once said. 'But back in 1974 you stated categorically that ...'"[41] These are direct statements in narrative that indicate a perception that research and portrayal of people is faulty and tenuous, and that there is a partial relationship between documentation, life, and writing, leaving the biographer/researcher with only clues to extrapolate from. In Edith-Esther's perception, freezing moments or comments of the living subject and giving certain details unnatural focus is the path of the biographer.[42]

At this point, I can only question my own use of the speeches Shields gave at various earlier stages of her life to illustrate my point in this paper. Given her exploration of the life/writing relationship and the inadequacy of documentation, it is difficult to quote comfortably and directly from the Carol Shields fonds to demonstrate the meaning of these details and the facts of her own life. On first sight, the implication for archives is that they lie close to biographical interpretation, close to an explanation of life and work processes, because they are produced in the living out of these processes. However, as we see in Shields's fiction, the biographical or deductive interpretation of documents is portrayed as flawed, fleeting, tantalizing, Gordian, though in certain senses inevitable. We are cautioned by her own work to know that the written word, the interpretation of others, and the documents and stray flotsam of life have a flexible and partial relationship to a lived reality. And yet the archives is that much more alluring for its associations and references. These references remain deliberately confounded by the approach to documentation, seen in her fiction. Where her narrative explores documentation, Shields the author appears fully aware of the irony of her archives.

56

Catherine Hobbs

NOTES

All archival material cited is from the Carol Shields fonds, LMS–0212, the first accession, 1994–13, or the second accesion, 1997–04; held in the Literary Archives of Library and Archives Canada. Archival material from the Carol Shields fonds is cited in the following manner: Carol Shields fonds, first accession, box 54, file 1, is cited as CSf I b.54 f.1

1 Shields, "Giving Your Literary Papers Away," 43.
2 Manuscript for *The Vortex*, CSf I b.23 f.1 p.1.
3 "Sense of Place" (autobiographical film script), CSf I b.3 f.10, sections 2 and 3. Details of setting also are selected carefully for their particular connotations by Shields, and she goes on in the film to describe why she chose the Manitoba Club as an all-male organization.
4 Speech on being a writer, CSf I 63 f.1, cards 5 and 6.
5 Ibid., cards 8 and 9.
6 "Sense of Place" (autobiographical film script), CSf I b.3 f.10 section 10.
7 First draft of *Larry's Party*, dated 10 July 1995, CSf II b.34 f.1 p.1.
8 "Edith Esther" (drafts with handwritten revisions), CSf II b.40 f.33.
9 Fax from Christopher Potter, 3 Feb. 1993, CSf I b.6 f.35.
10 Correspondence with Mindy Werner, 4 Jan. 1991, Viking Penguin file, CSf I b.17 f.2.
11 Trip diary of Inez Warner: trip to Great Britain, 6 May –12 June 1969, CSf II b.54 f.4 p.6.
12 Ibid., p.3.
13 Ibid., p.52.
14 Shields, *Larry's Party*, 23. The actual diary written by Shields's mother, Inez Warner, is a 5-by–3¼-inch "Collins Mini Memo" bound in red leather with narrow ruled pages.
15 Trip diary of Inez Warner: trip to Great Britain, 6 May 1969–12 June 1969, CSf II b.54 f.4 p.239.
16 Ibid., p.235.
17 "Our Trip," Aunt Edna's diary, 4 Sept. 1924, CSf I b.67 f.8 [first unnumbered page].
18 The references and influences of older women are most certainly also inspired by Shields's long correspondence with Louise Wyatt, a retired teacher and book reviewer in London, Ontario, who corresponded with Shields into her nineties. Wyatt provided details for *The Stone Diaries* and gave detailed feedback on many of Shields's works.

19 First scene of *Thirteen Hands*, described in an e-mail to Susan McPherson Ryan, CSf II b.42 f.1 p.2.

20 Ibid., p.5.

21 E-mail to Anne Shields Giardini, 23 June 1998, CSf II b.12 f.2.

22 Menu and seating plans for *Larry's Party*, CSf II b.37.

23 Hand-drawn maps for *Larry's Party*, CSf II b.36 f.1.

24 Seating plans for *Larry's Party*, CSf II b.37 f. 2,3,4. One of these is missing Polly.

25 Introduction by Blanche Howard to Shields and Howard, *A Celibate Season*, 3.

26 Letter to Bill Richardson, 10 March 1994, CSf I b.51 f.59.

27 "A Celibate Intro" (introduction for book reading of *A Celibate Season*), CSf I b.63 f.20 p.2.

28 Letter from Blanche Howard, 13 Sept. 1983, CSf I b.8 f.25.

29 Both quotations from letter from Blanche Howard, 16 Oct. 1983, CSf I b.8 f.25.

30 Fax to Christopher Potter, 7 March 1993, Fourth Estate file, CSf I b.6 f.25.

31 Fax from Christopher Potter, 18 March 1993, Fourth Estate file, CSf I b.6 f.25.

32 Shields, *Small Ceremonies*, 53.

33 The irony of the Swann Symposium and seeing the Shields's documents in this context was surely not lost on the attendees to the colloquium "Carol Shields et l'extraordinaire."

34 I have translated this quotation in part and taken part from Shields's notes in English, prepared for the French translation. It should be noted that a number of Susanna (Strickland) Moodie's rare early novels have since been obtained by the National Library (now Library and Archives Canada) for its Rare Book Collection.

35 Talk given in Paris concerning *Swann*, CSf I b.63 f.22. My transcription of Shields's English notes and translation of the French version that continues the text.

36 Shields, *Dressing Up for the Carnival*, 177–8.

37 In the early university paper "Three Canadian Women," Shields says, "It has always been acknowledged that diaries, whether intended for publication or not, reveal the side of the writer which he wishes to reveal; just as one turns his most interesting profile to the photographer's lens, the writers of diaries project themselves as they would prefer to be seen." In this document, she clearly outlines the intentionality of diary-writing.

38 Shields, *Small Ceremonies*, 154.

39 Quotation from "Speech on Being a Writer," CSf I b.63 f.1 card 20.

40 Loose note titled "Biography," found amid the manuscript for *Swann*, CSf I b.74 f.3.

41 Shields, *Dressing Up for the Carnival*, 132.

42 No doubt Shields's perceptions of biography come from her work on Susanna
    Moodie. There were early hints of the theme of writing's unclear relationship to
    life in a university paper Shields wrote in 1970s, which touches on Susanna
    Moodie's autobiographical/fictional accounts. In it she writes that "the writer
    knows that the self can never be washed out of his storytelling, just as his creative
    and imaginative impulse can never be separated from his personal history ... If one
    subscribes to the theory that it is not a writer's self which is revealed in his writ-
    ing, but a sort of second self, then the onus upon him to distinguish between the
    separate spheres of fiction and autobiography will all but disappear. At the very
    least the boundaries will soften to a less arbitrary and more flexible interpretation.
    Fiction and biography can here be seen to come closer together because each is a
    partial and creative overlay onto life" ("Three Canadian Women: Fiction or Auto-
    biography," university essay, CSf 1 b.60 f.7 p.2). At the end of the writer-in-resi-
    dence speech quoted earlier, Shields said, "But fiction is also one of the most
    rarefied forms of truthtelling. The truth we must leave out of biography, disguised
    perhaps and protected, finds its voice finally in our novels and short stories"
    ("Speech on Being a Writer," CSf 1 b.63 f.1 card 27).

WORKS CITED

Library and Archives Canada, Ottawa. Carol Shields fonds. LMS–0212, Accessions
    1994–13 and 1997–04. In 2003 the fonds included 23 metres of
    correspondence, manuscripts, proofs, and professional and personal
    memorabilia of the author Carol Shields from the period 1954–98. Since that
    time, additional material has been added, dating up to 2002.
Shields, Carol. *Dressing Up for the Carnival*, Toronto: Vintage Canada, 2001.
– "Giving Your Literary Papers Away." *Quill & Quire* 64, no. 11 (1998): 43.
– *Larry's Party*. Toronto: Random House, 1997.
– *Small Ceremonies*. Toronto: Totem, 1978.

3

(Es)Saying It Her Way:
Carol Shields as Essayist

CHRISTL VERDUYN

Carol Shields was widely recognized as a talented, imaginative, and accomplished novelist, playwright, and poet. It is not as well appreciated, however, that she was also an extremely competent and proficient essayist. What attracted her to this form of writing? What was she trying to accomplish in her essays such that she added the genre to her literary repertoire? What was the relationship between her essay-writing and the other genres she practised with so much success?

One of Shields's last and most substantial writing accomplishments was a Penguin Life of Jane Austen. Her decision to take on this project was somewhat surprising, given her views on the limits of the biographical form. Indeed, Shields was asked about this issue directly in a BBC radio interview in 2001. Her reply offers an insight into what attracted her to the essay form. "I thought of it as an essay," Shields explained, "with a biographical spine, and along the way I would talk about novels in general, novels of [Austen's] time, the writer's dilemma, particularly their day to day problems as fiction makers."[1]

This reply points us very much to "Shields territory" – the demands of writing, the details of writers' everyday lives, the exploration of the ordinary and the quotidian. Shields's genius and success lay in her exceptional capacity to synthesize the mundane with the profound and the ordinary with the extraordinary, in compelling, insightful, and satisfying ways. She used the essay form in a unique and expansionary manner.

It offered her another highly flexible mode of writing to reflect on and explore connections and contradictions in human experience. Her particular style of essay-writing represents a kind of symbiosis between the broad essay genre and her personal artistic vision. The essay form lent itself extremely well to her writing skills and, in particular, to her belief in the centrality of story or narrative to life and to its artistic representation. Shields's essays are convincing examples of Graham Good's sense of the essay as a sort of "non-fictional cognate of certain kinds of fiction."[2]

In this chapter I will consider and assess Shields's work as an essayist by focusing on four of her publications: "Eros" in the collection *Desire in Seven Voices* (1999), edited by Lorna Crozier; Shields's "Afterword" in both volumes of *Dropped Threads: What We Aren't Told* (2001, 2003), which she co-edited with Marjorie Anderson; her award-winning biographical essay *Jane Austen* (2001); and "Narrative Hunger and the Overflowing Cupboard" (2003).[3] The chapter will begin by sketching out a theoretical and intellectual context for the consideration and assessment of Shields's work as an essayist. Even a brief exploration of the essay as genre will reveal why, like many writers, Carol Shields was drawn to the form. This introductory framework will allow us to consider her work as an essayist from gender and political perspectives. Shields's use of the essay deftly combines or synthesizes what have historically been two competing historical traditions in essay writing.

THE ESSAY: CONCEPTUAL AND HISTORICAL FRAMEWORK

Assessments of the essay form have been infused with controversy, contradiction, and condescension. Indeed, one of the great ironies of considering the genre is this: while it is widely regarded as inferior in status to the novel, poetry, drama, and other literary forms, its practitioners have included some of the most influential thinkers of all time. Until recently, these practitioners have appeared to be predominantly men. This phenomenon has conferred a particular political resonance upon the essay in some quarters. What is generally accepted, though, is that in its history, evolution, and form, the essay has suffered from a kind of shapelessness. This negative impression – unfair, in many ways – has historical as well as conceptual roots.

The essay as genre has twin origins and adherents, one stemming from a personal and informal French tradition and the other from a more formal and empiricist English tradition. The interplay of these two traditions has generated a dynamic or dialectic, which mirrors the tension between Continental and Anglo-American empirical philosophy, with both negative and positive effects. On the one hand, the tension between the traditions has generated the impression of the essay's shapelessness, alluded to earlier. On the other hand, it has also created tremendous opportunities – political and otherwise – for experimentation and innovation in writing.

The origins of the essay lie in France, and its first practitioner was the sixteenth-century French writer Michel de Montaigne. Indeed, the very word itself – essay – is derived from the French. The verb *essayer* means to try or to attempt something. In 1580 Montaigne published a collection of writings entitled *Essais* in which he "tried" to express in prose his thoughts and feelings on a variety of different subjects. These writings or essays very much comprised an exercise in "giving it a try" or "having a say" on a number of subjects, which gave them a distinctly exploratory feel, form, and character. This style of writing was not unrelated to the substance of the issues or matter being discussed. Indeed, the latter more or less demanded the former. As in other transformative historical epochs, changed circumstances demanded changed modes of analysis and articulation if the new world was to be penetrated with any insight. Montaigne was a writer shaped by the Renaissance and the society in which he lived. His writings examined and interrogated the various political, religious, and scientific paradigm shifts of that era. The essay form allowed him the space and freedom to do so, unconstrained by traditional rules and expectations of writing. Montaigne adopted a highly personal and informal approach, infusing his writing about the era with his own experiences of the changing times. In this way, life and writing, content and form, converged in the new activity of "essaying." Graham Good's characterization effectively evokes this accomplishment: the Montaigne essay comprised "testing and tasting one's own life while experiencing it"; in this way, "the essay [w]as a sample of the self."[4]

Montaigne's essays were very much an exercise in "having a try." They were personal and informal in style. In this, his essays marked a radical departure from the prescribed forms of classical rhetoric of his day. What made the essays compelling and convincing – what gave them their "authority" – was the very experience upon which the text was based, which in turn encouraged a certain kind of format. The essays had a more "natural" form. This defied the limiting demands and constraints of traditional writing, such as unity in format, consistency in presentation and argumentation, and even relevance to the moment. The new form of writing was decidedly experimental for the times. It submitted to the essayist's flow of thought at the moment. Thus it embraced spontaneity in expression and in formulation. The essay offered liberation from a linear format and argumentation and provided a more free-form presentation that allowed unconventional connections of facts, arguments, and speculations. Indeed, the essay's speculative character was a substantive feature in itself. The essay did not have to bring "closure" to a subject. The exploration itself could be the substance of the essay. The emphasis was squarely on process and exploration, rather than a necessary conclusion.

Montaigne's essay style has come into and gone out of favour over the years. That it has done so is not surprising for such a radical and personal approach. On the one hand, critics have offered both formal and political objections. Many have complained that the Montaigne essay is self-indulgent – overly focused on the personal and under-concerned about facts. Others have seen the personal essay as being essentially apolitical and insufficiently attentive to the larger social, economic, and political forces that should inform any argument or assessment if it is to have any relevance or use. On the other hand, many have championed and supported the Montaigne essay form as an essentially radical form of writing. French feminists of the twentieth century, for example, such as Hélène Cixous and Luce Irigaray, practised a Montaigne-style essay. Germany's T.W. Adorno saw "the essay's freedom from specialization and genre boundaries as one way to destabilize [these] hierarchical divisions."[5] Thus Montaigne set the stage for the personal, polemical form of essay, as practised by Continental thinkers and activists to the present day.

Towards the end of the sixteenth century, England's Sir Francis Bacon tried his hand at the new essay form in a very different manner. His *Essays* (1597) were constructed in a diametrically opposite way to those of Montaigne. Instead of starting from personal reaction to changed or new circumstances, Bacon focused on the observable facts that made up these situations. His essays comprised sets of empirical observations that described with ostensible scientific accuracy the unfolding new world. These essays were to be offered to readers to help them understand their environment before reacting to it and making consequential decisions. In this way, the Bacon essay comprised advice and counsel to his contemporaries. This approach was in stark contrast to Montaigne's personal, open-ended speculations. A Montaigne essay might or might not have been "useful" to the reader, given its speculative nature, which typically drew no conclusions or calls to action. In contrast, Bacon's essays were essentially utilitarian exercises with a motive: to take the facts of the situation and draw a definitive, defensible conclusion. This conclusion would in turn delineate a line of action. The Bacon essay, then, aimed to provide guidance to improve individuals' conditions and attain their rational ends. The content or purpose of the essay demanded a different style. Where Montaigne's essays were personal and spontaneous, Bacon's took a more "detached" and scientific approach that required a degree of discipline and rigour to lead to a sought-for conclusion.

Ultimately, the two essay forms had very different purposes or strategies. The Montaigne essay was personally motivated, while the Bacon essay had a utilitarian public purpose. As Kirklighter suggests, "The didactic nature of [Bacon's] essays moves away from the inconclusive skepticism that pervades Montaigne's form. Bacon's essays were meant to reach a public audience that would act on his word."[6] In this sense, Bacon's essays had a more direct political intent than Montaigne's essays of "self-revelation."

To sum up, by the end of the sixteenth century there were two contrasting or competing ways of "trying to say" something in a new writing format, two ways of using the essay form to assess and evaluate new circumstances and prepare a call to action. The French-style essay can be characterized as personal, intimate, informal, or conversational. The English essay can be described as impersonal, objective, methodical, rational, and pedagogic. These are, of course, ideal types, and even Montaigne and Bacon themselves did not remain completely bound by their features. For example, Montaigne drew on empirical evidence and observation to argue the merits of experience. Similarly, Bacon resisted oppressive literary traditions; his essays were based on objective study and not the religious authority that formed the foundation for claims about moral conduct in earlier eras.[7] At bottom, both essayists were motivated by and interested in the same thing: how to generate knowledge that was derived from experience and observation rather than from preordained doctrine.

THE ESSAY: EVOLVING CHARACTER AND PRACTICE

Four centuries later, both the Montaigne and the Bacon essay traditions retain their modern adherents and practitioners. Over the years, intellectuals and activists around the world and across social circumstances have embraced the essay form to articulate personal response and advance personal insight or to assess circumstances and issue calls to action. How might this extensive, rich, and varied essay-writing experience be summarized?

A good starting point is to assess the critical issue of the essay's ostensible "shapelessness." Indeed, one can point to an almost universal observation consistent across the vast body of literature about the essay. Most observers agree that the essay is a very difficult genre to define. McCarthy characterizes it as an "enigmatic and elusive genre which seems to defy definition."[8] How can one make sense of something that is simultaneously associated with "the facetious, the trivial, and the anecdotal on the one hand and with the learned treatise and useful, effective expository writing on the other"?[9]

Some analysts have attempted to construct a typology or analytical framework for situating and analyzing the essay form. These attempts have had mixed and varying results. Some work has been done to create a continuum of genres that stretches from the essay to the novel, the play, and the poem.[10] Others have attempted to locate the essay within the poetics of French feminist practice, understood as "a movement of interweaving concepts that demand neither origin nor end, completeness nor continuity. The essay recognizes that there is no single reality but rather realities that are discontinuous and brittle, and that people are not 'lords and masters' of creation."[11]

It might be fair to conclude that the essay can be considered a non-genre, or a "non-generic" genre – in essence, an anti-genre. This characterization attributes to the essay form a powerful dialectical possibility. On the one hand, the essay is seen or depicted as a "lesser" genre because it cannot easily be marketed or branded as a specific form, with qualities, rules, and so on that highlight and confer authority upon mainstream genres. On the other hand, the absence of generic rules or qualities offers limitless possibilities and freedoms; providing the essay form with opportunities for innovation and transcendence.

The essay, then, encompasses numerous and different kinds of writing. Succinctly put, "the essay is the most adaptable of all forms."[12] This attribute in turn makes the form far more accessible than other literary genres. Indeed, many have characterized the essay as potentially the most democratic form of writing, because the genre lends itself to variation on all levels, including form, content, and purpose. First, the essay form is open to consideration of different kinds of material or substance, either in the subject matter being addressed or in the facts/evidence/observations/experiences used as the content of the essay. Second, it is open to different styles or modes of expression, as well as different kinds of argumentation and reasoning. Third, the essay is allowed to have different functions or to pursue different purposes. It can aim to persuade and convince or to present a story or history, real or imagined. It can take the form of a play or that of dialogue, poetry, or meditation. The essay can be dramatic, ironic, even "essayistic."[13] Good has commented that the initial thrust of the essay was "in the direction of formlessness."[14] Butrym, too, has remarked on the essay's ability to "draw us by indirection out of ourselves." The "formlessness" of the essay form is arguably one of its strengths, permitting individuals to "speak to each other across the boundaries of our narrower selves."[15]

The essay lends itself to a range of opportunities, from intellectual practice of the highest formal discipline and elegance to the most personal, soulful articulation in an open-ended and spontaneous manner. Good thus concludes that "the essay is neither an élite form nor a mass form ... it is a democratic form, open to anyone."[16] Kirklighter takes this point a step further. She extends her evaluation of the essay form across the traditional western European and American "borders" of the genre to evaluate and explore Latin American essay practice. "The leaders in Latin American essay scholarship consider the essay whether it be personal or not as paramount to understanding the historical, cultural, and political complexities of these nations,"[17] Kirklighter reports. In Latin America the essay has comprised a form of political and social writing that aims to further democratic changes.

The democratic character of the essay form is not to be confused with the particular substance or practice of the essay. The genre has been used for reactionary as well as for progressive purposes and by elitists as well as democrats. In *The Politics of the Essay: Feminist Perspectives*, editors Ruth-Ellen Boetcher Joeres and Elizabeth Mittman challenge the exuberantly over-ambitious claim that the essay is non-elite. The essay has been marked by elitism, they argue, not only of social class but also of gender. In this regard, where gender and class are considered, the essay has had no different a historical track record than other genres. For the first three hundred years of its existence as a genre, Joeres and Mittman assert, the essay lay firmly outside the domain of the woman writer and her concerns. That said, they note that the genre has been malleable, accessible, and open enough to ultimately allow non-traditional writers such as women and minorities to use the essay's form. In their practice, these essayists have contributed to the transformation or extension of the genre to meet their personal and political needs.[18]

Over the past century in particular, women essayists and women's essays have begun to be acknowledged. What is particularly intriguing is the extent to which the essay form has provided a good "fit" or practice for gendered writing. In simple terms, the more personal, informal style of the Montaigne essay has been characterized as "feminine," while the rational, objective Baconian essay has been aligned with the masculine. In this manner, notwithstanding their historical exclusion from essay practice, the essay form lends itself to the discourse and practice of feminist writers. As Joeres observes:

Whereas essayists, the actors and agents, are almost always defined very clearly as "masculine," the essay itself is placed over and over again into a space that is uncannily feminine, at least as the qualities adhering to the "feminine" have been defined since the eighteenth century. Essays are called a mixture of anecdote, description, and opinion. Essays are said to focus on a little world, on details. Essays seem, according to Theodor Adorno, to form patterns of relationships "rather than a straight line of necessary consequences ..." Essays stress process rather than product.[19]

The essay sits on a seam between acculturated assumptions and social constructs about women and women's writing and what seems actually to characterize women's essays in general. The latter is not easily pinpointed or proved, as Joeres and Mittman point out.[20] Thus, for example, such a well-known essayist as Virginia Woolf may be considered to "essay" in the Montaigne mode. But women write many different styles of essays. The Latin American tradition of essay-writing by women understands the form as primarily a political instrument.[21] This is a far cry from the view of the "feminine" essay that is highly introspective or deeply removed from the hard edges of daily reality.

To sum up, the essay form has become a kind of anti-genre, defying rules and regulations. This space allows freedom to "try things out" in terms of the form of writing, the subject matter addressed, and the purpose of the writing. The essay form's accessibility has created a space to investigate and interrogate changing conditions and circumstances, where new content requires new form and purpose in writing. This accessibility has offered productive opportunities for non-traditional writers such as women to explore and address their condition and to propose change and action.

Within the Canadian context, women writers have taken up this opportunity to great effect. The Canadian literary scene boasts a rich and lengthy female tradition of essay-writing. This extends from the writings of Emily Carr, Nellie McClung, Margaret Laurence, Adele Wiseman, Jane Rule, and Miriam Waddington to more recent collections by women such as Dionne Brand, Di Brandt, Nicole Brossard, Elly Danica, Smaro Kamboureli, Lee Maracle, Daphne Marlatt, Nourbese Philip, Gail Scott, Lola Lemire Tostevin, Aritha van Herk, Bronwen Wallace, and Phyllis Webb. Recently, two of Canada's foremost women writers added major essay publications to their oeuvres, both in 2001: Margaret Atwood's *Negotiating with the Dead: A Writer on Writing* and Carol Shields's *Jane Austen*. Essay-writing by Canadian women writers has been and continues to be integral to their work. This dimension of their writing comprises an ongoing challenge to literary traditions and to the societal status quo alike. Indeed, Canadian women's essay-writing deserves as much critical attention as their texts of fiction and poetry.[22] This is certainly the case for Carol Shields.

CAROL SHIELDS AS ESSAYIST

Where does Carol Shields fit in this long tradition of "essaying"? To what extent did she take advantage of the opportunities provided by the essay form? And how did she make use of the genre, in terms of form, content, and purpose?

The second of these questions is fairly straightforward, although readers may be surprised by the extent of Shields's use of the essay form. A search of the Shields fonds at Library and Archives Canada reveals that the author "essayed" extensively.[23] Not surprisingly, given their form and the continuing low authority of the essay, most of Shields's essays did not appear in academic journals or in "serious" publication outlets. Many of her essays were presented as conference papers or public talks, and they remain unpublished (and ready for an edited collection!). Others were published, albeit in popular and mainstream venues such as magazines and newspapers. Altogether, Shields's essays provide excellent, evocative examples of the author as essayist, "having a try" or "a say" on a variety of topics.

The four texts selected for consideration here – "Eros" in *Desire* (1999); Shields's "Afterword" in both volumes of *Dropped Threads: What We Aren't Told* (2001, 2003); *Jane Austen* (2001); and "Narrative Hunger and the Overflowing Cupboard" (2003) – illustrate how she used the essay form on a variety of topics, in various ways, and for multiple purposes. By way of foreshadowing and illustration of the cross-bordering involved in the essays, this section begins with an analysis of Shields's piece entitled "Eros." First published in Lorna Crozier's collection *Desire in Seven Voices*, "Eros" was subsequently included in Shields's collection of short stories *Dressing Up for the Carnival* (2000). This publication history reveals how the author made use of the essay form in a "de-regulated" way, drawing as readily on fiction as on fact. Shields moved easily between the Montaigne and Bacon forms of essaying – indeed, combining or synthesizing the two traditions.

"Eros"

The first example of Shields's work as an essayist is her contribution to a collection of works exploring the topic of desire. The collection includes essays by Susan Musgrave, Evelyn Lau, Lorna Crozier herself, Bonnie Burnard, Shani Mootoo, Dionne Brand, and finally Carol Shields. Shields contributes what editor Crozier terms a "fictionalized essay."[24] She chooses an imaginary situation to address the theme of desire, which presents a variety of analytical and methodological challenges. The purpose of "Eros" is to explore desire in more than a bloodless or analytical way, drawing on real-life details and experiences to make a transcendental point. In the process, "Eros" transforms the ordinary into the extraordinary and the fictional into reality.

In the essay, Ann and Benjamin have come to Paris to rescue what has become a passionless marriage. Like others in the hotel where they are staying, their window opens onto an inner courtyard. Their time in Paris is disappointingly sedate until the last day. Through the open windows, they hear a woman cry out in orgasm. A "half-singing, half-weeping, wordless release"[25] seems to block out all of the competing and distracting mundane sounds of the hotel, of Paris, and indeed of France. Like a call to action, it triggers the reawakening of Ann's and Benjamin's desire for each other. Shields writes: "This must be it, this force that funnelled through the open air, travelling through the porous masonry and entering her [Ann's] veins ... She imagined that each room on the air shaft was similarly transformed, that men and women were coming together ecstatically as she and Benjamin were doing" (165).

Even a brief excerpt from "Eros" illustrates how Shields makes use of the transformative work of imagination. She regularly calls on the imagination to work on or process the observable and mundane facts of everyday life to the cause of action and explanation. She is Baconian in that she uses observation and the real to draw a conclusion and to offer a utilitarian call to action. At the same time Shields follows Montaigne, for she uses language and personal imagination to transform the ordinary facts of life into something extraordinary – a speculative and open-ended vision. "The combined sounds they made," she writes, "formed an erotic random choir, whose luminous, unmoored music was spreading skyward over the city. This was all they ever needed for such perfect happiness, this exquisite permission, a stranger's morning cry" (165).

Of course, writers typically draw upon their imagination and command of language to transform reality for some purpose. This is a writer's stock and trade, practised to differing degrees of skill and success. What is remarkable in Shields's writing is how this strategy of transformation is as characteristic of her essays as of her fiction. "Eros" is a powerful and evocative example. Recalling that long-ago morning in Paris, Ann is seated at a friend's dinner table. Her hand extends beneath the table to rest in the crotch of the guest beside her, a man she scarcely knows. Earlier in the evening, Ann had taken issue with the man's Baconian position that the sexual act required an authoritative verbal gloss in today's world. "These days explication is required," the man had insisted, "in order to sanction the commands of the blood" (146). For Ann, this is an old-fashioned and retrograde position, and yet she finds herself connected to the man and "part of the blissful and awakened world" (166).

"Eros" contains all the elements of the essay from both Bacon and Montaigne and beyond, as characterized above. In the first instance, its purpose is to address new territory or circumstances that have not typically been addressed so openly, in particular women's erotic desire. Its mode of operation combines the objective or descriptive – the facts of everyday life – with feelings and imagination – the personal. And it addresses the topic in a speculative way while drawing a conclusion and prescription. The notion of being awake to the world is a theme that recurs in Shields's writing.[26] It complements her determination "to say what had once been unsayable."[27] This was the project of the enormously successful two-volume *Dropped Threads: What We Aren't Told*. With this project, Shields the essayist expanded her practice to editing the essays of other women.

Dropped Threads: What We Aren't Told

Shields edited *Dropped Threads* (2001 and 2003) with her friend Marjorie Anderson with a view to exploring new territory – the "what" in life that we are not told. Their focus was women's experience of reality, articulated in an open and collective way. The ultimate aim of the collection was to open up and understand the world as "told" by women.

For Shields, this project required a different form if the new territory was to be explored to effect. She wanted women's experiences and lives to be presented in a fluid shape, which itself would say something about women's lives. A collection of short essays was the ideal solution. *Dropped Threads* afforded "the apprehension of a structure," Shields wrote in her "Afterword" to the 2001 collection,[28] a shape with enough fluidity and form to (es)say something about women's lives. In effect, the volume is an example of the strategy adopted by Montaigne, to use the essay form in a highly personal and "feeling" manner as a way of breaking through into understanding and (self) discovery. "There were the things our mothers hadn't voiced," Shields wrote, "the subjects our teachers had neglected, the false prophetic warnings (*tempus fugit*, for example) we had been given and the fatal silence surrounding particular areas of anxiety or happiness. Why weren't we told?" (1:246). Replies poured in. "The essays expressed perplexity at life's offerings: injury and outrage that could not be voiced (*Woman, hold thy tongue*), expectations that could not be met, fulfillment arriving in unexpected places, the need for touchness, the beginning of understanding, the beginning of being able to say what had once been unsayable. Or, in my case, the apprehension of a structure that gave fluidity and ease" (1:346–7).

The short essay allowed women, many of them first-time essayists, to "try out" writing, to use the open-ended, fluid form to break through and explore, analyze and critique, their world. This is the achievement of the essays in *Dropped Threads*. Women from a variety of walks of life contributed to the volume.[29] Their varied experiences constitute the empirical (Baconian) facts of the subject matter. Their essays embrace a wide variety of themes, issues, and (Baconian) conclusions, as the essayists express the surprise of self-discovery, insights, and truths, or as Shields put it, "the beginning of being able to say" (1:347). For these writers, this is also the beginning of the essay.

Dropped Threads, then, combines elements of both the Bacon and the Montaigne essay strategies. This experiment in essaying recalls Butrym's observation about the genre's ability to "draw us by indirection out of ourselves ... [to] speak to each other across the boundaries of our narrower selves."[30] The very form of the collection allows a substantive exploration and far-reaching readership.

Jane Austen

Shields's award-winning *Jane Austen* is an extended biographical essay that employs the same empirical evidence used by the biographer, but in a different way. Shields starts with the facts – dates, situations, events, and so on – and transforms them into an imaginative narrative and speculative form. This process allows her to draw a conclusion and to bring resolution, meaning, and insight to the substance of everyday life. In this way, she combines Baconian empiricism with the speculation of the Montaigne method. She transforms the personal and empirical into the collective and moves from the speculative to a conclusion. This study of the writer Jane Austen adopts the fluid form noted by Shields in *Dropped Threads* and allows a remarkable and innovative interplay between imagination and facts.

Shields begins her essay on Jane Austen's life and literary work with an account of a paper that she and her daughter Anne Giardini delivered at a conference in 1996. The paper focused on "the politics of a glance."[31] The authors argued that, through the "glance" of her characters, Austen was able to inscribe the political and historical background of her times, which some Austen critics claimed was lacking in her work. For Shields and Giardini, Austen was clearly and deeply engaged with her time and place, her eyes wide open on the world.[32] The glance serves as a double metaphor and framework. On the one hand, it demonstrated the fact that women lived – and still live – constrained lives in the world. On the other hand, this reality does not imply that they were unaware of their circumstances. The glance is the medium through which this awareness is conveyed.

In her subsequent long essay about Jane Austen for the Penguin Lives series, Shields departs from traditional biographical practice. Austen biographers typically have read the facts of her life (birth, travels, death, and so on) into the substance of her novels. "In so doing," Shields comments, "the assumption is made that fiction flows directly from a novelist's experience rather than from her imagination" (11). Shields proposes instead to "read *into* [her] own resistance, instead of seeking a confirmation or denial embedded in the fiction" (11). The resistance she has in mind is not entirely clear to the reader early on in her analysis. It quickly becomes apparent, however, that the imagination plays a key role. As noted above, Shields has been celebrated for the way in which she uses and transforms the ordinary and everyday in her fiction. In her essay on Jane Austen's life, she builds substantially on the imagined and imaginative to transform the facts into something greater. This process can be seen in the very language of the essay.

An early historical fact or event in Austen's life will illustrate Shields's technique. In the context of presenting some basic information about Austen's date and place of birth, physical appearance, and so on, Shields turns to two topics that she favours in her own writing: family and home life. Austen's childhood spurs Shields's imagination. Jane's mother, Cassandra Austen, placed her babies with a local family until they could walk and talk. For Shields, this fact has meaning beyond the empirical reality:

It can be *imagined* that the abrupt shift from mother's breast to alien household made a profound emotional impact on the child. This early expulsion from home was the first of many, and it is *doubtful* whether she had much to say about such later separations, just as she had little power over her other domestic arrangements ... Her fictional expression can be *imagined* as a smooth flow of narrative deriving from her confined reality, but a flow that is interrupted by jets of alternate possibility, the moment observed and then repositioned and recharged. (13, emphases added)

This passage parallels the excerpt from "Eros" discussed above. It replicates the textual movement from factual reality (babies fostered out; the limited power of women of Jane Austen's class, time, and place) to imagined and imaginative thought. From the constraining confines of reality, Shields produces a smooth narrative flow. From a moment observed – a glance – the world is repositioned and recharged. This is the pattern and technique that she uses to create textual movement and to generate insight. Upholding the pattern is the author's transformative prose. *Jane Austen* abounds in phrases that hold facts at arm's length and transforms them in the process: "it can be imagined" (13); "it is doubtful" (13); "it can be thought" (14); "May or may not have" (18); "on the whole it can be said that" (21): "we can only guess" (29); "[it] can be assumed" (29); "[it] may be imagined" (32); "must have" (34); "may have" (34); "it cannot have been a surprise" (38); "it must have offered" (38); "must at times have imagined and projected"(39); "it is commonly believed" (82); "there can be little question" (99); "it might be thought" (102); "everything we know of her during this period [the middle of her life] is a guessing game, a question that leads around and around [to an even greater silence]" (110).

This is not to suggest that Shields's biographical essay on Austen is short on facts or information. Indeed, it still carries a full factual load.

The concrete, empirical reality of Austen's situation in life is clearly delineated and firmly established. Like other women of her circumstances, Austen was dependent on the goodwill of family and friends for life's needs. Her writing depicts women trapped by social barriers and barred from active lives. Shields's essay shows that such conditions applied in Jane Austen's own life as well. Thus there is considerable biographical substance as traditionally understood. But there is something more substantial and consequential as well: the way in which Shields uses the interplay of fact and imagination to push the study into deeper waters.

Like the two volumes of *Dropped Threads*, Shields's *Jane Austen* sold extremely well. It met with the favour of critics (e.g., jurors of the 2002 Charles Taylor Prize for Literary Non-Fiction, which it won) as well as mainstream readers. Readers everywhere seem to find a great deal of satisfaction in what Shields's writing often offers, including her essay on Jane Austen: a resolution of the day-to-day, with all its petty demands and details, and the world of the imagination, with its promise and pleasure. There is comfort and reassurance in such resolutions – for readers as for characters: Ann and Benjamin resolving to revive their relationship in a Paris hotel; Jane Austen pole-vaulting class prejudice through reading and writing. Like Shields and through her writing, the reader resists dissolution and the defeats incumbent on the acceptance of dichotomy. In her essays as in her fiction, Shields resolves dichotomy by transforming the ordinary into the extraordinary.

"Narrative Hunger and the Overflowing Cupboard"

The final essay under consideration here, "Narrative Hunger and the Overflowing Cupboard,"[33] offers an exceptional insight into the purpose of Shields's writing and how and why she used the essay form. This essay also suggests why writing is itself the subject of so much of her work, a theme that lends itself particularly well to the essay form. Finally, "Narrative Hunger and the Overflowing Cupboard" very clearly inverts the typical fictional narrative, turning facts in on themselves to form a speculative narrative. In raw form, this process illustrates how Shields uses the essay genre to take empirical facts and transform them through speculation into wide-reaching conclusions.

Her point of departure in "Narrative Hunger and the Overflowing Cupboard" is the sight of a street person in Paris. A man sits on the city sidewalk with a sign around his neck that reads, "J'ai faim" (I am hungry).

An hour later, the essayist sees the man eating a large sandwich. She reacts first as a writer and lover of language and remarks that the sign should be corrected to "J'ai eu faim" (I was hungry). On second thought, though, it occurs to her that she is seeing something else altogether. What she sees is "a man momentarily satisfied but conscious of further hunger to come, and gesturing also, perhaps, toward an enlarged or existential hunger, toward a coded message, a threaded notation, an orderly account or story that would serve as a witness to his place in the world" (19). This passage evokes the strategic purpose and character of the essay genre as Shields practised it: an account or story that serves as witness to the world. Like the preceding examples, "Narrative Hunger and the Overflowing Cupboard" privileges the narrative component of the account as Shields reflects on the human need for story. People have a natural, healthy longing for story, she maintains, from letters to Ann Landers to obituaries in the newspaper, from primary school texts to civilization's most prized pieces of writing.

For Shields, narrative is all-important. It is the necessary ingredient both of life and of writing – essays included. Form and matter in Shields's essay-writing are not limited to empirical description or the manipulation of observable facts. Her essays move fluidly into the realm of fiction, and she makes ready use of the tools and techniques of fiction-writing, including characters, dilemmas, metaphor, the narrative pause, exaggeration, word-work or language, and imagination. There is no irreconcilable difference between fact and fiction, between the observable and the speculative in Shields's essays. Hunger here is both "real" and the substance of the narrative, in a manner akin to how hunger exists even when cupboards overflow with food. In her essays Shields discounts and discourages the acceptance of conventional wisdom and the received notion of the dichotomy between reality and fiction. She perceives instead that fiction is not strictly mimetic. In "Narrative Hunger and the Overflowing Cupboard" she declares that fiction springs out of and illuminates the world, rather than mirroring it back to us. Narrative, she asserts, "questions experience, repositions experience, expands or contracts experience, rearranges experience, dramatizes experience, [and] brings, without apology, colour, interpretation and political selection" (24). This is a compelling description not only of narrative but also of Shields's conception of the essay. Narrative, she declares in this essay, gets "*inside reality* rather than *getting reality right*" (35).

For Shields, then, an essay may draw as comfortably and usefully on fiction as it does on fact, whether the subject matter is Jane Austen or desire or narrativity. This feature of her essay-writing allows her to pursue her fascination and faith in writing itself. It accounts for the fact that so many of her essays have writing as their main focus. Shields's essays regularly provide her with opportunities to (es)say something about writing and writers and the details of their own daily lives. In this way they assert a wholehearted affirmation of – indeed, insistence upon – the centrality of narrative in life and in writing. This affirmation extends to her essay-writing as well. For Shields, this exercise and articulation takes full advantage of the freedom and opportunity provided by the essay form.

CONCLUSION

Shields's accomplishments as an essayist are considerable though generally under-acknowledged. On the one hand, they offer a number of transparent insights into what she was trying to do as a writer and how she accomplished her objectives. On the other hand, the substance and strategies of her essays are as compelling and in many ways as satisfying as her fiction.

The essay form offers writers freedom and opportunity – in how they write, in the subjects they choose and observe, and in the purpose of their writing. The realm of the essay can reach from the world of Montaigne to the world of Bacon, from feelings to facts, from the subjective to the objective, from spontaneity to discipline, from speculation to science, from dreaming to action. Carol Shields's essays comprise all of the above. They synthesize the approaches set out by Montaigne and Bacon in intriguing and innovative ways, typically using fiction to illustrate facts in the aim of finding resolution. A central reason why she was attracted to the essay genre was that it allowed her greater freedom, particularly to explore the nature of writing itself.

NOTES

1 Mark Lawson, "Interview with Carol Shields," *Front Row*, BBC Radio 4, 6 March 2001, 7:15 p.m. Quoted in Faye Hammill, "My Own Life Will Never Be Enough for Me: Carol Shields as Biographer [Jane Austen]," *American Review of Canadian Studies* 32, no. 1 (spring 2002): 143–148.

2 Early in his study of the genre, *The Observing Self*, Good discusses the essay as "a sort of fiction, in the context of the novel" (12), "a non-fictional cognate of certain kinds of fiction" (13).

3 Archival copy, dated 15 March 1995, later revised 31 August 1995 and delivered
   as an address at Hanover College, 26 September 1996. I heard a version of the
   essay as a keynote speech at the Nordic Association for Canadian Studies conference in Reykjavik, Iceland, in August 1999. A final version of the essay is featured
   in Eden and Goertz, *Carol Shields, Narrative Hunger, and the Possibilities of Fiction*.
4 Good, *Observing Self*, 32.
5 Kirklighter, *Traversing the Democratic Borders of the Essay*, 3.
6 Ibid., 10.
7 Good, *Observing Self*, 46.
8 McCarthy, *Crossing Boundaries*, ix.
9 Butrym, *Essays on the Essay*, 4.
10 See Scholes and Klaus, *Elements of the Essay*.
11 Brugmann, "Between the Lines," 75.
12 Dobree, *English Essayists*, 47.
13 Scholes and Klaus, *Elements of the Essay*.
14 Good, *Observing Self*, 1.
15 Butrym, *Essays on the Essay*, 1.
16 Good, *Observing Self*, 186.
17 Kirklighter, *Traversing the Democratic Borders of the Essay*, 4.
18 Joeres and Mittman, *Politics of the Essay*, 2–3.
19 Ibid., 19–20.
20 Ibid., 16.
21 See Kirklighter, *Traversing the Democratic Borders of the Essay*.
22 When, in April 1997, *Toronto Star* literary reviewer Bert Archer complained that
   he could not remember the last time he had read a good essay published in Canada, he apparently had not been reading the essays of the country's women writers. See Bert Archer, "The Art of the Essay," *Toronto Star*, 5 April 1997, M16.
   "Essay writing is an art and a skill," Archer stated, lamenting what he saw as a lack
   of good essayists in Canada.
23 Shields, "Giving Your Literary Papers Away"; "Framing the Structure of a Novel";
   "Making Words/Finding Stories"; "What's in a Picture"; "The Personal Library";
   "Leaving the Brick House Behind"; "Jane Austen: Images of the Body"; "Creative
   Writing Courses"; "'Thinking Back through Our Mothers'"; "Marian Engel
   Award Acceptance Speech 1990"; "News from Another Country"; "A View from
   the Edge of the Edge" (in this volume).
24 Crozier, *Desire*, 27.
25 Shields, "Eros," 164.
26 This is a topic worth exploring further. Speaking with Ann Dowsett Johnston
   about writing *Unless* (*Maclean's* 115, no. 15 [15 April 2002]: 48–51), Shields

remarked how she was "more at ease with writing this novel than with others. Cancer makes one serious, and awake." Speaking earlier with Jennifer Jackson ("'Soft-spoken Subversive' Doing What She Loves," *Kingston-Whig Standard*, 13 March 2001), Shields observed that "this state of being awake [following the birth of her first child, at the age of twenty-two, which snapped her out of a 'rather sleepy girlhood'] spread to the rest of my life and, I believe, made me more alert, more perceptive, more aware of the shades of feeling, of the large and small collisions of personality." Earlier still, "in her 1996 address at the graduation ceremonies for the Balmoral Hall School for Girls in Winnipeg, Shields, as Lesley Hughes recounted in *Chatelaine*, stated ... 'Just wake up and be yourself'" (quoted in *Contemporary Canadian Biographies*, August 1997).

27 *Dropped Threads* 1: 347.

28 Ibid., 347.

29 The contributors include writers, academics, ranchers, politicians, homemakers, journalists, and lawyers.

30 Butrym, *Essays on the Essay*, 1.

31 See Shields's 15 March 1995 draft of "Narrative Hunger and the Overflowing Cupboard" (LAC, Carol Shields fonds) for more on "the glance": "Such a wealth of material to draw on, but never ... quite ... enough. And never quite accurate either, glancing off the epic of human experience rather than reflecting it back to us" (4). The opening image of this essay – a Parisian street person with a sign that reads "J'ai faim" around his neck – seems to anticipate the narrator's daughter in *Unless*.

32 Shields, 15 March 1995 draft of "Narrative Hunger and the Overflowing Cupboard," 4.

33 In Eden and Goertz, *Carol Shields, Narrative Hunger, and the Possibilities of Fiction*, 19–36.

WORKS CITED

Brugmann, Margaret. "Between the Lines: On the Essayistic Experiments of Hélène Cixous in 'The Laugh of the Medusa.'" In *The Politics of the Essay: Feminist Perspectives*, ed. Joeres Ruth-Ellen Boetcher and Elizabeth Mittman, 73–84. Bloomington and Indianapolis: Indiana University Press, 1993.

Butrym, Alexander J., ed. *Essays on the Essay: Redefining the Genre*. Athens and London: The University of Georgia Press, 1989.

Crozier, Lorna, ed. *Desire in Seven Voices*. Vancouver: Douglas & McIntyre, 1999.

Dobrée, Bonamy. *English Essayists*. London: Collins [n.d.]

Eden, Edward, and Dee Goertz, eds. *Carol Shields, Narrative Hunger, and the Possibilities of Fiction*. Toronto: University of Toronto Press, 2003.

Good, Graham. The *Observing Self: Rediscovering the Essay*. London and New
    York: Routledge, 1988.
Joeres, Ruth-Ellen Boetcher, and Elizabeth Mittman, eds. *The Politics of the Essay:
    Feminist Perspectives*. Bloomington and Indianapolis: Indiana University Press,
    1993.
Kirklighter, Cristina. *Traversing the Democratic Borders of the Essay*. New York:
    State University of New York Press, 2002.
Lynch, Gerald, and David Rampton, eds. *The Canadian Essay*. Ottawa: University
    of Ottawa Press, 1991.
McCarthy, John A. *Crossing Boundaries: A Theory and History of Essay Writing in
    German 1680–1815*. Philadelphia: University of Pennsylvania Press, 1989.
Scholes, Robert, and Carl H. Klaus. *Elements of the Essay*. New York: Oxford
    University Press, 1969.
Shields, Carol. "Art of Darkness, World of Wealth" Rev. of *When the Sons of
    Heaven Meet the Daughters of the Earth* by Fernanda Eberstadt. *Globe and Mail*,
    15 March 1997, D14.
– "Creative Writing Courses: A Lecture Given in Trier, April 1990." (LAC, Carol
    Shields fonds, first accession, B. 63 f.12 p.87).
– "Eros." In Crozier, *Desire in Seven Voices*.
– "Fiction or Autobiography," *Atlantis* 4, no. 1 (1978): 49–54.
– "Framing the Structure of a Novel." *The Writer* 111, no. 7 (1998): 3–6.
– "Giving Your Literary Papers Away." *Quill & Quire* 64, no. 11 (1998): 43.
– "Harvard Seminar: A View from the Edge of the Edge." (LAC, Carol Shields
    fonds, second accession f–8 p. 90).
– *Jane Austen*. Penguin Lives series. New York: Viking, 2001.
– "Jane Austen: Images of the Body: No Fingers, No Toes." (1991) (LAC, Carol
    Shields fonds, first accession B. 63 f.16 p.87); later in *Persuasions: Journal of the
    Jane Austen Society of North American* 13 (16 Dec. 1991): 132–7.
– and Marjorie Anderson, eds. *Dropped Threads: What We Aren't Told*. Toronto:
    Vintage Canada, 2001.
– *Dropped Threads 2: More of What We Aren't Told*. Toronto: Vintage Canada,
    2003.
– "Leaving the Brick House Behind: Margaret Laurence and the Loop of
    Memory" (26 September 1991) (LAC, Carol Shields fonds, first accession f.24
    p.84); later in *Ranam: Recherches anglaises et nord-américaines* 24 (1991): 75–7.
– "Making Words/Finding Stories." *Journal of Business Administration* 24
    (1996–98): 36–52.
– "Marian Engel Award Acceptance Speech 1990." (LAC, Carol Shields fonds,
    first accession f–13 p.87).

– "Narrative Hunger and the Overflowing Cupboard." In *Carol Shields, Narrative Hunger, and the Possibilities of Fiction*, ed. Edward Eden and Dee Goertz, 19–36. Toronto: University of Toronto Press, 2003.

– "News from Another Country." In *The Second Macmillan Anthology* (Toronto: Macmillan); reprinted in *How Stories Mean*, ed. John Metcalf and J.R. Struthers, 91–3. Erin, ON: The Porcupine's Quill, 1993.

– "The Personal Library." *Globe and Mail*, October 1992. (LAC, Carol Shields fonds, first accession B 62 f.34 p.85).

– "'Thinking Back through Our Mothers': Tradition in Canadian Women's Writing." With Clara Thomas and Donna Smyth. In *Re(dis)covering Our Foremothers: Nineteenth-Century Canadian Women Writers*, ed. Lorraine McMullen, 9–13. Ottawa: University of Ottawa Press, 1990.

– "What's in a Picture," *Civilization* 3, no. 5 (1996): 112.

4

"Dolls, Dolls, Dolls, Dolls": Into the (Extra)ordinary World of Girls and Women

CHRISTINE LORRE

Various Miracles, the title of Carol Shields's first collection of short stories, encapsulates her attitude towards the everyday: she sees it as a mix of the ordinary and the extraordinary – "various" usually refers to different things but often within the same general category, while, in contrast, "miracles" hints at the religious and the sacred. The short story "Dolls, Dolls, Dolls, Dolls," which is part of the collection, is a unique experiment in Shields's overall design to reveal the extraordinary – be it synonymous with magic, myth, or mysticism – contained in the ordinary. The aim of this paper is to analyze how, in "Dolls," in order to fathom the meaning and power of such commonplace objects as dolls in the lives of women, Shields pursues her "quest of the ordinary." The phrase is borrowed from Stanley Cavell, who traces the origins of this search back to Romanticism. The Romantic poetical agenda was famously formulated by Wordsworth in his "Preface to Lyrical Ballads" of 1800: "The principal object, then proposed in these poems was to choose incidents and situations from common life, and to relate or describe them, throughout, as far as possible in a selection of language really used by men, and, at the same time, to throw over them a certain coloring of imagination, whereby ordinary things should be presented to the mind in an unusual aspect."[1] Cavell considers "this perception of the everyday as of 'the extraordinary of the ordinary,' a perception of the weirdness, or surrealism, of what we call, accept, adapt to, as the usual, the real."[2] In "Dolls,"

Shields treads the line that separates the ordinary from the extraordinary, and she looks at both sides by resorting to a hybrid genre – between essay and short story. Through the telling of Roberta's middle-age mystical experience with dolls in Japan, the narrator points to the enduring need for the projection of the self beyond the reality of the everyday. She then tells four more separate but related stories, thus pursuing her epistemological search into the extraordinary role of dolls in the lives of girls and women.

CROSSING GENRES TO REACH THE POINT WHERE THE ORDINARY AND THE EXTRAORDINARY INTERSECT

Various Miracles, as a collection of stories, may be seen as an expression of Shields's stance that the ordinary is extraordinary: the "various miracles" related, the short stories told, have an accumulative effect that points towards this conclusion. The short story "Dolls, Dolls, Dolls, Dolls" also relies on an effect of accumulation: in it, five loosely connected doll stories are told in succession, driving towards the closure of the short story as a whole, which is comprised in the narrator's clearly phrased conclusion: "Human love, I saw, could not always be relied upon. There would be times when I would have to settle for a kind of parallel love, an extension of my hidden self, hidden even from me. It would have to do, it would be a great deal better than nothing, I saw. It was something to be thankful for."[3]

Reading back, one realizes that this conclusion echoes a hypothesis formulated by the narrator at the beginning of the narrative. Although the story opens with the narration of Roberta's doll experience in Japan, this quickly becomes part of the exposition of the narrator's point, a way for her to introduce "one of [her] previously undeclared beliefs. Which is that dolls, dolls of all kinds – those strung-together parcels of wood or plastic or cloth or whatever – possess a measure of energy beyond their simple substance, something half-willed and half-alive" (72). This paragraph of reflection, usually "an essay signal,"[4] plays a key role in structuring the narrative, which, with hindsight, one may equally well read as an essay or as a short story. Similarly, the narrating "I" may be the voice of a first-person short story narrator or that of an essayist examining the extraordinary character of dolls, trying to unveil some general truth about it. It should be noted that generic boundaries are porous, so that certain forms of the essay and of the short story may have related characteristics. Charles May, in his analysis of the epistemological value of the short story, proposes a definition of the genre that matches well the narrative of "Dolls": "the short story is mythic and spiritual ... intuitive and lyrical ... [it] exists to 'defamiliarize' the everyday."[5] But Aldous Huxley's description of the essay equally corresponds to Shields's narrative: he describes the genre as the vehicle of "free association artistically controlled," in appearance "one damned thing after another," but in reality the attempt "to say everything at once in as near an approach to contrapuntal simultaneity as the nature of literary art will allow of."[6]

Because the genre of a narrative shapes the reader's mind frame, it is worth analyzing further the effects of Shields's playing on the two genres of the short story and the essay in "Dolls," particularly in structural terms. It is generally agreed that narratives have, and are perceived by the reader as having, two dimensions – a horizontal, chronological one and a vertical, paradigmatic one – the two often being intermingled. Paul Ricoeur describes these two dimensions as follows: "Every narrative combines two dimensions in various proportions, one chronological and the other nonchronological. The first may be called the episodic dimension, which characterizes the story as made out of events. The second is the configurational dimension, according to which the plot construes significant wholes out of scattered events ... To tell and to follow a story is already to reflect upon events in order to encompass them in successive wholes."[7]

In "Dolls" the two dimensions of narrative are in a complex fashion intertwined.[8] The five doll stories each have a horizontal dynamic: events are related chronologically, and the focus is on "the way things happened." Yet the overall structure of the short story is vertical: the five stories are juxtaposed, they are not told chronologically, and as the narrator's exposition suggests, they are revealing of a larger truth. From this perspective, the focus is on "the way things are." By playing on the two dimensions of the narrative, Shields maintains the reader's focus on an in-between point, somewhere midway between what happened and what the stories mean, between facts and their significance. This structuring of the narrative can be read as the formal projection of her sense of the double dimension of the everyday: it is both ordinary (made up of commonplace facts, objects, and goings-on) and extraordinary (commonplace goings-on have unsuspected meaning and power). Shifting the ground on which narrative is usually constructed by crossing genres and narrative dimensions, Shields forces us to look at what is there from two sides, to look beyond the line that separates the ordinary and the extraordinary.

The narrative starts with the mention of Roberta's letter about dolls. The fifth and last section of the story, which deals with the narrator's growing up and discarding dolls, also refers to a Roberta: Roberta Callahan, who, along with JoAnn Brown and the narrator, formed a detective club when they were ten years old. No explicit link is established between the older and the younger Roberta, but one is inclined to think that they are two versions of the same character, considering that the narrator says of Roberta at forty-eight that "she is one of my oldest friends" (71).

Roberta's letter – "another pilgrimage to the heart's interior"(71), the narrator's husband ironizes – brings more proof of "her problem," as the narrator sees it; that is, to sum up, she tends to get overexcited at her discoveries and experiences during business trips with her husband. The narrator's lucidity stands in contrast with Roberta's naïveté and inability to explain or understand herself: the latter's letter ends "with a statement that is really a question. 'I don't suppose,' she says, 'that you'll understand any of this'" (75). The narrator could have dismissed Roberta's experience as being insignificant or devoid of interest. But on the contrary, she uses it as a springboard to start an engaging story, picking up on Roberta's question to investigate her own belief in the mysterious power of dolls. Furthermore, Roberta's letter also acts as one of the discrete leading threads of the narrative, making it come full circle with the reappearance of Roberta as a girl in the fifth story. She is not the focus of that final story, though; the narrator's experience of growing up is. So Roberta's story contributes to giving the narrative coherence and substance by acting as a mirror to the narrator's experience and her reflection on it, at the same time giving them depth.

Roberta's letter is the narrator's entry into the topic of dolls. Her focus on dolls as objects from ordinary life leads her into the world of female childhood and the early development of the female imagination and personality. The five stories focus on female characters: Roberta, a forty-eight-year-old childhood friend of the narrator's; the narrator's mother and her two small daughters; the narrator's own daughter at the age of seven; the narrator's adult sister; and the narrator and two girl-friends at the age of ten. These five stories show various facets of the role of dolls in the development of the imagination, without creating a single unified picture of little girls playing with dolls. Rather, they sketch the range of possibilities that imagination enables. The narrator's hypothesis is a "previously undeclared belief," rather than a dogmatic creed, and her conclusion emerges from her own experience. What is achieved through

the combination of the short story and essay genres is a puzzling narrative, one that is "neither transparent nor opaque but translucent, holding our attention as [a meaning-full event], not just as [a see-through
container] of points."[9]

The female world of dolls that the narrator explores is one in which,
on the whole, males and females do not communicate well. In fact, they
do not seem to share the same imaginary world, as the narrator's husband's reaction to Roberta's letter shows, for instance; he finds her letters inappropriate for a grown-up woman.

PROJECTION BEYOND THE ORDINARY: ROBERTA'S "MYSTICAL" EXPERIENCE

In her letter, Roberta writes about a visit she took to a doll factory in
Japan, while on a business trip with her husband, and the mystical experience she had when holding the finished head of a doll: "What she *had*
felt was a stirring apprehension of possibility. It was more than mere
animism; the life, or whatever it was that had been brought into being
by those industriously toiling women, seemed to Roberta to be deliberate and to fulfill some unstated law of necessity" (75).

To a rational mind, it is unlikely that a doll's head should come alive.
Roberta's reaction seems inappropriate, and the narrator diagnoses "the
heart of her problem" as follows: "she is incredulous, still, that the colour and imagination of our childhood should have come to rest in nothing at all but these lengthy monochrome business trips with her
husband ... ; but that is neither here nor there" (71). In the narrator's
eyes, Roberta's imagination tends to overflow during her trips abroad in
a somehow immature way. The fact that her mystical experience in
Japan was focused on a doll points to the connection between Roberta's
problem and her girlhood. In his essay on psychoanalytic philosophy,
Sami-Ali defines the commonplace – the ordinary – as a problematic
concept, arguing that "what poses a problem with the commonplace is
that the real, which is both rational and technical, tends more and more
to take the place of the imaginary. The imaginary is fundamentally
linked with projection, so that, through the intervention of the commonplace, the whole problematics of projection is approached again
through its negative aspect of absence of projection; now the real is only
what it is."[10] Roberta speaks of a "mystical experience," while the narrator refers to her friend's "problem." So her experience seems to stand
somewhere between mysticism and pathology.

The situation depicted in Roberta's letter looks commonplace: a touring group visits a local workshop in a foreign country. Everything separates the tourists from their environment: the bus is air-conditioned; the use of the passive voice underlines their passiveness ("They were taken," "Roberta's party was brought," "they were led [72]"). They assume the standard position that voyeuristic Western tourists often hold when travelling outside the West: "The tourists – hulking, Western, flat-footed in their bare feet – watched as the tiny white doll heads were passed around the circle of workers" (73).

The tour guide, "a short and peppy Japanese" (73), is equally a caricature, which Roberta uses to liven up her letter: "(Roberta writes that he rose up on his toes when he reached the words *finest* and *purest* as though paying tribute to the god of superlatives.) … (another toe-rising here)" (73). Various markers (dashes or parentheses in the quotations above) indicate the presence of Roberta's voice in the account of her letter that is given by the narrator or the report by Roberta of the Japanese guide's voice in indirect speech ("– the guide vigorously repeated this statistic –" [72]). The effect created by the presence of these voices is one of contrast between the guide's and Roberta's perspectives on the situation: the opposition is male/female, Eastern/Western, tourist industry worker/tourist. The guide speaks in figures and superlatives, emphasizing the most striking technical aspects of the doll-making process. Roberta is sensitive to the more mysterious atmosphere of the place: "The air was musty from the mingled straw and dust, but the light from a row of latticed windows was softly opalescent, a distinctly mild, non-industrial quality of light, clean-focused and just touched with the egg-yellow of sunlight" (72).

In contrast with the guide, Roberta is focusing on the spirit that surrounds the making of the dolls, looking for impalpable clues in order to try to reach beyond the banality of simple technical facts, beyond the literal meaning of dolls as objects. The fact that she is in a foreign country, confronted with cultural otherness, creates a context that is cut off from her everyday life and that stimulates her imagination. But at the same time, her mystical experience has a lot to do with the ordinary fact that she is a woman and that the doll-makers are all women; in other words, it is linked to the ordinariness of the female body, which is mediated by the doll's head that Roberta is handed.

The house (as opposed to a factory) that the touring group is visiting is a place where dolls are made according to a certain tradition. But beyond this literal perception of the situation, it is also a house where women reproduce symbolic representations of human beings. For Roberta, entering the house means stepping into the symbolic and extraordinary sphere of female procreation. Whether she has children or not (the narrator's discretion on that topic suggests that she has not), Roberta is nostalgic for the age of procreation in her life; this is what the narrator hints at when she observes sparingly: "Forty-eight, an uneasy age" (71). All these aspects of Roberta's life come together when she holds the doll's head.

Her way of communicating with the other women in the room is subliminal. It may even be a one-way act of communication, perceived as such by Roberta only. In fact, it is the guide, rather than any of the female workers, who hands the head to her, not out of perception but by chance, "because [she] was standing closest to him" (74). No words are exchanged with the Japanese women; there is a line separating them from Roberta as far as verbal communication goes. But eye contact abolishes the cultural and linguistic barrier. So Roberta's "mystical" experience may also be analyzed as an exchange in which women who were culturally alien become universally familiar,[11] through the mutely shared understanding of their (perhaps subconscious) desire for motherhood and beyond their differing communicational codes:[12] "[The women who had created this little head] smiled, bowed, whispered, miming a busy humility, but their cool waiting eyes informed [Roberta] that they knew exactly what she was feeling" (74).

At that moment, projection replaces perception in Roberta's mind, and the world is transfigured: the Japanese women stop being simply the polite but entirely inaccessible workers that Roberta, like the other tourists, first saw. Projection enables her to communicate irrationally with them through eye contact, the doll acting as a catalyst. Is this projection a mystical experience or a sign of Roberta's (mild) pathology? Sami-Ali explains that "what is missing in the pathology of the commonplace is the possibility offered by the body's excessiveness to be what one dreams of being and what one doesn't dream of being ... What characterizes this pathology is that it consists mostly in a successful social adaptation but it leaves the problematics of projection up in the air."[13]

One may consider that Roberta has failed to come to a clear articulation between the everyday and the projections of the imagination. According to Sami-Ali, the body, as an essential element of representation, mediates the projection of a dynamics of the imagination, playing a crucial role in this articulation. So in an ordinarily exotic situation, Roberta has a "mystical experience" because she is trying to reach beyond the everyday, the mystical element being "the other side of the everyday."[14] But what she is really after is the (extra)ordinary possibility offered by her body of having a child.

Roberta's reaction may be read in various ways. It may be a stubbornly childish way of apprehending her body, as is suggested by the mention in the last story of her attachment, at the age of ten, to animals rather than people. It may also be the sign of her loneliness within her marriage. It is intimated that she and her husband live in two different imaginative worlds: she in the domestic sphere and he at work, outside the house; he in the real world and she in the sheltered world of the housewife. He does not seem to understand her desires well at all: "Tom always says I make too much of nothing" (74). And the narrator does not go to the trouble of characterizing him ("her husband, a man called Tom O'Brien" [71]), possibly leaving him to his unimaginative blandness. This lack of projection in Roberta's married life is compensated for by the appearances of a successful but conformist life as an American wife: during a business trip with her husband, she goes on a touring trip while her husband is "tied up in meetings, as per usual" (72).

Having reported on Roberta's experience, the narrator suddenly dives back into her own childhood and life to show the crucial role dolls play in the early development of the female personality. The epanadiplosis – "*Dolls, dolls, dolls, dolls*" (75) – announces the four childhood doll stories to come, although the original meaning of the formula remains entirely mysterious to the narrator. Egged on by Roberta's letter, she dives into the mysterious world of the female imagination, claiming back some space for its expansion through the telling of the stories.

THE DOLLS OF CHILDHOOD: CRISS-CROSSING FOUR MORE STORIES TO PURSUE THE EPISTEMOLOGICAL QUEST

The four doll stories the narrator tells in the wake of Roberta's appear as "fragments and scattered pieces of Truth,"[15] separated as they are from each other by blanks, yet all pointing to the simultaneously ordinary and extraordinary character of dolls. Through these four stories, the narrator criss-crosses several threads, highlighting how dolls at once pertain to myth and rituals and participate in the structuring of the self, in a dual process of projection and reflection.

The narrator first remembers the Christmas dolls of her own childhood, the magic that surrounded them, and the ritual of her mother buying them. She easily imagines the part of the ritual she was not allowed to witness as a child: "We never, of course, went with her on these shopping trips, but I can see how it must have been" (76). She recreates the spirit of care and love in which the dolls were bought, the sacredness in which they were held, and the mother probably asking for them to be wrapped separately and with extra caution, "persuaded already, as we would later be persuaded, by the reality of their small beating hearts" (76–7). By association, another seasonal ritual is remembered, that of the mother canning peaches in summer, "each peach half turned with a fork so that the curve, round as a baby's cheek, gleamed lustrous through the blue glass" (77). These seasonal rituals have more than simple parental or domestic significance. The care and love the mother puts into these gestures gives them an almost religious character, but they are more akin to pagan rituals than to religious rites, despite the Christmas association in the case of the dolls; more linked to myth than to religious belief. They are symbolic gestures in which images of procreation (the "birth" of the dolls) and nurturing (the canning of the peaches) are repeated.

The second framed story, which takes place in a French museum, focuses on the narrator's daughter and acts as a reminder that, as artifacts, dolls are closely linked to humankind's timeless attempt at representing the mystery of life. While visiting an archaeological museum, the family – mother, father, and daughter – is exposed to a primitive form of dolls, officially "icons," which underlines their contrasted reactions to the artifact. Through the figures – icons or dolls, depending on who is looking – primitiveness and childhood seem to collapse into one. Before they acquired symbolic value, icons, like rituals, were originally "re-presentations": the believers thought that the divinity was literally present in the sacred object or during the ritualistic performance.[16] So the evolution from primitive belief to religious or mystical faith is contained in them. The narrator reports that, after a day of touring in Paris, "the juxtaposition of time – ancient, medieval and modern – affected us powerfully" (79). She and her husband have a sense of historical time. But their seven-year-old daughter does not; she perceives the figures (the icons) as dolls, in a curious time-collapsing move that speaks for their mythical power of representation.

Besides their power to evoke myth and mystery, dolls play a key role in structuring the development of little girls into social, cultural, gendered subjects. In the third framed story, when the sisters remember their childhood dolls, the mimetic function of dolls is emphasized.

When first given, the dolls are presented "exactly the way real children are presented" (81), and they then play their role as props in the two little girls' imitation of adult behaviour. Typically, the girls used to project parental love onto their dolls – "We always loved them on sight" (81) – and to experiment with a range of feelings and moral states – the dolls were vulnerable and at their owners' mercy. It is strictly a one-way relationship: the dolls do not respond, and there is no animism, magic, or mysticism to speak of.

The "Christmas dolls / Nanette" story evokes both myth and the process of social structuring. The adult narrator cannot help wondering at her mother's naïveté; the latter's attachment to ritual leaves the grown-up daughter clueless and slightly bewildered, a possible sign of the generation gap in the two women's aspirations and beliefs. The narrator finds the female sphere infantilizing, having outgrown the early beliefs she readily adopted as a child. Or it may be a sign of her refusal to acknowledge in hindsight that her mother's world was constraining; she prefers to keep intact her memory of family bliss. What she does see clearly is how dolls fitted into the world of childhood and contributed to structuring it, being "one of the certainties of life" (75), as if part of some natural order of that world, like the seasons. Dolls were a link in the protective family circle, defined by the house and outside which lay the potential terrors of the larger world.

In the "French museum" story, the mother is more aware than the father of the need for her young daughter both to have firm, familiar bearings and to follow the lead of her imagination. The daughter perceives the figures she sees very differently from the way her father does. The enthusiastic father points at them, explains, translates, and finally protests when his daughter, for all his talking, clings to her feeling that the figures are dolls. The father's approach is historical and psychological: for him, the figures mostly have to do with the manly business of hunting and waging war, with controlling one's fear of danger. In contrast, the daughter sees the figures as dolls, projecting the familiarity of her world onto what is in front of her, following the lead of an imagination shaped by play. The mother is angered by her husband's stubbornness in rationalizing the meaning of the object for the little girl's benefit. Eventually the father gives up and accepts the possibility that his daughter's interpretation of the object might be closer to reality than his, leaving definite knowledge about the figures open to question: "Who knows" (80).

Dolls play a role in structuring the self both inside and outside the family circle. Stepping outside the family house and beyond the familiar

neighbourhood of "real and continuing people" (77) to attend a birthday party, the child narrator encounters otherness in the form of
Nanette's family, and this experience is mediated by a doll. Nanette's
family is part of a lower social class ("These people only rent, our father
had told us" [77]) and probably of a different ethnic group, as the name
Nanette suggests (she may have been from a French Canadian family),
in contrast with the familiar Celtic and Anglo names of the neighbourhood. The lack of "reality" – that is, of ordinariness – of the people who
lived in "The Apartments" engenders the child's distrust of them, a reaction to the social and cultural homogeneity of her well-established
Euclid Avenue community.

The contrast between the familiar and the alien reappears in dramatic
form a few years later, in the last framed story. An extraordinary event
has taken place in the city where the narrator lives: "a little girl was mur-
dered ... [The killer] cut off her head and her arms and her legs. Some of
these pieces were never found" (84). The narrator and her friends start
playing detectives, and she recalls how she learnt to tame her fear of
being killed. The dichotomy between "neighbourhood heroine" and
"this shallow-breathing, rigidly sleepless coward" (87), between days of
brave determination and sleepless, fearful nights, parallels the opposition between the known and the unknown, the ordinary and the extraordinary. The night becomes the backdrop onto which the girl's fear is
projected: the fear of being stabbed by the killer, of being dismembered,
taken apart, disintegrated, taken away from her family. In contrast, her
daily surroundings consist of the familiar neighbourhood on which the
expanding world of childhood remains centred. The narrator's play-
mates at ten – Roberta Callahan, JoAnn Brown, and Terry Shea – are
the children of "the Browns, the McArthurs, the Sheas, the Calla-
hans"(77), who were mentioned in the first framed story. Outside this
neighbourhood are people from other ethnic backgrounds (that is to say,
non-Celtic, non-Anglo), such as the "suspicious-looking men ... swarthy
men" (86) the three girls choose to follow, being once again influenced
by their reading of the early Nancy Drew stories, in which "dark-
skinned immigrants" were often "suspicious and criminal-minded."[17]

The "detective club" story illustrates how, as girls grow up and discard
their dolls, the latter stop functioning as objects onto which the self is
projected, but may start functioning as objects that reflect the self. By
the time the narrator is ten years old, "Dolls, which had once formed the
centre of [her] imagination, now seemed part of an exceedingly sissified
past, something [she] used to do before [she] got big" (84). But as different

games and activities are adopted, the process of projection of the imagination onto objects remains at work, the girls treasure "pictures of horses
and baseball stickers and collections of bird nests. Rough things, rugged
things, tough things" (85). These things and games are as many ways
into the larger outside world, away from the intimate world of motherhood that dolls represent and closer to the world of adulthood and sexuality – "Perhaps it was our approaching but undreamed of puberty"
(85). The narrator's mother adjusts to the unrolling of this natural cycle:
she reluctantly gives up buying her daughters dolls for Christmas the
year they are ten, giving the girl narrator a watch instead – a sure sign of
time passing – and she eventually gets rid of the old dolls one spring
cleaning.

The girls grow up, their bodies change, and so do the objects that act
as mediators between their bodies and the world. The girls want to be
acknowledged as strong and tough, but they also want to prove their
identity as smart girls, in a combination of the best of both genders.
Inspired by Nancy Drew, the children's detective story heroine who
always overcomes her fears through her capacity for analysis and her
physical courage,[18] the girls form a detective club. They muster their
strength in the hope of becoming "the capturers of the crazed killer"
(85), a feat that would astonish their parents, "who all summer supposed
that their daughters were merely playing, believing that [they] were children, girls, that [they] were powerless" (86). However, even though
Nancy Drew is an extraordinary girl whom her young readers find more
exciting than their own everyday lives, murders do not occur in Nancy
Drew stories (they usually do not, in fact, in children's detective stories);
that would be truly extraordinary and a little too gorily real. Inwardly,
the narrator feels out of her depth.

The desire to build oneself a new, tough, independent personality is
what keeps the narrator from confessing her nightly fears to her mother
or anyone else: it would have meant "to surrender the tough new self
that had begun to grow inside me" (87). Then Nancy Lynn, the old doll
that had been shoved into a closet, rescues the girl. "She had no clothes
on, only her soft, soiled, mattressy body and the flattened joints where
the arms and legs were attached" (87). The doll's wholeness and togetherness is reassuring. Despite signs of wear and tear, her bodily functions
(eyes opening and shutting) are intact. Although the girl has grown out
of her earlier belief and knows that the doll is "lifeless, [knows] there [is]
no heart fluttering in her soft chest and no bravery in her hollow head"
(88), Nancy Lynn has the magic power of reassuring the child, of keeping

her alive. The contact with the doll's familiar texture and smell brings
the girl back to the comforting reality of her home environment, making
her realize that although a killer has entered the ordinary world in which
she lives, killers remain extraordinary, while caring families continue to
form the core of her everyday life. Her old doll acts as a reminder of her
familiar environment, a mirror reflecting what her life really is about.
This is how she overcomes her fear and finds courage and hope; how she
enters the parallel, impalpable, and therefore extraordinary world of
faith.

The process of reflection that dolls enable may take place retrospec-
tively. In the "Christmas dolls / Nanette" story, Nanette is given a doll
for her birthday, in complete disregard of the implicit rule according to
which dolls can be given at Christmas only. The narrator wonders if her
belief as a child in this rule was ascribable to culture ("Was it the rigidi-
ties of my family that dictated this belief") or nature ("or some obscure
and unconscious approximation to the facts of gestation?"), before real-
izing, "clearly enough now" (78), that it resulted from envy. This reali-
zation can be traced in her way of remembering the scene. She first
recalls the doll through the eyes of a child, how "her bronzed hair
gleamed with a richness that was more than visual; … [how she was]
pressed to Nanette's smocked bodice" (78). But looking back again as
an adult, she sees a slightly different reality: "there sat Nanette, rocking
back and forth in her spun rayon dress, stroking the doll's stiff wartime
curls" (78). The magic has drained away, and what is left is the doll as a
sign of poor parents' love for their daughter on her birthday, as well as
the girl narrator's not entirely charitable feelings. The narrator's first
experience of otherness was mediated by a birthday doll that, years later,
acts as a mirror held at her.

Dolls indirectly continue to play a part in the ever-changing definition of the self later in life. The story of the sisters remembering dolls is
pervaded by a sense of time passing, be it marked by the two women's
potential loss of memory of childhood scenes or by the mention of "the
time [our mother] made [the doll] Brenda a velvet cape trimmed with
scraps of fur from her old squirrel collar" (83), a detail that echoes the
description of the mother at a younger age, "in her claret-wine coat with
the black squirrel collar" (76). The narrator's and her sister's children
are listening in, "open-mouthed, disbelieving" (81), or howling at stories of their mothers' delicate attentions to their dolls. Among these six
children must be the narrator's daughter, the very one who was so taken
by the icons in the French museum some time before. Like the narrator

and her girlfriends playing detectives at the age of ten, she would by then disown her earlier, doll-loving self. These changes are signs of the passing of time: the narrator's and her sister's parents, seemingly absent from the family gathering, have probably passed away, and the two women are learning their part as members of the older generation. This process implies evolving from the nurturing role of a mother to that of memory bearer, telling family history, telling her-story, with dolls acting as triggers of memories. The scene also focuses on the sisterly bond and the female sphere, centred on the symbolic but also very real kitchen table where women's conversations take place. Men (the two husbands) stay on the margins of that world, considering the doll conversation an "ordering of trivia" (81).

   The sisterly conversation, even though it is a source of amusement, is central to the family gathering, but it is also crucial for the speakers. In this conversation, the important thing seems to be not so much the details about the dolls but the actual process of remembrance at work. They both love most to "reconstruct, frame by frame, the scenes of [their] childhood" (81). Besides, the narrator finds it hard to deal with her memories on her own: "My own recollections, not all happy, are relentlessly present, kept stashed away like ingots, testifying to a peculiar imprisoning, muscularity of recall" (81). The drawer lined with a blanket that she has forgotten about is probably tied to subconscious childhood fears, as is suggested by her association of the "fleecy pink drawer" with "the dark night" and the good-night saying "Don't let the bedbugs bite" (84), which is meant to keep equally at bay pests and bogeymen. Forgetting is part of growing up and letting go, but "[c]hildish things can be put aside vengefully." So it is important to forget in a way that constitutes a birth, "forgoing the grief and anger in abandonment." Consequently, remembering childhood is not synonymous with nostalgic eternal re-enactment; here it means "to recollect, to call back and to gather together."[19] As the narrative unfolds, the twin dolls, Shirley and Helen, gradually come to be synonymous with an antidote for childhood fears, much as sisterly kitchen-table conversations are a way to reconstruct not only the scenes of childhood but also the vanished family circle that offered protection. The reconstruction of these memories, through the dolls, is a way to re-member childhood, to put it back together, in order, before letting it go.

   In "Dolls, Dolls, Dolls, Dolls," Carol Shields relates moments of truth linked to the role that dolls play in women's lives. Dolls – such ordinary artifacts – have a soul,[20] in the sense that they have an enduring life as objects onto which human feelings are projected and which reflect human feelings. They are part of the ordinary rituals of life's seasons, the rituals that establish the landmarks of domesticity, shaping the time and space in which personal identity is defined. Dolls partake of a system of markers of time – the time of birth, growing up (which includes discarding dolls), becoming an adult, and aging – and markers of space, as structured by human relations – with family members, friends, and others. Dolls are also connected to myth and the mystery of origins, and they have a role in the building of faith. Shields does not consider them in terms of animism or mysticism, but holds that they are important keys to understand the shaping of the female psyche and imagination and the complex range and depth of feelings of the female soul. And this quality makes them (extra)ordinary things.

NOTES

1 Wordsworth, "Preface," 3–4.
2 Cavell, *In Quest of the Ordinary*, 9. Warmest thanks to Françoise Palleau for sharing with me her readings on the theoretical context of the ordinary.
3 Shields, *Various Miracles*, 88.
4 The phrase is used by Hesse in "A Boundary Zone," 89.
5 May, "The Nature of Knowledge in Short Fiction," 133. Further in his argument, May links the genre of the short story to the early nineteenth-century Romantic effort "to regain through art what had been lost in religion ... what many anthropologists have called 'the sacred origin of storytelling'" (139–40).
6 Huxley, quoted in Chadbourne, "A Puzzling Genre," 136. In conclusion to his survey of the essay throughout several literary traditions, Chadbourne gives a comprehensive characterization of the genre which may serve as a general definition: "The essay is a brief, highly polished piece of prose that is often poetic, often marked by an artful disorder in its composition, and that is both fragmentary and complete in itself, capable both of standing on its own and of forming a kind of 'higher organism' when assembled with other essays by its author ... [It] is a unique vehicle of 'thought,' of the pondering of experience" (149).
7 Ricoeur, "Narrative Time," 178. These two dimensions have been analyzed in various terms, as Douglas Hesse points out: one – the horizontal – is also variously called diachronic, syntacmatic, linear, successive, and chronological; the other – the vertical – synchronic, paradigmatic, spatial, configurational, and achronological. See Hesse, "A Boundary Zone," 89. Tzvetan Todorov speaks of narratives

of substitution (for the "vertical" ones) as opposed to narratives of contiguity (for the "horizontal" ones). See Todorov, *Poétique de la prose*, 73.

8 On Shields's play on the two dimensions of narrative in *Various Miracles*, see Vauthier, "Closure in Carol Shields' *Various Miracles*," 115.

9 Hesse, "A Boundary Zone," 105.

10 Sami-Ali, *Le Banal*, 9–10. The translation is mine: "Ce qui fait problème dans le banal, c'est que le réel, qui est à la fois le rationnel et le technique, tend de plus en plus à prendre la place de l'imaginaire. L'imaginaire qu'un lien fondamental unit à la projection de sorte que, par le truchement du banal, c'est toute la problématique de la projection qui se trouve de nouveau abordée sous son aspect négatif d'absence de projection: le réel n'est plus que ce qu'il est."

11 The Japanese have a yearly Day of the Dolls, also called Girls' Day, on 3 March, which had its origin in a purificatory rite – additional proof that dolls have universal symbolic functions in the lives of girls and women. Thanks to the Japanese student who pointed out this fact following my presentation on "Dolls" at the Centre for Canadian Studies of Université Paris 3 on 15 March 2003.

12 The point is supported by the passage on Roberta's feeling when holding the doll: "The life ... seemed to Roberta ... to fulfil some unstated law of necessity" (75).

13 Sami-Ali, *Le Banal*, 137–8. The translation is mine: "Ce qui fait défaut dans la pathologie du banal, c'est la possibilité offerte par la démesure du corps d'être ce dont on rêve et d'être ce dont on ne rêve pas ... [Le propre de cette pathologie est] d'être essentiellement une adaptation sociale réussie mais [de laisser] en suspens la problématique de la projection."

14 Sami-Ali, *Le Banal*, 160: "L'élément mystique, c'est l'autre face du banal."

15 Sir Thomas Brown, quoted in Chadbourne, "A Puzzling Literary Genre," 135.

16 See Danto, on representation, in chapter 1 of *The Transfiguration of the Commonplace*.

17 Erica Noonan, "Readers Remain Captivated by Nancy Drew," *Augusta Chronicle*, 2 July 1999; quoted in Roblin, "Aux frontières des littératures enfantine, féministe et policière."

18 On Nancy Drew and children's detective stories, see See Roblin, "Aux frontières des littératures enfantine, féministe et policière."

19 Cavell, on Wordsworth's "Intimations of Immortality from Recollections of Early Childhood," in *In Quest of the Ordinary*, 73–4.

20 See Heidegger, "The Thing," 163–86, and Cavell (on Heidegger), *In Quest of the Ordinary*, 50–75. See also Eliade, *The Sacred and the Profane*, 12: "By manifesting the sacred, any object becomes something else, yet it continues to remain itself, for it continues to participate in its surrounding cosmic milieu."

WORKS CITED

Cavell, Stanley. *In Quest of the Ordinary: Lines of Skepticism and Romanticism.* Chicago and London: University of Chicago Press, 1988.

Chadbourne, Richard. "A Puzzling Genre: Comparative Views of the Essay." *Comparative Literature Studies* 20 (1983): 133–53.

Danto, Arthur. *The Transfiguration of the Commonplace.* Harvard: Harvard University Press, 1981.

Eliade, Mircea. *The Sacred and the Profane.* Trans. Willard R Trask. New York: Harper and Row, 1961.

Heidegger, Martin. "The Thing." In *Poetry, Language, Thought,* trans. and ed. Albert Hofstadter, 163–86. New York: Harper and Row, 1971.

Hesse, Douglas. "A Boundary Zone: First-Person Short Stories and Narrative Essays." In *Short Story Theory at a Crossroads,* ed. Susan Lohafer and Jo Ellyn Clarey, 85–105. Baton Rouge and London: Louisiana State University Press, 1989.

May, Charles. "The Nature of Knowledge in Short Fiction." In *The New Short Story Theories,* ed. Charles E. May, 131–43. Athens: Ohio University Press, 1994.

Ricoeur, Paul. "Narrative Time." *Critical Inquiry* 7, 1 (1980): 169–90.

Roblin, Isabelle. "Aux frontières des littératures enfantine, féministe et policière: l'exemple de Nancy Drew." *Confluences* 20 (2002): 129–43.

Sami-Ali. *Le Banal.* Paris: Gallimard, 1980.

Shields, Carol. *Various Miracles.* London: Fourth Estate, 1994.

Todorov, Tzvetan. *Poétique de la prose.* Paris: Seuil, 1978.

Vauthier, Simone. "Closure in Carol Shields's *Various Miracles.*" In *Reverberations: Explorations in the Canadian Short Story,* 114–31. Concord, ON: Anansi, 1993.

Wordsworth, William. "Preface to Lyrical Ballads" (1800). In *The Prelude: Selected Poems and Sonnets,* 1–32. New York: Holt, Rhinehart and Winston, 1954.

5

Carol Shields's *The Republic of Love,* or How to Ravish a Genre

TAÏNA TUHKUNEN

Among the attempts to give shape to a republic, a state in which supreme power is held by the people and not by a pre-eminent ruler, Carol Shields's novel *The Republic of Love* is undoubtedly one of the most extraordinary essays at voicing one's wish to live in peaceful, yet not necessarily placid, coexistence with one's fellow creatures, even in our bleak and boastful modern times. Both a serious meditation on love and a playful, novelistic exposé of one of the least beloved subjects of artistic expression – that of an ordinary happy life – Shields's novel leaves the reader puzzled at the ostensible impossibility of inserting the worn-out term "love" under any reassuringly fixed definitions. A delightfully oscillating word that is kept frolicking between the legendary and the real, the mythical past and the trivial present, between Canada and Europe, Winnipeg and Paris, "love" is cleared of its most compelling predeterminations, while it is reviewed as an obstinate sign of the inaccessible, just like the mermaids and various other sea sprites and odd ocean creatures that populate Shields's plot.

However, as we open *The Republic of Love*, nothing seems to point at mystery, any more than at secrecy or the prospect of an out-of-the ordinary topos of any kind. On the contrary, it is the dreariness and drabness of everyday existence that predominates in the calm and cold, bleakly composed Canadian city of Winnipeg. As one of the multiple minor characters of this novel, whose narrative structure relies on a dense network

of voices, affirms, "Routine is liberating. It makes you feel in control."[1]
There seems to be very little more a Winnipegger can do than grumble
about the lack of heated bus shelters or "just plain old-fashioned live
[t]here" (169). This scantiness of options is reinforced by the narrator's
factual comment: "The population of Winnipeg is six hundred thousand, a fairly large city, with people who tend to stay put. Families overlap with families, neighbourhoods with neighbourhoods. You can't
escape it" (77).

I wrote most of this text while in my native Finland last winter. It was
freezing cold, and I knew it was the best possible place in Europe for
anybody wishing to understand Carol Shields's wintry Winnipeg, the
Canadian city where nearly all the events of *The Republic of Love* take
place. As I was fighting my way through the icy Nordic winds and the
merciless sub-zero chills, I felt in my bones that the elements of mystery
Shields wove into her text have *absolutely nothing* to do with the inspiration provided by a chilly and snowy landscape, for while up in the
north I certainly caught no sight of the mermaids and other extraordinary Mediterranean-bred presences that warm up the atmosphere in her
novel.

The question I therefore put to myself was simply this: how does
Shields do it? How does she manage to weave mystery, secrecy, and intercontinental mermaid mobility into what could so easily be reduced to a
trifling tapestry of Nordic bleakness, snowed-in city streets, and unheated
bus shelters? In other words, the fixed and frozen day-by-day existence
of ordinary people. My own wonderment was further heightened by
Shields's deliberate choice of a minor genre, that of romance fiction, to
lead the readers of *The Republic of Love* into probing the rhetoric of love in
itself as a deep-frozen area of human expression, congealed beneath ready-
made linguistic patterns, fixed schemes, and rigid scenarios.

SHIELDS'S SOLITARY HEROES

Emblematically enough, Shields's fluctuating story, initially entitled
"Bodies of Water," begins at a time of thaw, on a Good Friday. But just
like the Christian holiday whose pagan roots Fay, the associate folklorist, mermaid scholar, and central female character of the novel, is seized
wondering about on the first pages of the novel, the text itself seems to
plunge its referential roots into pagan iconography and legendary lore.
The spinning movement of Fay's thoughts while she is made love to by
Peter Knightly, a man whom she is getting ready to leave, provides the

reader with an early indication of the revolving, overlapping, and entangled structure of the novel: "She tries to concentrate on the reverberations of Good Friday. The thoughts spill and roll. Does he know, she wonders, rocking him gently back and forth, that Good Friday has pagan roots? That it is the ultimate day of contradictions? Celebration mixed with gloom. Suffering with satiety. The dolorous and the delightful. Winter and spring. Cold and hot" (5).

Even if elements of renewal and resurrection there certainly are in this tale where two lonely hearts are slowly but surely brought together into modern wedlock, one based on fission rather than on fusion, it is useless to look for any biblical miracles in a text where the hero and the heroine keep, in the vein of Jane Austen, ignoring each other until their perfectly predictable encounter.

Already in the previous, numberless chapter entitled simply "Tom" we have briefly encountered the male protagonist, Fay's neighbour Tom Avery, a forty-year-old divorced radio host whom Fay will not meet until the middle of the narrative during a curiously naive falling-in-love scene that includes "rainbow-colored balloons" (175), Hollywood-type slow-motion embraces, and other irritatingly customary romantic trappings.

The alternating third-person viewpoint that keeps shifting from Fay to Tom and back to Fay again, even after Fay has embarked on a mermaid research journey to Europe, is only one of the subtle narrative choices, including self-reflexive commentary, that upset, without totally transgressing, the codes and modes of a seemingly traditional love plot. As we shall see, Shields's text frequently flirts, often quite strikingly, with the easily recognizable generic features of romance fiction, while making ample use of irony and parody. Thus, for instance, at one point in this novel, we learn about Fay's fondness for the nineteenth-century novels she likes to curl up with, for they offer "predicament, resolution, a happy ending, always a happy ending" (158). Whether there *will* be a happy ending in Shields's novel is quite another matter, perhaps because the definition of "happiness" has considerably changed in the minds of women since Victorian times.

Both Fay and Tom, Shields's two childless protagonists, have gone through sentimental failures and fiascos and share equally mixed feelings about utterances that include the word "love." Tom Avery has been married thrice (to Sheila, Clair, and Suzanne), while the fruitless love affairs of Fay McLeod, the thirty-five-year-old folklorist, with three different male partners have merely allowed her to avoid stretch marks and various other "agony lines" (216) on her slender body. Solitude is repeatedly at rendez-vous, but as Shields's narrative tactics underline, the solitary man or woman who is equally "lousy marriage material" (48) is never deserted or definitely dropped from the love plot.

While a romantic novel would be brought to a predictable end, a more or less foreseeable closure at the marriage altar, where the female heroine would sacrifice her doubts to a presumably and eternally blissful standstill, this scenario carries on to explore the very structure of what we tend to call a "love story." As Faye Hammill convincingly argues in her fine essay "*The Republic of Love* and Popular Romance," highlighting the intertextual links between Jane Austen and Carol Shields's fiction, the Canadian author humorously reworks the codifiable forms of romance writing, reflecting at the same time upon its very structures. While the early nineteenth-century British author challenged some of the formulaic genres of her era, namely, the sentimental novel and the gothic romance, Shields questions, just as surely, the popular fiction of her own times. The basic romance pattern remains visible, but as Hammill writes, Shields "removes the love story from the realm of doctor-and-nurse books by adding a dimension of sophisticated intellectual analysis to the traditional focus on emotional and sexual experience."[2]

It was undoubtedly this focus on the emotional and the sexual that resulted in the limited critical interest received by *The Republic of Love*, which, unlike Shields's other novels, was mostly ignored by the critics. Whether it is the ongoing tendency to label even alternative versions of love stories as "feminine" and therefore as inferior writing or the mere impossibility to fix into words "What We Talk about When We Talk about Love" – to borrow a title used by Raymond Carver – it is true that love is not desired as an object of critical study. This viewpoint seems to be shared by the major protagonist of Carol Shields's novel, who is caught thinking that "love is not, anywhere, taken seriously. It's not respected. It's the one thing in the world everyone wants – she's convinced of that – but for some reason people are obliged to pretend that love is trifling and foolish" (248).

Whether a distant echo of gothic fiction parodied by Jane Austen or a sign of a modern mindscape marked by broken-down relationships, the inflated, deliberately embroidered language of love of Shields's republic hardly conceals the contemporary man or woman's fear of the thing that still cannot be named: "'I'm having,' said Fay, 'I'm having ... I don't know what I'm having. A romance, I suppose. What a word! Do you know what my sister-in-law, Sonya, calls romance? She calls it 'the love that dares not speak its name'" (250).

In this novel of solitary longing and reviewed matchmaking, where the "ultimate horror" consists in, as Fay believes, "ending up alone" (132), the emphasis remains undoubtedly on language. This focus is confirmed by passages where Shields's writing suddenly ceases or freezes in order to stop and scan the possible variations or extensions provided by language. An illustration can be found in chapter 1, called "Breaking," where the attention of the writerly "I" is suddenly seized by the word "single": "Occasionally during these walks, the word 'single' presents itself. [Fay] makes herself sigh it out, trying hard to keep her mouth from puckering – single, singleness, singlehood, herself engaged in a single-ish stroll" (7).

A curious contract seems to be established between the storyteller and the reader who willingly surrenders to such incongruous words as "[m]ermaiding" (152) and "Fay-ness" (154), which, curiously enough, start making sense in the middle of the narrative. To enhance the impression of communication between the writing "I," the two major protagonists, and the reader, we find a number of minor characters, frequently left without a face or a name of their own. They form a curious chorus, a protective network of singular voices whose lengthy monologues tend to alleviate whatever melancholy or solitary inflexions there might have been, preventing the inhabitants of the "big wide radioland" (119) in and around Winnipeg from falling into deleterious pathos. Indeed, one of the greatest mysteries of Carol Shields's novel is that while speaking out of a lonely locus, her characters remain capable of establishing vivid connections.

The extraordinary and the fantastic, but never the "ghastly," "freakish," let alone the "weird," start seeping in from the opening pages of *The Republic of Love*. Or at least since the appearance of Tom Avery, a late-night radio host whose "Niteline" program on the Winnipeg radio station CHOL attracts hundreds of lonely listeners every night. As if giving voice to speechless, otherworldly creatures, they seem to echo Fay's definition of the mermaids as providers of "fragments, blurred visions, partial accounts" (79). However, well before Tom's alluring radio voice reaches the readers of the novel, our attention may have been caught by another voice, that of an anonymous storyteller whose utterances frame and structure the story.

This is how she unfolds her tale:

As a baby, Tom Avery had twenty-seven mothers. So he says. That was almost forty years ago.

Ask me more, his eyes beg, ask me for details.

Well, then. At three weeks of age, there he was, this little stringy wailing thing, six and a half pounds of malleable flesh. His mother was sick, desperately sick, a kind of flu that worsened to pneumonia and then depression. In all, she was hospitalized for six months. Where was his father in all this? What father? Ha! That's another story. (1)

Familiar with the traditional codes and modes of storytelling, as well as with the contemporary narrative strategies that strive to shake up and subvert those very codes, we now know what is coming: "only" a story! or even worse, a mere "love story," a ready-made plot we may instantly and freely feel contemptuous and condescending about, especially after reading through the thirty-six deliberately soppy headings à la Barbara Cartland proposed in the table of contents ("I believe in One Thing," "Love Is the Only Enchantment," "The Pageant of Romance," "Love and the Absence of Love," "Seduction and Consolation," "I Love You," "I Love You Too," etc., etc.), which echo countless *déjà entendu* titles of "penny romances," "trashy novels," or (as the French would put it) "rose-water novels" (*romans à l'eau de rose*), to call forth the much disdained *littérature de gare* that has precipitated into a predictably gloomy destiny flocks of love-hungry women, even after Flaubert's calls for vigilance in *Madame Bovary*.

Those who nevertheless decide to keep reading this outrageously lightly written story in "woman-talk" are plunged into a cozy, dangerously blissful atmosphere of femininity, that of the neo-Georgian Department of Home Economics at the University of Manitoba, where the newborn Tom was entrusted to the loving care of no fewer than twenty-seven mothers, twenty-seven young women whose "pearly hands" (2) never ceased feeding, burping, kissing, oiling, powdering, rocking, tickling, rewarding, and wrapping the baby until the all-too-foreseeable outcome. A man whose pre-verbal beginnings in life had been so exceedingly sweet was bound to endure periods of subsequent sourness. Or as Shields's narrator lovingly puts it, "Such love, such love – ah God, he'd never know love like that again" (3).

Some of the elements of Shields's playful, yet never ludicrous or openly farcical, scenario thus made perceptible, the author leads her male hero away from the most treacherous songs of the sirens. Instead of being definitely drawn into the "remembrances of that charmed time" (2), the potentially traumatized and tragic oedipal hero, endowed with a peculiar voice that has got just "a bit of infrared in it" (138), is developed into a modern merman, a delightfully unpretentious male protagonist who shows amazing disinterest in "pen envy," in the power of the so-called male gaze, as well as what Shields's narrator sums up as the whole "business of being a guy" (44). A Burt Reynolds–like gender construction made up of muscle, nerve, and chest hair maintained by strong doses of protein, carbohydrates, burgers, and other earthly sustenance for manly men, Tom Avery nevertheless reverses a series of gendered stereotypes. Despite the appearances, it is more the man than the woman whose enchanting voice catches radio listeners from the dead of the night, and who also embodies the "dark continent," the object of discovery to be revealed.

On the other hand, although Tom Avery's face is displayed on a huge billboard outside Winnipeg – the kind of North American road culture sign that Jay Gatsby keeps dashing by in his motorcar in Scott Fitzgerald's doomed love story inspired by a disillusioned generation – there are no overblown bespectacled or non-spectacled looks or other godlike visions in Shields's novel. Quite conversely, instead of being intensely visual, the fascination and love lure in her novel seem of a different order – of the kind that by defamiliarizing the ordinary reality, both bends towards and reaches beyond what Antoine de Saint-Exupéry's *Petit Prince* claims as the essential that remains invisible to the eye.

The impossibility of rendering visible, of be-holding, that is, grasping and controling the perceived object by the mere act of eyeing, is highlighted by the fragmentary and always incomplete presentation of mermaids, mermen, merdogs, and mercats (I did not even know they existed before reading Shields's novel!), those peculiar fabled marine creatures with an upper body of a human being and the tail of a fish that fascinate Fay McLeod to the point that she wishes to write a scholarly study on them.

BEYOND THE IDIOMS OF LOVE

Although it could be easily claimed that as an attempt to resuscitate the "language of love" from the realm of dead clichés in order to restore some of its lost mystery, Shields's plot reads like a deliberate, premeditated flop, I wish to go on arguing that the Canadian author here deals with the subject in an indirect, slanted fashion, a mode of writing that may have been inspired by both Emily Dickinson and Jane Austen. At the same time, *The Republic of Love*, scarcely more than Raymond Carver's *What We Talk about When We Talk about Love* (1981), never pretends to capture the mystery of love in a few unambiguous, plain-spoken words.

Strikingly enough, it is out of the modern city-dwellers' repeated musings regarding the survival of love in the cynical world of urban anxiety
and solitude – "What does it mean to be a romantic in the last decade of
the twentieth century?" (35); "Love," she sniffed rudely, "Who needs it"
(49) and so on – that Shields's text stretches out its tentacles towards other
spaces and supposedly bygone times. By so doing, it establishes links not
only between North America and Europe, between contemporary popular culture and the legendary past, but also between history-telling and
more intimate storytelling or fantasy-telling; all examples of the true
"bonding strategy" that underlies this novel, whose reader is left to create
the links, or simply to ponder over the existence of potential relations,
between the juxtaposed elements forming the subtle puzzle.

It was finally only after my return from frozen Finland and while
caught up in the polar weather that had mysteriously crept over France
one night that I began to grasp the more secret mechanisms of Shields's
writing. Instead of expecting language to provide the longed-for, clear
answers – for Shields very well knew how treacherous words can be – the
author probes accidental experiences, events, and unforeseen wordings
to capture the unique, the solitary, and the singular beneath the common and the ordinary. By saying so, I do not suggest that her narrative is
a haphazard fabrication, but rather that its focus remains on the "here
and now" of the singular, the deliberately magnified "Anything May
Happen," as well as all those other seemingly insignificant "oddities of
language" (15) that render our mortal lives more sufferable.

Shields's awareness of the limits of language and of artistic expression
itself leads to a series of dislocations, the most conspicuous of which is
certainly the mermaid motif. At once a research topic, a slippery object
of the gaze, and a gap in a linguistic code that fails to represent the world
fully, the mermaid – together with the mer people or the mer folk that
surround her – becomes the entangled mirror image through which we
can see and hear something that our ordinary, everyday language may be
incapable of conveying. Of course, there are links between the legend
and Fay, herself a probable fairy ("une fée"), an imaginary creature
endowed with magic. Especially since the day she was presented with a
cryptic object in polished gray soapstone, an Inuit carving of a plump
and joyful mermaid "lying on her side propped up by her own thick
muscled elbow" (13). First invested with authenticity, presented as culturally rooted in mainland Canada, before turning out to be a cheap,
mass-produced avatar that could have been fabricated practically anywhere, the cross-cultural and cross-ethnic figure, which keeps oscillating

between authenticity and artifice, high and popular art, is pursued until the final pages of the novel through various references to representations of mermaids in the visual arts – in the art collections of the Louvre, at the buffet restaurant of the Gare de Lyon, and at the École des Ponts et Chaussées, up to mermaid sightings in the Nantes area – without a clearly established frontier between fact and fantasy.

Fay's mermaid research starts out as a feminist deconstruction project of the age-old temptress figure, but leads to the publication of her book *Mermaids of the Inner Mind* (365), a puzzling piece of scholarly writing whose Jungian contents the reader is given a few hazy hints of in the closing pages of the novel. In the course of this research, the hybrid, cross-continental figure of the mermaid is tracked but never literally traced down through various "sightings" and miscellaneous portrayals of sirens in the realm of the visual arts. Criss-crossing France during her research journey, Fay ends up near Nantes, a city where the author of this text is lucky enough to teach what the great American author Nathaniel Hawthorne once called "the damned mob of scribbling women,"[3] that is, North American women writers. It is indeed in St Pierre, a village near Nantes, that two teenage girls, Michelène Payot and Sophie Jaud,[4] are said to have spotted a "fishtailed woman" (34). While working on this text, I almost telephoned *Ouest-France*, the local daily newspaper that Shields mentions on page 206 of her novel, calling it "the local tabloid." But on second thought, I decided not to run the risk of making a fool of myself by asking whether such a sighting had ever been brought up on its pages. For although soundly and seriously told, mixing English and French – a "sirène," "Appelant de la main," or singing "Bonnée journée, bonne journée" (207, 208) – thus increasing the veracity of the sighting scene, the account is interspersed (just like Shields's entire novel) with what could be regarded as self-reflexive elements. Not only does the "sirène" leave behind a few "bubbles," "[a]nd a little hole, *un trou*, on the surface of the water" (208), just the kind of gaps and voids the reader is invited to fill while reading the novel, but right after Fay's interview with the two teenage girls, Fay herself refuses to go on taking any of the adolescent mermaid stuff seriously. Still, in the non-nihilistic universe of Carol Shields, even this outwardly nonsensical "rubbish" that bears the mark of teenage fantasies and popular culture is "preferable to nothingness," as we can read on page 210: "Anything is better than nothing, monsters, virgins, wild animals, film stars, rock singers, mermaids – whatever can be prised out of the available culture and given a transitory shape."

PARIS AND A FEW PALIMPSESTS

In an ultimate effort to understand Shields's world of transitory shapes and fleeting figures, which blend idolatry of former times with more recent forms of revelation and idolization, I visited one of the French locations mentioned in *The Republic of Love*, the Gare de Lyon railway station in Paris, to have a look at the mermaids of its *belle époque* restaurant's lavish decor: "[Fay] splurged one day on an expensive lunch at the Station Buffet at the Gare de Lyon, where the walls are covered with immense painted mermaids voluptuously wagging their full breasts and rounded bottoms, one of them wearing her hair in an endearing Gibson Girl mop" (202).

Not a specialist in mermaid anatomy, let alone sirenophelia, I can nonetheless guarantee that the buffet restaurant at the railway station, actually called "Train Bleu," displays no painted mermaids on its walls, just as surely as there are no villages called St Pierre near Nantes. There are mermaids in the immense rooms of the classy restaurant, over-charged with sculptures and paintings, but these ocean creatures are not painted beings or found in the middle of a canvas. Quite the contrary, they constitute fairly inconspicuous ornamental side-elements forming the gilt frame of the forty-one magnificent, somewhat pompous paint-ings recalling journeys to the Côte d'Azur, the French Riviera, in the heyday of train travelling. While sitting under the high-hung, brightly coloured paintings, beneath which many celebrated French and interna-tional artists are known to have dined, I did not perceive any "wagging" of breasts or bottoms, nor did I catch sight of any "endearing Gibson Girl mops," but that is probably because I am just too realistic a reader. Somewhat like Peggy, Fay's far less fairy-like Winnipeggian mother, who is writing a self-help manual for menopausal women. This lack of imagination did not, however, prevent me from being, once again, lured into the movable middle ground where the Shieldsian ordinary is left mingling with the extra-ordinary, the familiar with the foreign, the familial with the solitary and the singular, and the trivial and trifling with the legendary.

While contemplating the gilded mermaids of the Gare de Lyon, which remained exceedingly lifeless and soulless compared to the impression of activity provided by Shields's writing, it would have been tempting to explain the whole exasperatingly elusive female figure away by earmarking (or rather "tailmarking") it with a deliberately feminist rationalization. Indeed, the manner in which Shields reintroduces the fish-tailed goddess figure back to centre stage of the reader's consciousness could be viewed as yet another reminder of the way women have often been represented as mute, passive, and peripheral objects. But to do so would, of course, be an abusive reduction of the multiple, often quite contradictory moves of the mesmerizing sea nymphs, perilous sea sirens, and other mystical creatures in *The Republic of Love*.

The fascination of the mermaid figure would probably not work as well if the text did not at times read like a palimpsest, a manuscript on which later writing has covered the original one, while allowing the earlier version to be read through. This quality is quite obvious, for instance, in the closing scene marked by a fairy-tale denouement where the reader is abandoned with the final mermaid-like salute, bringing to mind the way Hans Christian Andersen's soul-searching Little Mermaid is left floating into Paradise, "longing for completion" (366); just as the closing paragraphs of the novel may themselves read as an expression of "longing" or "craving" for resolution. Through this ultimate mirror effect, Shields's text seems to acknowledge its very powerlessness to pull together all the threads connected with mermaid legends and/or images of sirens, the mermaid narratives thus proving to be just as elusive, slippery, and adaptable as the myth itself.

On the other hand, Fay's mermaid study seems far more ambiguous and dishevelled than the other ongoing writing venture, Peggy McLeod's menopause project, a completely different way of perceiving and representing the female body. Rather than approaching it as a mysterious half-human beast or a Circe-like sorceress, Fay's mother focuses on the loss of reproductive organs in a female being made of flesh and bone. Yet at the same time, one cannot but wonder to what extent the daughter's and the mother's seemingly different writing processes are related and finally intertwined by Shields's penwomanship. For both deal not only with abbreviated, unproductive female sexuality beneath the waist but also with the fear of transformation and aging and – as Peggy's suddenly perturbed love life underlines – with the descent into the unknown, into the depths of our more or less irrational impulses, where no siren's comb may help us unravel the entangled desires.

From a more general topographical perspective, Carol Shields's hybrid fable has two overlapping levels. One accounts for the immersed realm of knowledge, which, quite like Atlantis, seems to lie somewhere in the fictitious depths of the ocean sirens. Above this water land we find the more earthy and ordinary world of Winnipeg, with its real cankerworms that submerge the city after each winter, before the arrival of the just as authentic summer mosquitoes. In *The Republic of Love* these two narrative levels not only keep overlapping but spin and rotate so as to represent Winnipeg as a mysterious, both antediluvian and sunken city, the "other world" where, as it is repeatedly claimed in the novel, "anything might happen." Anything but truly nasty things, as some critics have underscored, calling attention to Carol Shields's undisguised reluctance to let anything foul break into her tale. Neither does her republic, which rotates around love and marriage, consider the revolutions shaped by same-sex couples and their marriages, the ardently debated issue tackled in the Canadian public forum the very summer of 2003, when Deepa Mehta's film version of *The Republic of Love* was waiting for its premiere at the Toronto International Film Festival. Carol Shields, who had passed away barely two months before the event, was no longer present to enjoy what would have been a well-merited stroll along the red carpet at Roy Thomson Hall, but something of the enchantment generated by Mehta's film made the audience doubt that she was entirely absent from the occasion.

Prolonging this testamentary tone, we may also wish to note that although in Shields's lovable and movable republic, there are no perfectly blissful marriages, marital (including post-marital) relations tend to remain, if not happy, at least jovial or cheerful. If need be, rather than blindly following predetermined scenarios, they come to an end *before* ceasing to be happy. Despite the perception of matrimony as a wavering institution, the institution is revisited in such a way as to liberate it from some of the severest social conformities and restrictions that have defined wedlock through history. In the process, the Shieldsian seascape, whirled through by supernatural creatures, remains strangely earthly in the sense of the terrestrial and the time-bound, offering alternative spaces – either simply next door or, in any case, within reachable bounds of our agitated, constrained daily world.

MERMAID MOBILITY

bell hooks, an American feminist theorist, cultural critic, and author of a trilogy of essays on love-related issues, begins her *Communion: The Female Search for Love* with the following words: "Women talk about love. From girlhood on, we learn that conversations about love are a gendered narrative, a female subject." The aching and burning of love, the always available gendered cultural narrative that indeed seems to participate in the shaping of female subjectivity, is undeniably one of the ingredients of Shields's own "love writing." However, the charm of her novel cannot be explained away by the romance-fiction or fairy-tale quality of her texts. While mirroring some of the typical features of romance fiction, including a love-at-first-sight scene and marriage as an inevitable resolution, Shields recoils from the more explicit similarities with what one of her characters repeatedly calls "those doctor-and-nurse things." Despite the premarital crisis caused by the breakdown of Fay's parents' idealized wedlock, Tom and Fay *will* get married with the same inescapability that couples are led to the altar at the end of Jane Austen's novels. What makes the difference is the future bride's sudden withdrawal from the arranged rituals surrounding a formally sanctioned union and her calling everything off at the last minute, which allows Shields to bring in more contemporary preoccupations, suspicions, and fantasies, namely, the fear of coupling, which nowadays seems to have overcome that of uncoupling. Strikingly enough, it is this part of *The Republic of Love* that is the least exciting to read. As Wayne Tefs remarks in his article "Cultivating the Middle-Class Garden," two-thirds of the way through, the novel seems to "slow to a crawl," as the reader is "treated to all the excesses of romance: love-letters, desperate waiting, morose self-examinations, brooding."[5] Shields then introduces what Tefs calls a "wrinkle," that is, a flaw in the form of Fay's father's unexplained refusal to go on with his previously perfect marriage. As Tefs suggests, however, this unexpected development energizes the remaining third of the narrative, bringing alive some of the other characters who would have been eclipsed by the central characters of the novel.

Whether anonymous or clearly named, the "mer people" of Winnipeg are presented as a more or less loosely knit yet movable network, a body of persons forming, as Deborah Keahey points out in her article entitled "Love = Winnipeg = Home," a double or dual republic, both a political and territorial unit and a state of being in love, akin to a "merry-go-round,"[6] a revolving mechanism that allows one to step in and out, fall in and out of love, without rejecting anybody definitely from the endless life and love cycle. The movable republic imagined by Carol Shields relies on no deleterious "combines" or other invisible systems that are capable of gulping down the individual, as, for instance, in Ken Kesey's *One Flew over the Cuckoo's Nest*. Quite as imperceptible, her mechanics of love rest upon a mysteriously functioning device that lays out a winding, snaky path from Fay to Tom via a number of former, would-be, or present-day husbands, wives, boyfriends, girlfriends, pals, and partners. Barely discernable, just like the game of hopscotch – another structural pattern that can be felt through the narrative, with its coupling and uncoupling players trying to move through magically numbered squares towards a place called "heaven"[7] – there is the ever-present invisible safety net, a curiously extended family relying on a beloved community that does not always protect, but at least helps with healing.

All this may of course seem quite different from the ordered and linear family history found in Jane Austen's novels, where wedlock is always a "wed-lock." Yet just as in Austen's microcosm, Shields's imaginary world seems – pardon me for the all-too-easy pun – "shielded" against the major upheavals and ruptures of modern society. For no matter how solitary, "singles-oriented" (63), or alienated the Winnipeggian man or woman may be, the community is ready to reach out a helping hand (or rather a voice) to stop him or her from falling into deeper doldrums. This quite outdated, not to say obsolete, view of society undoubtedly mirrors the reassuring rural society depicted by Austen, one that still has a centre as well as a feeling of belonging to someone or something – quite an exception or an oddity, one might argue, in our contemporary fiction. As is underlined by the humorous depiction of Tom Avery's disenchantment with the "coping strategies – bonding, rebonding, and disbonding" (61) – proposed by the "Newly Single Club," where the anti-heroic disc jockey dutifully listens to therapeutic talks about "The Ghettoization of the Single in Contemporary Urban Society" (61), Shields does not seem to believe in exclusively rational and/or deconstructive handlings of humankind's alienation, fragmentation, and other identity syndromes. On the contrary, it is a deeper magical, often less articulate and silent, process that even the most matter-of-fact character may blissfully fall a prey to which frequently seizes her imagination.

While allowing her personae to drift towards, if not a happy, at least a happi*er* ending (after all, mermaid stories rarely end up happily!), Shields explores the nature, the absurdities, and certainly also the limits of the language of love. The reader of *The Republic of Love* may share Fay McLeod's doubts about the whole love business as "a kind of perversion" (107), but the conventional, ironical, and mocking comebacks of the word "love" confirm that for Shields, the perverted business of love nevertheless remained serious business. As the French playwright Alfred de Musset put it in the title of his 1834 play *On ne badine pas avec l'amour*, there is no trifling with love! Never cynical or scornful towards those who still dare use the much-chastised term, Shields in her writing nurtures and multiplies the worn-out word in an attempt to restore some of its lost charm. This is at least what the reader assumes while try-ing to cope with the almost incantatory echoes that are made to ring through the novel. For the same gooey and sticky common noun is repeatedly found not only in biblical precepts and the openly sentimen-tal sentences where declarations of love are reflected upon afterwards, but also in more philosophizing, suspended passages where the old issue is briefly approached through the lenses of the ordinary and the com-monplace. This is the case, for instance, as Tom Avery, who, while gro-cery shopping one day, overhears a woman in a green blazer say: "Love is the only enchantment we know" (70). The fragment that includes this simple utterance is left lingering without further narrative comment, other than the following remark restating the already-heard maxim: "Later, as he was peeling oranges over a garbage bag, the phrase came to him again. Love is the only enchantment. This, he said to himself, is how a Chinese gong must feel when it's struck by a hammer in its abso-lute centre" (70).

Besides passages where the centrality of love is restated in this kind of offhanded, far-fetched metaphor, more often than not, the "language of love" is made to sound so customary and conventional that it is difficult to perceive anything original, let alone extraordinary, beyond its scrupu-lous adherence to prescribed forms. Oddly enough, the effect is similar to the normative, everyday use of the language of death, loss, and bereavement, which Fay McLeod has a particular liking for, together with her interest in mermaid legends and nineteenth-century novels: "Fay seldom reads the death notices in the newspaper, but when she's tired or dispirited or personally affected, as she was last week, she studies them closely. She likes the formalism of obituary language, what it sug-gests and conceals. Died suddenly while on vacation in Santa Fe, after a long struggle, after a difficult battle with, after a brief illness, as the result of a tragic accident, peacefully entered into sleep, into Our Maker's arms" (92).

In the gap-filled web worked out of the three strangely interrelated elements – the awareness of mortality, mermaid legends, and nineteenth-century novels – rather than on the end of love, the emphasis thus remains on the fleeting instances of renewal of the rhetoric of love. Even though a hardcore feminist scholar might prefer plugging her ears with the same beeswax with which Ulysses plugged his, so as not to hear the ravishing voice of Shields's storyteller, a closer reading of her text leads us into a movable, hybrid world of half-truths where not even meno-pause guides are devoid of interest. As for the mishaps entailed by love, caused by as improbable incidents as the falling out of the sky of an air-plane tire that triggers off Fay's parents' breakup, they may highlight that *"anything* may happen" in this republic. And at any moment or age!

Should we ultimately be disenchanted, baffled, or thrilled by the fact that Shields offers no actual keys to the mysteries and mishaps of love, any more than she provides clear answers to the question of "goodness" posed by her tenth and final novel, *Unless*, another peculiarly consoling story that soothes without tranquilizing the anguished, novelty-seeking modern readers that we tend to be? The answer is a probable "yes" to all three adjectives.

While looking for the words to account for Carol Shields's own application of what she regarded as the "texture of the quotidian"[8] and the dramatization of the commonplace in Jane Austen's works, the slightly subversive grounding in domestic reality that does not hinder wider insights into and commentaries on the workings of the society, I suddenly thought of the definition provided in *Le féminin et le sacré* (The Feminine and the Sacred) by Julia Kristeva about the work of the American painter Georgia O'Keeffe:

I adore this sober and sensual woman painter, her fleshy flowers, her egg visions (she too!), humid bones and cleaned-up skulls. Here's yet another modest explorer of the unnameable ... She does not hesitate to draw mysteries, but of what? Her body, a flower-sex, life, death, the cosmos, the human being? Secretly, modestly, she moves – she does not name but keeps quiet. And she draws. She does not draw what she draws but *something else* in *the same thing*, an insignificant thing, almost nothing.[9]

I believe that this kind of "O'Keeffian framing of the nearly nothing-ness," underlaid by the tacit acceptance of "silencing" instead of "nam-ing," intimating rather than fiercely designating the thing by its presumably "proper" name, can also be sensed through *The Republic of Love*. Indeed, the aesthetic activity perceptible in Carol Shields's novel may be read as an attempt to permeate, without immersing, the "same ordinary thing" with "autre chose"/"something else." The porous inter-space of fantasy thus outlined with the help of a mesmerizing story-teller's voice is neither a utopia nor a dystopia, but a sunken, rather than a fallen, republic, a "big wide radioland" (119) where the postmodernist view of the displaced, disillusioned, disconnected, and deeply distressed North American city-dweller is playfully yet no less critically challenged. Not entirely unlike the collective "love affair," which turns out to be a puritan nightmare in a text by another Canadian writer, Margaret

Atwood, whose novel *The Handmaid's Tale* deliberately blurs the distinctions between private and public fantasies, Shields's novel explores a fundamental, never a fundamentalist, religiously sanctified "power of love." Although written from completely different standpoints, these two novels seem to share the same conviction about an underlying, easily ridiculed, yet potentially transformative, capacity to love. At the same time they reveal an acute awareness of the risky reiterations of such worn-out assumptions and postulates, especially by women writers.

This is how, in the second half of the novel, Fay McLeod – conscious of the way women writers' love-related texts have often been passed over as something childish, womanish, "something to jeer at, something for jerks" (248) – is seized while pondering over the ambivalent and unresolved word "love":

It's possible to speak ironically about romance, but no adult with any sense talks about love's richness and transcendence, that it actually happens, that it's happening right now, in the last years of our long, hard, lean, bitter, and promiscuous century. Even *here* it's happening, in this flat, midcontinental city with its half million people and its traffic and weather and asphalt parking lots and languishing flower borders and yellow-leafed trees – right here, the miracle of it. (248)

Finally, after exploring some of the implications of the enigmatically and paradigmatically vibrant mermaid in *The Republic of Love*, we might wish to ponder what Carol Shields's figure of a merman – another "handmade" and "mer-made" creature – could suggest about masculinity as it is approached through this deliberately fishy, watered-down version of a love tale, before it plunges back into the primordial sea of memory.

But well, that's another story!

NOTES

1 Shields, *Republic of Love*, 42.
2 Faye Hammill in Eden and Goertz, *Carol Shields, Narrative Hunger, and the Possibilities of Fiction*, 61.
3 "America is now wholly given over to a damned mob of scribbling women, and I should have no chance of success while the public taste is occupied with their trash – and should be ashamed of myself if I did succeed. What is the mystery of these innumerable editions of *The Lamplighter* and other books neither better nor worse? Worse they could not be, and better they need not be, when they sell by

the hundred thousand" (Hawthorne's 1855 letter to his publisher William D. Ticknor, quoted in Fred L. Pattee, *The Feminine Fifties* [New York: Appleton-Century Co., 1940], 110).

4 Shields, *Republic of Love*, 207.

5 Tefs, "Cultivating the Middle-Class Garden," 34.

6 Keahey, "Love = Winnipeg = Home," 216.

7 Shields, *Republic of Love*, 39.

8 Shields, "That Same Ticking Clock," 258.

9 "J'adore cette femme-peintre sobre et sensuelle, ses fleurs charnues, ses visions d'oeufs (elle aussi!), d'os humides et de crânes nettoyés. Encore une exploratrice modeste de l'innommable ... Elle ne se prive pas de tracer les mystères, mais de quoi? Son corps, un sexe-fleur, la vie, la mort, le cosmos, l'être? Secrètement, modestement, elle se déplace – elle ne nomme pas mais se tait. Et dessine. Elle ne dessine pas ce qu'elle dessine, mais *autre chose* dans *la chose même*; une chose insignifiante, presque rien" (Julia Kristeva in the collection of letters *Le féminin et le sacré*, by Catherine Clément and Julia Kristeva, 65–6).

WORKS CITED

Atwood, Margaret. *The Handmaid's Tale*. London: Vintage, 1985.

Clément, Catherine, and Julia Kristeva. *Le féminin et le sacré*. Paris: Stock, 1998.

Donovan, Rita. "A Fine Romance: A Republic of Love." *Books in Canada* 21, no. 3 (1992): 40.

Eden, Edward, and Dee Goertz, eds. *Carol Shields, Narrative Hunger, and the Possibilities of Fiction*. Toronto: University of Toronto Press, 2003.

hooks, bell. *Communion: The Female Search for Love*. New York: HarperCollins, 2002.

Keahey, Deborah. "Love = Winnipeg = Home: Carol Shields's *The Republic of Love*." *Prairie Fire* 20, no. 2 (1999): 210–21.

Nodelman, Perry. "Living in the Republic of Love: Carol Shields's Winnipeg." *Prairie Fire* 16, no. 1 (1995): 40–55.

Shields, Carol. *The Republic of Love*. London: Flamingo, 1993.

– "The Same Ticking Clock." In *Language in Her Eye: Views on Writing and Gender by Canadian Women Writing in English*, ed. Libby Scheier, Sharah Sheard, and Eleanor Wachtel, 256–9. Toronto: Coach House, 1990.

Tefs, Wayne. "Cultivating the Middle-Class Garden." *Border Crossings* 11, no. 3 (1992): 33–4.

Thomas, Joan. "The Republic of Love." *Prairie Fire* 13, no. 2 (1992): 99–101.

6

Larry's A/Mazing Spaces

CORAL ANN HOWELLS

A/MAZING SPACE INC.
Laurence J. Weller – Landscape Architecture
Specialty: Garden Mazes

982 Lake Street, Suite 33, Oak Park, Il. 91045
Telephone: 312 999 2888
Fax: 312 999 8884

> At the age of thirty-eight Larry Weller finds himself a member of a rarefied and eccentric profession: he is a designer, and what he designs and installs are garden mazes. A simple maze maker is what he prefers to call himself.[1]

Larry Weller's first business card when he sets himself up as a specialist in garden mazes in suburban Chicago in 1988 provides an apt emblem for this essay, as it summarizes in visual profile all the issues related to mazes and spaces that I wish to consider in my reading of Carol Shields's fictive biography. That card advertises the maze as a physical feature in landscape architecture, while its miniature pictorial representation foregrounds the maze as an artificially constructed space where one can wander slightly disoriented and be amazed, so that the maze may be appreciated as a spatial design which will accommodate multiple symbolic meanings, varying from spiritual or sexual to psychological, all within an aesthetic frame. Moreover, the maze design on Larry's card is contextualized within the novel, being the same as the one featured at the beginning of chapter 1, suggestive of the principle of doubling back and repeating which is a characteristic feature of the narrative structure (the design itself is taken from Aidan Meehan's *Celtic Design Maze Patterns*, 1993).[2] The typographical device of the slash in "A/Mazing," which seven years later Larry comes to see as rather coy and outdated, may indeed be too 1980s, and "it absolutely won't begin to do for the year 1995" (260), though that break does open up the word for the space of a double pun on "maze" (the original meaning of which was "to stupefy or to bewilder") and "amaze," meaning "to overwhelm with wonder," thereby opening the way to a promise of new meanings via Larry's maze-making. That break also signals the important dimension of space, and in this essay I intend to use the spatial theories of Henri Lefebvre, spelled out in *The Production of Space*, with his dual consideration of "representations of space" (lived material space) and "representational (symbolic) space."[3] I shall argue that Shields's narrative continually plays across these two different concepts of space, situating Larry's a/mazing moments on the indeterminate borderlines between the two. By this means the mazes also thematize what is going on in his subjective life and so bring it into sharper focus.

The mazes in *Larry's Party* signal yet another of Shields's distinctive revisions of the genre of fictive biography, where she offers a spatial figuring of Larry's life story rather than staying within the constraints of a temporal pattern. Through her use of pictorial and textual maze imagery, she contrives to represent the mobility of her subject, as he moves through physical and social spaces while also negotiating the shifting planes of perception within his own interior life. Shields has always been fascinated by the challenges posed by biography, that problematical genre which is perhaps best summed up by the quotation used as a chapter head by Paula Backscheider in *Reflections on Biography*: "There are three rules for writing biography, but, unfortunately, no one knows what they are."[4] So shifting are the parameters of this genre that often biographies are favourably compared with novels, or on the other hand, a novelist may claim that "the only good biographies are to be found in novels."[5] Though she has written two biographies of literary women, one on Susanna Moodie and one on Jane Austen, Shields's radical skepticism about the genre has enticed her, like the protagonist of her first novel, into "that whorish field of biographical fiction,"[6] where her innovations within fictive biography and autobiography in *Swann: A Mystery*

(1987), *The Stone Diaries* (1993), and *Larry's Party* (1997) have challenged the very foundations on which the genre is structured.

Of course, Shields's thinking has been influenced by feminist theory, deconstruction, and postmodernism. As she says, "All of us in recent years have been inhaling the pollen of contemporary literary theory."[7] She credits postmodernism with giving writers a lens through which to see the limits of realism ("It was, perhaps, not real enough" – for the interesting reason that "it passed too quickly through the territory of the quotidian"),[8] though she also has arguments with postmodernism for its neglect of the human issues pertaining to embodied selves who live in and respond to specific historical and social environments. Biography, factual or fictive, is concerned with constructing a story of the life of its subject and that subject's individual identity, which is represented in the text. However, as Shields speculates, the very concept of identity may be a convenient fiction dictated by generic imperatives. We recall here Paul de Man's early deconstructive comment on life-writing that "the autobiographical project may itself produce and determine the life and that whatever the writer *does* is in fact governed by the technical demands of self-portraiture and thus determined, in all its aspects, by the resources of his medium."[9] Alternatively we have Judith Butler's gender-based critique of traditional conventions of identity construction: "What can be meant by 'identity' then, and what grounds the presumption that identities are self-identical, persisting through time as the same, unified, and internally coherent?"[10]

Shields as novelist is engaging with the same issues of instability and contradiction with her representation of identities always in process, as indicated in the title of chapter 9 of *Larry's Party*: "Larry So Far, 1990" ("So far, so good" [181]). Larry as biographical subject eludes traditional literary conventions of a "coherent, stable, singular, and sharply defined selfhood"[11] by assuming a surprising number of identities and roles. He is a son and a brother, a husband (twice), a father (once), a lover (three times), and he has two professions, first as florist and then as maze maker. This would seem to conform to postmodern concepts of multiple shifting identities that are always provisional and open to reconstruction, but Shields manages to keep her distance from postmodern theories through her construction of Larry as embodied remembering and feeling subject.

Her novel appears to conform to traditional biographical conventions while at the same time exposing their limitations, which is a strategy she adopted in *The Stone Diaries*. It begins with a portrait of the biographical subject, though as it is a photo of Larry at nine months old sitting in his high chair with his face "pulled into a knit of absorbed anguish" (48), its status is ambiguous: is it emblematic or is it parodic? The table of contents is arranged on a chronological grid that maps out a sequence of twenty years in Larry's life, starting with "Fifteen Minutes in the Life of Larry Weller, 1977," continuing through such chapters as "Larry Inc., 1988," and "Men Called Larry, 1995," to end with "Larry's Party, 1997," which marks both his mid-life crisis and another decisive turning point in his emotional life. The documentary evidence is there in the details of his career and his maze projects, but such formal arrangement is insistently undercut by the narrative's twists and turns, by its shifts of perspective and geographical location, and above all by the apparent randomness of Larry's memories and private associations, which are continually interspersed with the factual details. The biographer's presence is quite unobtrusive, and the reader has no idea how she got access to her evidence; indeed, Shields uses her freedom as a novelist to write about what is undocumented, in a deliberate flouting of biographical convention. There is certainly no omniscient narrator's voice, for Larry's is the main focalizing consciousness here, and the biographer's voice is elided into his indirect interior monologue. Yet one has the impression that the biographer is female, based mainly on the kinds of experience that are selected as significant in Larry's life story. Backscheider's comments on the influence of feminism bring this issue of the imperative of gender into focus: "The second effect of feminism on biography [the first being the increased number of women featuring as biographical and autobiographical subjects] is to assure that biographers will think about the significance and amount of space 'ordinary' aspects of life merit and that the importance of the private, domestic, or intimate sphere will be given attention,"[12] whether the biographical subject is male or female.

The main evidence of the biographer's interpretive role is shown in her mapping of Larry's interior life as a spatial one, of which the maze designs at the beginning of every chapter are a reminder to her readers. Inside every chapter the narrative wanders digressively within the marked time period, while looping backwards and sideways rather like the progress through a maze – always refusing a linear progression, just as it rejects any centring principle or a definite single meaning. Instead, it draws attention to the way Larry's experience is constructed as accidental, continually surprising to himself. We are reminded of Backscheider's question in her discussion of experimental biographies: "Should we demand that biographers recognize 'the accidental life' more often?"[13]

This time Shields represents in novel form the same enterprise in which she was engaged with her short stories in *Various Miracles*: "I wanted 'Scenes' to become a container for what it was talking about – which was the randomness of a human life, its arbitrary and fractured experiences that nevertheless strains towards a kind of wholeness."[14] Reviewers and critics have all commented on the mazes in the novel, either in terms of narrative design, which mimics the backward and forward loopings of a maze,[15] or in relation to maze symbolism.[16] Goertz's excellent essay contains detailed documentation of the sources for all the maze designs in the novel, together with an extended critical commentary, which emphasizes Shields's postmodern playfulness in her deployment of maze images for varying purposes – sometimes as thematic illustrations, sometimes as symbols, sometimes as narrative jokes on the reader: "Shields plays the postmodern game of never letting us forget that we are reading."[17] Goertz also records Shields's remark on the narrative structure of *Larry's Party*: "In a radio interview, Shields said that she 'wanted to design each chapter as a little maze in itself.'"[18]

Turning back to the chapter "Larry Inc, 1988," from which I borrowed the emblem for the opening of this essay, we find a perfect illustration of the maze structure in his retrospective narrative of his life. If we bear in mind his distinction between a labyrinth as a "predetermined conveyor track" and a maze, which is "designed to deceive" (81), with its twists and turns, dead ends, and constant doublings back on itself, we can see this pattern traced in his nighttime musings. Here is a man who has apparently reinvented himself, relocating from Canada to the United States, changing jobs, and marrying a second time; yet through his private history, certain continuities of the affective life emerge which form the basis of his individual selfhood. Though the narrative begins in the present tense as Larry mulls over his recent experiences as a professional maze designer, it soon doubles back in time as he recapitulates the history of his nine completed maze projects, beginning with his first experimental maze in his own backyard in Lipton Street, Winnipeg, before moving on to the memory of his first maze commissions in Manitoba and Saskatchewan. After a leap forward in time with a rare shift to the biographer's voice referring to a snow maze that he would build many years later in Siberia, Larry's narrative circles back again to his old Winnipeg maze and memories of his first wife, Dorrie, and his son, Ryan, and then further back still to his original maze experience at Hampton Court. A break at this point in the text signals Larry's professional breakthrough with the Barnes maze in Illinois and the break in his life with his divorce, his move to Chicago, and his meeting with his second wife. That is followed in chronological order by their honeymoon in Tennessee, where Larry was beginning work on a new maze, and a glance at his other projects ranging across America from upstate New York to Colorado. Perhaps surprisingly, Larry's mazing ends with a doubling back for the third time to his Lipton Street maze before returning to the present. However, the chapter ends with a last backward glance at that first maze, now half-destroyed but still flourishing.

From this brief account, the strategies of a narrative maze structure will be evident, where the "turnings" are signalled by temporal shifts, the "looping paths" by the digressions of associated memories that may lead to "dead ends," and the "doubling back" by the insistent return to the Winnipeg maze. Through this net conflation of space, time, and memory, Shields adds a human dimension to Lefebvre's comment: "In space, what came earlier continues to underpin what follows."[19] What is perhaps less evident is the way that the details of Larry's affective life are interspersed with his professional history – his developing passion for mazes, his thoughts about his two marriages, and the cluster of inarticulate emotions centred on his first maze. That mutilated maze in no way conforms to the "teasing mysteries" of traditional design, and yet what it symbolizes in terms of a human relationship constitutes "the most unexamined mystery of his life" (180).

This apparently digressive but very self-consciously designed fictive biography takes into account the oscillations and oddities of Larry's subjective life, constructing someone who experiences life as a maze (as the extracts from the two poems at the beginning and end suggest) and who makes his living as a maze maker. Just as the maze artifact goes far back through human history into Greek mythology with the story of Theseus and the Minotaur in the Cretan labyrinth, so Shields argues that storytelling and stories too have "deep structures": "You can go straight to Ulysses to see an early model: the tale of the wanderer, the homeless, the picaresque hero with an unsteady eye and an inability to effect change, a being helplessly adrift ... Today, we might describe such a person as being incompletely socialized, someone who stands outside of events, who in fact chooses that position ... The outsider is the most persistent of literary heroes in our tradition."[20] And so to the life of Larry Weller, who describes himself as "touring in his own life adventure" (245), always wondering "was this the life that Larry Weller had signed up for" (165), and like Ulysses, experiencing a homecoming at the end of the story.

However, my emphasis in this essay is only indirectly on Shields's revisions of the biographical genre. Instead, focusing on the "extra-ordinary," I shall pay attention to three epiphanic moments in an attempt to analyze how she negotiates between the everyday world of fact and the subjective world of the creative imagination. Arguably it is via the a/mazing spaces in Larry's life story that Shields finds a language to open up her realistic fictional frame to accommodate a squint-eyed view "that distorts but also sharpens beyond ordinary vision, bringing forward what might be called the subjunctive mode of oneself or others, a world of dreams and possibilities and parallel realities."[21] It is this power to represent the subjunctive mode that Shields sees as the feature which distinguishes fiction from the genres of biography and history: "Biography and history have a narrative structure, but they don't tell us much about the interior lives of people. This seems to me to be fiction's magic that it attempts to be an account of all that cannot be documented but is, nevertheless, true."[22] The three "a/mazing spaces" which I shall consider are constructed inside a text that seeks to catch those undocumented moments of Larry's subjective life: his first visit to Hampton Court maze in 1978, the experience that he later comes to view as his creative awakening; his construction of the McCord maze in Toronto in 1997, which he sees as "the most creatively adventurous of his life" (289); and finally, the mirage effect of his reconciliation with Dorrie in the social space of his dinner party, which might be interpreted as the centre of Larry's life maze.

It would seem that these three moments represent progressive stages in Larry's mazing through life, in a way comparable with Laurence Sterne's eighteenth-century autobiographical fiction *The Life and Opinions of Tristram Shandy, Gentleman*, where a similarly errant subject describes his narrative as "digressive, and it is progressive too, – and at the same time."[23] Shields and Sterne both use visual resources as well as words – her mazes, his marbled pages and doodlings – for both writers recognize "the stubborn resistance of language to certain modes of meditation."[24] There are other Shandean parallels as well, such as the teasing textual games that these authors play with their readers, while there is something decidedly hobby-horsical about Larry's "maze craze" as he builds his first scaled-down maze in his small Winnipeg garden, an activity not unlike Sterne's Uncle Toby, who stages his mock-ups of Marlborough's campaigns on the bowling green at Shandy Hall. Even Larry's name echoes Sterne's; both of them were christened Laurence, though so far as we know, Sterne was never called Larry. Such shadowy parallels may lead to dead ends, though they "pleasure heart and head" (339) as they float like "wayward chips" in the novel, their suggestiveness remaining as unaccommodated as some of the minor perverse pleasures in Larry's own life: "These wayward chips of himself are hard to look at, so mainly he doesn't" (237). To return to Larry's a/mazing moments, Shields manages in all these episodes to create parallel realities within the seemingly safe spaces of realism. Larry continues to be himself: "He could be someone else, but he's not. He's Larry Weller, an ordinary man who's been touched by ordinary good and bad luck" (249), while he also negotiates connections between himself and the world outside and makes discoveries about his most secret desires.

In analyzing these sideways slippages away from the ordinary into the extraordinary, one could explain them as shifts in narrative perspective (which they are), or an alternative approach would be to view them as a/mazing spaces, using Henri Lefebvre's spatial theories as a lens, bearing in mind Shields's own figuring in spatial terms of the relation between words and the world: "But we need to remember that the labyrinth of language stands beside reality itself: a somewhat awkward, almost always distorted facsimile or matrix."[25] When Lefebvre writes about the purpose of art, his speculations might include both Shields's narrative art and Larry's art of maze-making: "What is the fantasy of art? To lead out of what is present, out of what is close, out of representations of space [material space], into what is further off, into nature, into symbols, into representational spaces."[26] That statement suggests why mazes are so significant in Shields's narrative. Situated in the material world as a feature of landscape architecture, a maze offers the aesthetic equivalent to Lefebvre's example of an ancient Roman city: "Inserted into nature, occupying its own site, in a well-defined situation clearly distinguishable from its surroundings, it gave rise to a particular representation of space."[27] Both the maze and the city are circumscribed sites that may be transformed into representational spaces, though in comparison with the Roman city, an *image mundi* (image of the world),[28] the maze offers a playful fantasy in miniature.

As a purely decorative space, a maze design invites that it be read as a symbolic space, and Shields's novel entertains both conceptualizations of space, never losing the dimension of realism based on the materiality of earth and shrubs, but also playing with the multiple symbolic meanings that mazes have assumed. In her narrative, mazes and maze production belong to the world of paid work; they may be Larry's passion, but they are also his profession, and he spends years studying books about maze design, learning about shrubs, and acquiring a maze vocabulary, while as a maze maker he is engaged in the mathematics of the artifact as well as delighting in the "miracle of it, making something out of nothing" (68). He is also involved in maze construction, planting, and maintenance and in dealing with clients, for like Shields, Larry never neglects the human dimension: "(Yes, Mr Barnes. Of course, Mr Barnes)" (146). As two of Larry's rich patrons phrase it, "In the abstract, there's no reason for these mazes. They're wrapped in privilege, they do nothing"; "And we were so taken by the, the mystery of them" (312).

The maze, like a painting, has an ambiguous relation to the real world, being space set apart onto which are projected multiple cultural meanings, so that it becomes what Lefebvre would call a "representational space." In the novel, mazes are variously interpreted by the characters, so that Dr Eric Eisner, Larry's mentor, rejects the traditional spiritual interpretation of the maze as a simulacrum of life's pilgrimage towards salvation in favour of a sexual interpretation with orgasm at its centre (139), whereas several of Larry's clients favour psychological interpretations centred on an "encounter with oneself" (313) or as a figuring of dream and awakening (which I shall discuss in relation to the McCord maze). For Larry, on the other hand, the possible interpretations of these "mere toys and riddles" (152) are always shifting and elusive, so that the multivoiced chorus of symbolic interpretations makes it plain that the meanings of the maze are developed from different subjective perspectives. The boundary between realism and the symbolic is insistently blurred, and Larry lives his life on that borderline, slipping quite unexpectedly through the quotidian grid into moments of clarity and insight. All his a/mazing moments are situated within artificially constructed spaces, either of the hedge mazes or of the social space of his dinner party, which is "a kind of interpersonal maze," as one recent critic has suggested.[29] In every case the familiar everyday world represented through the discourse of realism opens up momentarily to reveal a parallel plane of subjectively apprehended reality. That extra-ordinary other dimension is always figured through or closely related to maze imagery.

Shields begins her exploration of the paradoxical relation between art and nature, sight and vision, together with notions of perceptual distortion and willed abandonment, with Larry's first visit to Hampton Court maze on his honeymoon trip to England back in 1978. The maze design at the head of the chapter is indeed the Hampton Court maze, though as it is not named, that fact is left for the reader to discover. This is typical of Shields's authorial games, while the chapter title "Larry's Love" casts a deliberate ambiguity on where the centre of Larry's affection really lies. It is in the maze that a moment occurs which might be traditionally described as the revelation of the artist's vocation. Here we may notice one more move in Shields's intertextual games, in the parallel with Stephen Dedalus's revelatory moment on the beach in James Joyce's *A Portrait of the Artist as a Young Man*. That parallel is all the more provocative when we consider that Stephen's surname evokes the mythic figure of Dedalus, creator of the Cretan labyrinth and Icarus's wings.

However, Shields leaves those intertextual threads hanging, for Larry's own name, Weller, has only ambiguous origins (253), and for him the revelatory experience at Hampton Court is apparently accidental. Only later does he recall it as "what he supposed he must call a transformative experience" (217). Larry, the young floral designer from Winnipeg who had been overcome with wonder at the greenness of England in early March and had bought a second-hand book about shrubs in Manchester, has already discovered in "the greenness of hedgerows" his first means of escape from daily life: "It was like switching channels. Holly, lime, whitethorn, box, a string of names like the chorus of a popular song. He let their shrubby patterns press down on his brain" (31). This is the young man who has his moment of "unexpected rapture" on the last day of his honeymoon, not with his young wife, Dorrie, who makes him anxious, but by himself when he manages to get lost among the living shrubs of Hampton Court maze. Dorrie says that he looks "dizzy" when he finally comes out, only to find the rest of the tourist bus party waiting for him. That word "dizzy" is a sly reminder to the reader of the Middle English meaning of "maze," and it is this deliberate skewing of perception, the subjective experience of being "mazed," which comes to characterize all Larry's a/mazing moments, beginning with this one in the "closed, expansive contrivance" of the oldest hedge maze in England.

At Hampton Court Larry is aware of himself not intellectually but sensationally as a body moving through space, experiencing a *dérèglement de sens*. For the first time in his life he feels beside himself, split into his own double, as he "observed how his feet chose each wrong turning, working against his navigational instincts" (36). Slipping out of the shell of his own identity, he manages for a moment to transcend the socially scripted boundaries of his identity, with all its restrictions and responsibilities, as he slips across the borders between realism into spaces of imagination and desire. His activity of "circling and repeating" in a state of "feverish detachment" bears striking similarities to Freud's figurative language as he speculates on the Death Drive, "the most universal endeavour of all living substance – namely to return to the quiescence of the inorganic world."[30] Freud's comment on the regressive character of the instincts seems to be echoed in Larry's awareness of an "old greedy grammar flapping in his ears: lost, more lost, utterly lost." (36). This secret desire spells release from life's pleasures and tensions, epitomized here in the "curved space" of his new marriage (after his divorce referred to as "a cramped crawlspace"), which he must learn to fit into in his life of daily obligation. It is through Larry's indirect interior monologue that we are made aware of his sudden perception of his own doubleness, which opens up undreamed-of possibilities and new freedoms. Though he does not realize it at the time, Larry's maze experience will be the shaping force in his life as a creative artist. Paradoxically ("A paradox. You know, like ironic" [82]), his passion for mazes gives him his identity, where "his freakish profession is the only thing that keeps him from disappearing" (180), while it also frees him from the limits of personal identity.

Ten years later, when working on the Barnes maze, Larry is able to formulate his objectives as a maze designer and why he creates those boxed-in, shrub-lined winding paths: "In a maze you had to feel doubly lost, with exterior sensation cut so cleanly away that nothing remained except for the sound of one's own breath and the teasing sense of wilful abandonment" (153). His formulation, now expressed with professional detachment, echoes almost word for word his Hampton Court experience (see 36–7). Then he had found himself surrounded by "green walls too high to see over," which generated those delicious feelings of being lost and "unplugged from the world," all culminating in a "moment of willful abandonment." His unconscious compulsion to repeat the details of that experience through his own created artifact long afterwards has a slightly uncanny effect which emphasizes the significance of that transformative moment of Larry's creative awakening.

Larry, whose international celebrity as a maze designer is based on his Hampton Court experience, does not understand the significance of what is happening at the time, and fourteen years later, when he returns to England, the greater part of the mystery still eludes him: "He has never been able to identify what happened to him during the hour he wandered lost and dazed and separated from the others" (217). Larry himself is a different person by then, and ironically, on that second visit, the maze does nothing for him, since he is too professionally involved with the mechanics of mazes; the magic has drained away. However, his interior monologue at this time is mingled with a narrative voice-over that translates his largely inarticulate feelings for the reader: "He remembers he felt a joyous rising of spirit that was related in some way to the self's dimpled plasticity; he could move beyond what he was, the puzzling hedges seemed to announce, he could become someone other than Larry Weller, shockingly new husband of Dorrie Shaw, non-speculative citizen of a former colony, a man of limited imagination and few choices" (217). This moment "in the subjunctive mode" has strong affinities with Magnus Flett's transformative experience in *The Stone Diaries* of reading *Jane Eyre* for the first time, on which Shields commented in an interview: "I think he took the book into his body and soul, and made it his. It was a whole other dimension, another world to live in besides the one he was stuck in. Then, later, it gave him a sort of celebrity."[31]

These experiences of maze-making and reading are both versions of what Shields has described as "narrative hunger," that imaginative need which is not satisfied by our ordinary everyday lives: "Judith Gill in *Small Ceremonies* talks about 'narrative hunger,' why do we need stories? Her conclusion – and mine [says Shields] – is that our own lives are never quite enough for us. They're too busy, too dark, too circumscribed, too bound by geography, by gender, by cultural history."[32] In her 1996 Hanover College address, entitled "Narrative Hunger and the Overflowing Cupboard," Shields elaborates on her theories of writing and reading stories as "a hunger for narrative, for storytelling, that is, is probably about 40,000 years old."[33] For Larry, a man who never has enough words, that lack is supplied not by stories but by mazes, and given Shields's keen, double-edged awareness of the powers and limits of language, it is not surprising that we find other characters like him in her novels who prefer alternative narrative constructions to more obviously verbal ones. In an essay entitled "Filling the Creative Void," Sarah Gamble writes about how "those characters who express themselves through craft transcend the limitations of narrative convention and linguistic structures,"[34] citing examples from *Small Ceremonies*, where Judith Gill's husband reworks his literary criticism of *Paradise Lost* as a tapestry in coloured wools, or Brenda Bowman's quilts in *Happenstance*.

However, it seems to me that the person who comes closest to Larry is Daisy Goodwill Flett, whose lovingly tended garden in *The Stone Diaries* shares common ground with Larry's mazes: "Entering it is to leave the troubles of the world behind. Visitors standing in this garden sometimes feel their hearts lock into place for an instant, and experience blurred primal visions of creation – Eden itself, paradise indeed."[35] Larry's mazes, with their pulsing vegetable growth, are paralleled in the "stubborn vegetable will" and "green secrets" of Daisy's garden. Mazes and gardens present similar refuges from everyday confusion, and being inside a hedge maze brings Larry as close as he ever comes to paradise: a maze sends his spirit "soaring" (72).

Larry's maze craze is his way of living "outside his life story as well as inside it,"[36] but when his passion becomes his livelihood, he is forced to think about mazes more realistically: "He plans, he constructs, he hires and subcontracts" (152). The reader is constantly reminded of Larry's growing professional expertise in a narrative that follows the shape of his career with detailed accounts of the mazes he designs and builds and the prizes he wins, notably his Guggenheim Fellowship in 1992, which enables him and his second wife, Beth, to spend several months visiting mazes all over Europe and beyond: "In the spring of the following year they would find themselves in Japan's teasing, contemporary wooden mazes, and then on to Australia. So many wonders to see" (226). Through Larry's mazing, Shields contrives a recapitulation of maze history, though that word "wonder" is a reminder of the constant oscillation between the realistic and the symbolic. Larry is endlessly fascinated by the mystery of mazes, where "the path to a maze's goal is always shortened by turning away from the goal" (152), one of the secrets that keeps him "reverent, awestruck, faithful" – all words that tend to describe a sacred mystery hidden paradoxically within the structure of the quotidian.

Perhaps one should say "hidden within the structure of the hedge maze," for it is the "greenness and growth" of shrubs, "the vital plant tissue when it had been coaxed into new shapes, so that it offered up one surprise after another, confounding human perception," which Larry loves, "presenting the opportunity to locate oneself in the living world" (150–1). The most extraordinary feature of mazes is their sense of enclosure, for being inside a maze is a sort of personal exclusion zone, a space for self-transcendence. It is a space created by art on the earth, rooted in the earth but not of the earth, a space of wonder at the conjunction of art and nature. That location in the living world is itself paradoxical (as Lefebvre points out), for the sacred space "continues to be perceived as part of nature" even though art has "wrenched the area from its natural context," creating a simulacrum of the natural through artificial means, which is exactly what a maze does. My reading of mazes here is a variant of Lefebvre's description of sacred places, though his emphasis, unlike mine, is on the exercise of political power: "A moment comes when, through the actions of masters or conquerors, a part of this [natural] space is assigned a new role and henceforward appears as transcendent, as sacred ... as magical and cosmic."[37] Art, on the other hand, exercises an intimately imaginative power, and there are elements in my reading which owe more to Bachelard's meditations on the poetic appeal of images of "felicitous space" as he seeks "to determine the human values of the sorts of space that may be grasped, that may be defended against adverse forces, the spaces we love."[38]

And so, by the twists and turns of narrative, we come to the second of Larry's a/mazing spaces that I shall discuss, the McCord maze, commissioned by a wealthy Toronto industrialist. For Larry, it signals new departures, not only in terms of his relocation from Illinois back to Canada but also in terms of maze design and conceptualization, for this is the largest garden maze he has ever made and his first three-dimensional maze, built not on a flat site but over a Toronto ravine. It is also the "most creatively adventurous of his life" in its deliberate attempt to straddle the border between reality and dream, the material and the imaginary. With its *trompe l'oeil* effects, it represents a reconfiguring of space in a triumph of artifice, designed to create the illusion of an organic relationship between the human and non-human worlds. The ravine site has given Larry the opportunity to play with maze conventions, "to bring the tradition home to Toronto," as Garth McCord phrases it (312): "He's pulled the rug out this time, but subtly, softly. Instead of the stiff, formal plantings of traditional mazes – holly, box, yew – he's employed dozens of dense but informal hedges – such gently sprawling plants as five-leaf aralia (tolerates polluted air well) ... rose of Sharon, caragana because of its feathery lightness, winged euonymus, and forsythia" (289). Here is evidence both of the craftsman's detailed planning and of the artist's vision, for the shrubs Larry chooses are designed to blur the boundaries between the maze-walkers' awareness of their physical bodies and the natural world. He has created what Bachelard would call a "poetic space" where "two kinds of space, intimate space and exterior space, keep encouraging each other, as it were, in their growth."[39] The varied plant forms, with their "gently sprawling" growth or their "feathery lightness," disperse any awareness of a solid material world, inducing an imaginative liberation from fixed boundaries of identity in a kind of mimicry of the dream state.

By skilfully manipulating the way the walkers register their progress down the ravine and up again, Larry is using the space of the maze as a visual figuring for psychological process: "The descent into unconscious sleep, followed by a slow awakening" (290). Larry has been constructing a dreamlike maze narrative that resembles Shields's description of the art of storytelling: "The remarkable Wendy Steiner, in her book *The Scandal of Pleasure*, tells us that art – and I'm thinking of narrative art here – lures us into a dreamlike world of radical freedom where the rules and habits of our consciously regulated lives are suspended, and where we remain capable of reflection and judgement and from which we return with heightened awareness of the tastes and choices that ordinarily define and confine us."[40] Speaking of the imaginative possibilities of fictional narrative that challenge the limits of realism, Shields suggests the close connections between different forms of verbal and visual art in enhancing the range of human experience.

Larry's image of the "dreamy organic world" which he has created (and which all the reporters at his press conference assiduously but uncomprehendingly note down) expresses the tension endemic to pastoral in the always ambiguous relationship between nature and art, and I wonder if Shields is not being gently ironic here. Has Larry fallen into the trap of thinking organically about something that is really very artificial? And is there also an implied irony in the fact that such a private dream space should be converted into a public space, for the McCord ravine property has been "generously donated to the city parks system" (289) and will be opened by the mayor of Toronto, who will "cut the ribbon" and "lead the first party through" (313). The juxtaposition between civic arrangements and the metaphysics of mazes is undeniably comic, though perhaps through the sharp contradictions drawn between private and public spheres, Shields's emphasis here is on "parallel realities" in the acknowledgment that the closest most city-dwellers can come to a sense of harmony with nature is through its simulacrum in the maze.

However, it is in the final chapter that Larry himself moves towards "a slow awakening" in a parallel narrative which is as dreamlike as that which he has envisaged for his maze-walkers. Here the maze becomes entirely metaphorical, having its reality only as a topic of conversation, and it is within the contrived social space of Larry's Toronto dinner party, given in honour of his two visiting ex-wives and to celebrate the completion of the McCord maze, that my third example of an a/mazing space is situated. This is the moment of reconciliation between Larry and Dorrie after their separation of fourteen years, and it is the image of the mirage that I wish to focus on here. For as Lefebvre remarks,

"Mirage effects can introduce an extraordinary element into an ordinary context."[41]

Yet that impression of ordinariness is extremely deceptive, for their moment of mutual recognition is really as carefully contrived as any scene in a play. In fact the image of a theatrical event prepares the reader for the climactic scene: "If this party were a play the curtain would come down … Right now" (327). Instead, the exchange of looks and smiles between Larry and Dorrie across the dinner table signals the resolution of a plot that belongs to the genre of popular romance. Realism is tinged with self-conscious narrative artifice as boundaries blur between material and subjective reality when Larry's position shifts from spectator to actor in his private emotional drama:

Something has happened in the room, he understands that; there are two densities present, suspended one inside the other, and the air around the table, candlelit, soft, breaks up into shimmering bars of heat. A perceptual accident perhaps, a mirage, but here they are, suddenly, Larry and Dorrie, the Wellers, husband and wife. This is their party. They are, in this alternate version of reality, partners in a long marriage, survivors of old quarrels long since mended. The journey they appear to have taken separately has really been made together. After all, after all. So this is what has happened. Their parents are dead, the years have flown, and they themselves are parents of a beloved son who is in difficulty. It is they, Dorrie and Larry, who have brought this evening into being, and here, arrayed around them as though in a holographic image, are their friends and family, warmly invited, encouraged to talk, comforted with food and wine, adored, embraced. (328)

Larry's mirage is a dramatic reconstruction, a little narrative "in the subjunctive mode" of parallel unlived lives and possibilities that shimmer in a dimension just beyond diurnal surfaces in the spaces of imagination and desire. Shields uses the image of double densities, thereby creating an enclosed space where emotion has effected a subtle dislocation in both space and time, so that what is real and what is imagined change places. We are brought close to the subjective refiguring of two people's life stories, which collapses the spatial and temporal separation of a broken marriage. What is evoked is intimate familial space, with the story of parents and children rooted in a long historical process, imaging the reconstitution of a shattered family unit. Notions of centres and peripheries have shifted here, so that Larry and Dorrie are together at the centre and everyone else is on the periphery, arranged around them in a kind of realistic illusion as insubstantial as a hologram, which is no more than a changing play of lights upon a surface. Within this visual vocabulary, reality becomes a matter of shifting perspectives where real and imaginary worlds are briefly reversed in the "mirage."

A mirage is nothing but an image of virtual reality in space, an optical illusion where something at a great distance or even over the horizon appears to be close. What is happening at the dinner table may be a "perceptual accident" brought about partly by the shimmering candlelight, partly by the social interaction of the guests, and partly by Larry's refusal (surprising even to himself) to be foster father to Beth's baby, but principally it is a manifestation of the unspoken connection between Larry and Dorrie. Again this is a thematization of what has already happened in the realistic narrative through the passage of time: "The old resentments and angers of his life with Dorrie have faded from view, leaving a circle of radiance behind" (141).

So the mirage serves as a blurred vision "of what rightfully is theirs," poised between fantasy and truth, seeming to be already present and indeed retrospective but really opening up possibilities of the future – like that slash in "a/mazing," which promised new meanings. As an image that conforms to Larry's and Dorrie's unspoken desires, it is a projection into what Margaret Atwood would call "another dimension of space."[42] It also offers a possible explanation for that indecipherable cluster of emotions around the old half-maze that Dorrie has kept in her garden in Winnipeg like an open secret, defined most elusively by Alice Munro as "something not startling until you think of trying to tell it."[43] The telling of that secret negotiation between Larry and Dorrie is a perfect illustration of the blurring of borders between fiction and biography, for what role does a biographer have at such an extremely private moment? Hermione Lee provides an answer in her discussion of Shields's story "Mirrors"[44] when she refers to a similar incident involving an exchange of glances between a man and a woman: "The storyteller goes out of herself and disappears into such secret moments, and there are a number of references to floating out of oneself into other people's stories."[45]

I think we can read that blurred vision of a shared life as the centre of the maze for Larry's life story, his own secret goal, though the aura of popular romance is tempered by a realistic awareness. Later, when Larry and Dorrie are speaking over coffee about their honeymoon visit to Hampton Court maze, the reader may also recall Larry's youthful moment of insight there when he perceives the vulnerability of love: "Love was not protected. No, it wasn't. It sat out in the open like anything else" (37) – indeed, very like the half-destroyed Lipton Street maze. Yet that conversation is also the time of Larry's enlightenment, when he is able, at least tentatively, to voice his desire not to be "lost" anymore but to be "found." The prospect opens out to a middle-aged romance for ex-husband and ex-wife, which is both a new beginning and a looping back into old familiar spaces. We could see the sequence as his slow awakening, which has been prefigured in the McCord maze, and an enactment of "the essential lost-and-found odyssey of a conventional maze" (289). It is certainly not an exit from the maze, for the only exit is death. As long as life lasts, "we will go round and around. Watching where we're going. Where we've been" (336). These are Larry's last thoughts after the party when he and Dorrie have confessed that they have always loved each other, but they are encoded so obliquely within free indirect discourse that we cannot be sure if it is Larry's perspective or his biographer's. (Are they his thoughts any more than the mistaken coat at the beginning was his or than the party is his? And is it his decision or Dorrie's? Throughout the party he has been waiting for "something more" to happen, though it is Dorrie who smiles at him first.)

The novel offers a spatial figuring of Larry's life inside the a/mazing space of the text, where Shields refashions two conventional life-writing metaphors, the journey and the maze, to take into account the vagaries of the subjective life, registered through a narrative combination of surface reportage and changing perspectives. Incidentally, she also relocates the romantic experience of the sublime, with all its rapture and self-transcendence; no longer is it situated in the vast, overwhelming natural settings of rugged mountains or wilderness, but it is miniaturized within the artificial space of the maze, imaging a shift from nature to culture. It is only inside a maze or when designing a maze that Larry comes closest to a kind of transcendental experience: "All this ignites Larry's sense of equilibrium and sends him soaring" (172). Larry as maze maker and Shields as novelist employ similar oscillations between realistic representations of space and symbolic spaces of the subjective life, those two densities "suspended one inside the other" (328), where ordinariness contains the extra-ordinary. By the control and shifting of perspectives within their created artifacts, both artists are able to reveal the dimensions of "the subjunctive mode of being" within everyday experience. As a final recognition of their affinity, I shall end not with Larry's words but with Shields's own, as she celebrates the art of the fiction writer who "prises open the crusted world and reveal[s] another plane of being, which is similar in its geographical particulars and peopled by those who resemble ourselves."[46]

NOTES

1 Shields, *Larry's Party*, 145.
2 Goertz, "Treading the Maze of *Larry's Party*," 250.
3 Lefebvre, *Production of Space*, 230–3.
4 Backscheider, *Reflections on Biography*, 163.
5 Eden, "The Subjunctive Mode of One's Self," 165.
6 Shields, *Small Ceremonies*, 53.
7 Shields, "Narrative Hunger," 28.
8 Ibid., 34.
9 De Man, "Autobiography as De-facement," 920.
10 Butler, *Gender Trouble*, 16.
11 Donaldson, "Gathering and Losing the Self," 2.
12 Backscheider, *Reflections on Biography*, 153.
13 Ibid., 176.
14 Shields, "Arriving Late," 249.
15 See Trozzi, *Carol Shields' Magic Wand*, 33–6.
16 See Goertz, "Treading the Maze of *Larry's Party*," 231–5.
17 Ibid., 241.
18 *Bookclub*, Radio 4, 5 March 2000, in Goertz, "Treading the Maze of *Larry's Party*," 253.
19 Lefebvre, *Production of Space*, 229.
20 Shields, "Narrative Hunger," 28.
21 Shields, "Arriving Late," 247.
22 Anderson, "Interview with Carol Shields," 71.
23 Sterne, *Tristram Shandy*, 1: 95.
24 Shields, "Ticking Clock," 87.
25 Shields, "Narrative Hunger," 23.
26 Lefebvre, *Production of Space*, 231–2.
27 Ibid., 244.
28 Ibid., 243.
29 Cariou, "*Larry's Party*: Man in the Maze," 88.
30 Freud, *Beyond the Pleasure Principle*, 336.
31 Denoon, "Playing with Convention," 12.
32 Anderson, "Interview with Carol Shields," 71.
33 Shields, "Narrative Hunger," 25.
34 Gamble, "Filling the Creative Void," 52.
35 Shields, *Stone Diaries*, 196.
36 Ibid., 123.
37 Lefebvre, *Production of Space*, 234.

38 Bachelard, *Poetics of Space*, xxxi.
39 Ibid., 201.
40 Shields, "Narrative Hunger," 34.
41 Lefebvre, *Production of Space*, 189.
42 Atwood, *The Blind Assassin*, 9.
43 Munro, *Open Secrets*, 160.
44 In Shields's *Dressing Up for the Carnival.*
45 Lee, "Reading beyond the Fridge Magnets," 26.
46 Shields, *Unless*, 314.

WORKS CITED

Anderson, Marjorie. "Interview with Carol Shields." *Prairie Fire* 16, no. 1 (1995):
   139–50. Reprinted in *Carol Shields: The Arts of a Writing Life*, ed. Neil K.
   Besner (Manitoba: Prairie Fire, 2003), 57–72.
Atwood, Margaret. *The Blind Assassin*. London: Bloomsbury, 2000.
Bachelard, Gaston. *The Poetics of Space*. Trans. Maria Jolas. Boston: Beacon, 1969.
Backscheider, Paula R. *Reflections on Biography*. Oxford: Oxford University Press,
   2001.
Besner, Neil K., ed. *Carol Shields: The Arts of a Writing Life*. Manitoba: Prairie
   Fire, 2003.
Butler, Judith. *Gender Trouble: Feminism and the Subversion of Identity*. New York
   and London: Routledge, 1990.
Cariou, Warren. "*Larry's Party*: Man in the Maze." In Besner, *Carol Shields*,
   87–96.
de Man, Paul. "Autobiography as De-facement." *Modern Language Notes* 94
   (1979): 931–55.
Denoon, Anne. "Playing with Convention." *Books in Canada* 22, no. 9, (1993):
   8–12.
Donaldson, Ian. "Gathering and Losing the Self: Jonson and Biography." In
   Shaping Lives: Reflections on Biography, ed. Ian Donaldson, Peter Read, and
   James Walter, 1–20. Canberra: Humanities Research Centre, 1992.
Eden, Edward, and Dee Goertz, eds. *Carol Shields, Narrative Hunger, and the
   Possibilities of Fiction*. Toronto: University of Toronto Press, 2003.
Eden, Melissa Pope. "The Subjunctive Mode of One's Self: Carol Shields's
   Biography of Jane Austen." In Eden and Goertz, *Carol Shields*, 147–71.
Freud, Sigmund. *Beyond the Pleasure Principle*. Penguin Freud Library, vol. 11.
   London: Penguin, 1991.

Gamble, Sarah. "Filling the Creative Void: Narrative Dilemmas in *Small Ceremonies,* the *Happenstance* novels, and *Swann*." In Eden and Goertz, *Carol Shields*, 39–60.

Goertz, Dee. "Treading the Maze of *Larry's Party*." In Eden and Goertz, *Carol Shields*, 230–54.

Lefebvre, Henri. *The Production of Space.* Trans. D.Nicholson-Smith. Oxford: Blackwell, 2001.

Lee, Hermione. "Reading beyond the Fridge Magnets: Review of Carol Shields's *Collected Stories.*" *Guardian Review*, 3 July 2004, 26.

Munro, Alice. *Open Secrets.* London: Vintage, 1995.

Shields, Carol. "Arriving Late: Starting Over." In *How Stories Mean*, 244–51.

– *Dressing Up for the Carnival.* Toronto: Random House Canada, 2000.

– *Jane Austen.* New York: Viking Penguin, 2001.

– *Larry's Party.* London: Fourth Estate, 1997.

– "Narrative Hunger and the Overflowing Cupboard." In Eden and Goertz, *Carol Shields* 19–36.

– "The Same Ticking Clock." In *How Stories Mean*, eds. J.Metcalf and J.R. (Tim) Struthers (Erin, Ontario: Porcupine's Quill, 1993), 87–90.

– *Small Ceremonies.* London: Fourth Estate, 1995.

– *The Stone Diaries.* London: Fourth Estate, 1994.

– *Susanna Moodie: Voice and Vision.* Ottawa: Borealis, 1977.

– *Unless.* Toronto: Random House Canada, 2002.

Sterne, Laurence. *The Life and Opinions of Tristram Shandy, Gentleman.* Harmondsworth: Penguin, 1967.

Trozzi, Adriana. *Carol Shields' Magic Wand: Turning the Ordinary into the Extraordinary.* Rome: Bulzoni, 2001.

PART TWO

Margins of Otherness:

Reflection, Subjectivity, Embodiment

A Knowable Country: Embodied Omniscience in Carol Shields's *The Republic of Love* and *Larry's Party*

LORNA IRVINE

Of all the elements of point of view, stance has been the most frequently discussed but also the most narrowly defined. The concept of stance traditional to the study of point of view has been almost entirely technical and skeletal, a question of "how" with very little attention to "what" is conveyed.

Susan Lanser, The Narrative Act

In *The Republic of Love*, Tom Avery, one of two central characters in a novel narrated in the third person, briefly addresses his body, observed, as always, by a narrator who mingles voice and perspective with those of Tom: "'You wimp,' he said to his dusky penis, but in a friendly tone. He dried carefully between his toes. It had been some time since he had regarded his toes closely. Years."[1] *Larry's Party* is also narrated in the third person. In it, we are presented with a series of questions by a narrator who likewise mingles voice and perspective with those of the main character, Larry: "Were penises funny then? Or such a serious business that they had to be roughly masked in backyard humor. Was a penis an event? Was it history? Was it sacred or profane? As a boy Larry didn't know. And at age thirty-six he still doesn't know."[2]

These two passages illustrate several characteristics of Carol Shields's narrative content and style that, as I will discuss in the following essay, include a virtually simultaneous presentation of opposing points of view, a mingling of third-person narration and first-person focalization, precisely detailed descriptions of physical bodies, and considerable experimentation with complex characterization. Indeed, Shields's democratic narrative tendencies affect the way she approaches perspective. In the passages quoted above, while the somewhat voyeuristic narrator controls both scenes, observing Tom and Larry from a third-person distance, the reader also sensually experiences the characters' bodies and hears both Tom's and Larry's voices. The passages slide back and forth between a past time and a present moment in which each of the characters mentioned examines his own male body. This writer's interest in all the parts of the human body and, in particular here, her intimate approach to male sexuality simultaneously distance readers so that they objectively observe these bodies while also being drawn close to them.[3]

These illustrations of Shields's experiments with point of view and voice are certainly not unique; indeed, they are reminiscent of a writer such as the eighteenth-century Laurence Sterne, whose novel *Tristram Shandy* plays with narrative perspective and voice, using an erudite and witty omniscience along with a limited insider's view to allow the central character to comment even on his own birth, just as Tom does at the beginning of *The Republic of Love*. Such ambiguous and often contradictory approaches to perspective clearly intrigue Carol Shields. She allows her characters uncommonly free use of their own point of view. In *The Stone Diaries*, for example, while employing what is traditionally referred to as a first-person narrator, she has Daisy gain insight into other characters' thoughts, and even into her own approaching death. Partly, it is through opposing and sometimes even contradictory ways of telling that Shields self-consciously draws attention to the act of narrative construction and to the underlying absurdity of an author's constructing logical, causally developed plots and characters bounded by narrative convention. Simone Vauthier, a critic who has devoted much time to complex analyses of Shields's narrative constructions, argues, in an article discussing the title story of the collection *Various Miracles*, that the story exhibits an "enigmatic continuity" which results in spite of the author's presentation of the miracles without any apparent "causal link."[4] Such continuity, Vauthier argues, results partially from the coincidence in "both place and time" of the written subject and the reading one, a certain "synchronicity" that obviates the usual plot causality.[5]

OXYMORONS AND THE PLEASURES OF PERSPECTIVE

Adjectives such as "enigmatic" and nouns such as "synchronicity" certainly describe Shields's approach to point of view and voice in the two novels that I am discussing. For example, "enigmatic" can be applied to the peculiar slant from which many of the stories are told, an omniscience that often contracts into the conventions of first-person narration, while "synchronic" can be used to describe the simultaneous outer and inner views that dramatize Shields's proclivity for presenting characters who are narrated both objectively and subjectively. I would like to add another word, a rhetorical device. The author has come close to perfecting the art of presenting apparently opposing methodologies simultaneously, thus exhibiting the appeal of the oxymoron. In many of Shields's narratives, oppositions clash together, abruptly jumping back and forth without resolution. This authorial penchant for the oxymoron offers narrators the freedom to cover a spectrum of possibilities, without their trying to create hierarchies among them. Shields's universe thus comes across as notably democratic, a paradoxical cosmos in which all points of view and voices achieve a certain equivalency.

Apart from giving Shields opportunity to experiment playfully with differences in narratorial perspective between private and public spaces, the immediate and the distant, the inner and outer points of view, such flexibility also allows the author the freedom to devote considerable attention to the human body, a locale that often situates Shields's fiction in the sensuous world of her characters. Attentive to the body's earthiness, and singularly uninterested in its more spiritual and esoteric manifestations (indeed, her narrators often make fun of spiritual excesses),[6] Shields uses the body as a location for her narrators and narrative focalizers to create a surprisingly sensual and exposed physical world. In *Larry's Party* we are told that "the sealed body was, after all, a knowable country, with its folded hills laid open to view" (138), and it is to the unsealing that Shields often turns her attention, using her narrators to move back and forth (or up and down), from omniscience to limitation, usually without transition.

Larry's Party is a particularly striking illustration of the body-text. Sandra Martin tells us that Shields "called up the image of the CAT-scan as a way of structuring her approach."[7] Throughout the novel, the author slices through Larry's memory, metaphysics, and body, allowing the reader repeated glimpses of a character viewed both objectively from above, sideways, and even underneath and more intimately and subjectively from inside the very body tissues the CAT-scans are meant to illuminate. While a very differently structured and focused novel, *The Republic of Love* also experiments with playful physical disjunctions that occur between the exterior world and the interior world of the human body, and between the "here" and "there" and the "now" and "then" of the novel's Zeitgeist. Addressing itself ironically to conventions of the romance, where a necessary objectivity distances narrator and therefore reader from some of the more excessive expressions of the genre, *The Republic of Love*, like *Larry's Party*, establishes an oppositional approach to an omniscient focus and voice – a storyteller who sees all and tells all – and a limited focus and voice emerging from the physical perspectives of the two main characters, Fay and Peter. In a number of ways, the ever-moving narrator encourages the reader to experience what the short story "Various Miracles" calls "the randomness and disorder of the world,"[8] emphasizing within the strategies of plotting and characterization the role of chance in ordinary lives. The frequently focused and limited perspective and voice of the two main characters create immediacy, giving the reader the sense of being inside the bodies of the main characters, experiencing life through their eyes. Romance, too often presented esoterically and written about in abstract and often metaphysical language, is, in this novel, often changed into a physical, though not necessarily sexual, force. As Fay suggests, it "grabs on to people like a prize deformity; it keeps them on edge, taunts them, and slitheringly changes shape and withdraws" (37). Such personification is but one of the ways that the novel's narrator gives to abstract concepts a sensuous and physical presence, a contradiction that reflects those of perspective and voice.

The kind of flexible omniscience chosen by Shields suits the teller in these tales. From all we learn about her narrative style, we understand that the author seems neither psychologically nor philosophically authoritarian. She often allows her all-seeing narrators striking proximity to narrative events through the characters' eyewitness accounts of the physical universe. Wallace Martin, in his analysis *Recent Theories of Narrative*, discusses writers who attempt to "dissolve the barriers between narrator and character, between outside and inside views ... and between the past and the present."[9] Certainly, a considerable amount of this kind of dissolution occurs in Shields's fiction. But it seems to me that there is a marked difference between the conventional narrative alterations that occur in fiction to create variety and what Shields is attempting to do. Hers, I argue, are more than technical choices; rather, they are psychological and even philosophical: they reflect a need to present life's contradictions in the very way her fictional universe is observed. The often abrupt clashing of points of view and voices, and therefore of spaces and times, is never brought into balance, the paradoxes never resolved, allowing a simultaneously both limited and omniscient focus that hovers somewhere between being "here" and "there." It is as if the author is exaggerating the artifice of storytelling, both the moment of creating and the space of the story itself, again and again allowing the narrator to enter the story in order, maybe, to give broader generalization to specific events and characters or to squeeze breadth and depth into an apparently bounded, physical dimension.

"ASK ME MORE": NARRATORS AND FOCALIZERS

The opening of *The Republic of Love* illustrates such artifice. "As a baby, Tom Avery had twenty-seven mothers. So he says. That was almost forty years ago. Ask me more, his eyes beg, ask me for details" (1). Here the reader can see how the character's – the focalizer's – point of view and voice join the narrator's (the voice that uses the third-person pronoun), not at all dissolving the difference between limited and omniscient telling but maintaining both together. As in free indirect discourse, third- person report can be turned into first-person accounting ("[I] had twenty-seven mothers") and is shortly thereafter ("Ask me more"); the latter can also be turned into third-person report: "Ask him more." The visualization of the present scene ("his eyes beg") brings the past into an indefinite immediacy. Readers are allowed to hear Tom's, the focalizer's, voice at the same time as they hear the narrator's, and they can see the scene from an omniscient as well as a limited perspective. "Well then. At three weeks of age, there he was ... Where was his father in all this? What father? Ha! That's another story" (1). Just as Shields periodically gives the first-person narrator, Daisy, in *The Stone Diaries* a peculiar third-person omniscience ("1965 was the year Mrs. Flett fell into a profound depression"),[10] so too in *The Republic of Love* the reader sometimes accepts Tom as the storyteller, perhaps speaking to a listener just out of sight.

Changes in person, time, and space happen so often that the reader is encouraged to forget, repeatedly, that both *The Republic of Love* and *Larry's Party* are not in fact first-person narratives, but are controlled by an all-seeing narrator who is free in time and space to jump forward or to move backward at will. However, the authority of the telling remains quite ambiguous. In *The Narrative Act*, Susan Lanser argues that a public narrator usually has more "diegetic authority," a focalizer more "mimetic authority."[11] Such is usually the case. Yet it seems to me that Shields plays with diegesis and mimesis, creating fictions in which the status of each is unclear and where syntactic markings for different narrative levels are sometimes misleading and often contradictory.

As well, distances between external and internal perspectives are frequently purposefully muddled, as this example from *Larry's Party* illustrates: "Larry and his mother went to Hector's, which she swears by, and that's where they found the Harris tweed, this nubby-dubby wool cloth" (7). Here we begin with a narratorial report, move almost immediately into Larry's frame of reference, and then on into his mother's voice. "Nubby-dubby" are her words, we assume, not Larry's nor the narrator's. In addition, this complex matter of voice, distance, and perspective seems to be further emphasized in Shields's use of parenthetical and italicized comments. Sometimes such comments appear to be coming from some indeterminate space outside the narrative universe, at others from immediately inside it, and at yet others apparently inside the story, but ambiguously situated. As Larry thinks about himself in the chapter entitled "Larry So Far," an italicized voice speaks a question: "*Who is this guy? Give me a break*" (166). This typical outburst, a bit disorienting, has no specific locus. Is this Larry's voice speaking from outside himself and observing his self from the outside? Or is this the narrator's voice, insisting on entering the narrative world and making judgments about the characters therein? Or is this a generalized third person, a composite of the many various voices that constitute Larry's world? A similar exchange happens earlier, as Larry thinks about the cupped flower he holds in his hand: "*It toils not, neither does it spin*" (76). The quotation, for it is one, is also ambiguously located and spoken, a distant echo from the Bible, a joint venture, as it were, between the narrator and the focalizer.

In *The Republic of Love* italicized passages seem to be used more sparingly, but here too quotations occasionally spring up in the text as, for example, the excerpt from the wedding ceremony recalled by the often-married Tom: "*To have and to hold from this day forward*" (281). Such ambiguously and erratically remembered quotations tend to fracture storylines, abruptly breaking into the internal spaces being created, on the edge of suggesting an intrusive narrative voice, though, in fact, the reader always hears the character's voice as well. It seems, then, that Shields does not want her readers to settle into a relaxing fictional environment, but prefers to unsettle them, persistently using perspectives and voices that abruptly jump back and forth between internal and external spaces and between past, present, and even future tenses. Such narrative devices make it difficult for readers to figure out where narrative authority, status, and stance are located. Readers of Shields's fiction need considerable flexibility; their position as narratees is repeatedly thrown into question.

The chapter titles offer another example of what I mean. In *The Republic of Love* these titles range from quotation ("Love Is the Only Enchantment"; "Everything They Say Is True"), ambiguously located in the same ways as the italicized passages in the already referenced passages, to first-person statement: "Put That on my Tombstone" or "I Believe in One Thing," to second- and third-person questions such as "What Has Befallen Him?" or "How Are You? How Are You?" The Contents is encased by the given names "Tom" (at the beginning) and "Fay" (at the end), as if these nouns were a signal denoting a certain, though unclear, embodiment. In fact, none of the titles offers clues referencing particular characters, appearing almost ironic, as if the reader were being let in on – but not quite – some private joke.

In *Larry's Party*, on the other hand, instead of having no specific given-name references, the chapter titles have nothing else: "Larry's Work"; "Larry's Friends"; "Larry's Penis." Such repetition is, however, just as unsettling and ironic as the unreferenced titles in *The Republic of Love*, confusing specificity – which the given name should be asserting – and generalization – the result of repetition and apparent distance. While it seems evident that some external narrator is announcing various temporal ("Fifteen Minutes in the Life of Larry Weller"), physical ("Larry's Living Tissues"), familial ("Larry's Kid"), and metaphysical ("Larry's Search for the Wonderful and the Good") perspectives to be taken on the novel's central character and, through a listing of dates, giving a controlled chronological progression of the forthcoming story's events – events known by the all-seeing narrator – as the titles re-emerge as chapter headings in the text, they often abruptly shift into the limited perspective of the central focalizer, Larry. Take a section from "Larry's Work," some of which is obviously narrated externally ("Larry had no idea that technology was about to bulldoze the market"), some of which moves into an ambiguous present tense ("And now, ever since Viv Bondurant's left Flowercity, Larry's been in charge down at the store"), and some of which shifts to an embodied perspective in which we hear Larry's own voice: "Brides want roses nine times out of ten. You can't talk them out of it. They think flowers, and, bingo, roses come to mind" (74) and so on. At this point, the chapter headings take on a physical immediacy that, in turn, reconfigures the narrator's position. While omniscience allows prescience (Larry is, at this moment in the text, ignorant about technology), at the same time, the name Larry increasingly embodies both external and internal perspectives as well as a heteroglossia of voices.[12]

While we are dealing here with, among other problems, ambiguous spatial and temporal locations in narrative perspective and voice, ambiguity is also built into the text for the narratee. Such ambiguity has partially to do with Shields's extensive use of questions. In *Larry's Party* many of the questions used connect the external narrator both to the reader and to the central character, Larry, though no clear demarcations exist. Some questions are apparently directed to Larry's body, while at other points they seem to be situated inside his body, as this question illustrates: "The curious rarefactions of his body ... have these been printed in his genes or did *he* imprint them *himself*?" (206). The italicized words, as they do elsewhere, simultaneously (and in apparent contradiction) suggest both the narrator's and Larry's voices, thinking of Larry in the third person, though the questions are ambiguously directed. Then occurs the characteristic shift to a generalized cultural voice: "As for the politics of a universal health care plan, Larry is noticeably silent. A topic best avoided. Ah, but (changing the subject) the Canadian wilderness, the famed train journey across the western continent – this is everyone's dream, is it not? Would Larry agree?" And then on to Larry's own voice, as we move into semi-direct discourse: "Yes. Emphatically. Oh yes. Absolutely," and so on (206). On the following page, the question "Is Larry cool?" leads to a whole series of questions: "So how is it he projects such an air of confidence when at the same time living a fraction of an inch from public humiliation?" and "Do other people exist this close to the flame of extinction?" (207). A public, omniscient narrator would probably suggest answers to these questions, while a limited narrator would not see the self from the outside, as in the first question. The questions involve a particular relationship with the reader as well, requiring a certain "conversation" that opens up the borders of the fictional world.

The variety and effect of the pronouns used further complicate both the status and the stance of the narrative point of view. Sometimes the external narrator addresses the reader in the second person: "He's been jogging for two years now, ever since his divorce papers came through. Ask him about it – he'll be glad to tell you" (18). This kind of address to the reader again underlines the way Shields's fiction plays with distance and closeness, with report and question, with writerly versus readerly construction. Roland Barthes argues, "Opposite the writerly text, then, is its countervalue, its negative, reactive value; what can be read, but not written: the *readerly*."[13] Again, then, I detect here another kind of contradiction favoured by Shields; on the one hand, as Barthes further suggests, the "metonymic labor"[14] of the readerly text, subverting and inter- rupting, on the other, the metaphors of the writerly text. I argue that Shields uses questions for such purposes, repeatedly interrupting the narrative line in order to open up simultaneously both the readerly and the writerly possibilities of her texts.

GEOGRAPHIES OF THE BODY

Apart from the abrupt and paradoxical movement between interior and exterior views, Shields's work also, as I have already indicated, reveals a passionate and extremely detailed attention to the physical bodies of her characters. Indeed, it is not too far-fetched to suggest that the all-seeing narrator discovers many ways of inhabiting the inside of the body, so that the fictional world can be seen through the characters' own eyes. The jumps made throughout both novels from report to experience seem, then, not merely intellectual exercises but, rather, embodiments that shift the narrative perspective and voice quite dramatically. Such movement happens in *Larry's Party* when the narrator moves to the inside of Larry's head, asking a parenthetical question from inside that head that ties together, again without boundaries, reader, character, and narrator: "(Hidden there, on the back wall of his retina, is a quizzing caption in flowing script, his own handwriting most likely, which asks: how did I get here? How did this happen?)" (208). Here again, the embodied narration gives the sense of the central character's thinking of himself in the third person.

Such anti-hierarchical dynamics are repeated over and over. In *The Republic of Love* the two focalizers, Fay and Tom, frequently embody the external narrator. We are told, about Fay, that "the solitude of living alone *does* worry her" (7), the italicized "does" signifying the mingling of Fay's and the narrator's voices. Then the passage moves on to Fay's speaking to herself in the first person (Shields does not often use first-person narration in these two novels): "I, Fay McLeod, have every right to breathe this air, to take possession of this stretch of pavement," and, in a parenthetical remark, the narrator seems to focus, sensually, on Fay's mouth, its proclivity to "pucker," her effort to sigh out the word "single" (7). Such physical details literally situate the reader inside Fay's body, where, as she walks, we can feel the "blasts of wind," see the weak yellow sun through her eyes, and expand with her as her lungs fill up with chilly air. A similar embodiment occurs during Tom's run on the "last Saturday before he turns forty" (18) when, at this temporally

distinctive moment, the reader is pulled into Tom's body, experiencing
the chill of the day, Tom's movement, the traffic he waits for, and his
shortness of breath, all emphasized by the use of the pronoun "your":
"Breathe in, then out, count your breaths, it makes the time turn over.
And think of your feet rounding on the pavement, the heel, first. Bending, rolling up to the toes," and the exhortation to the reader to "keep
that image in your mind" (19). Here the sentences echo the rhythm of
Tom's breathing, giving even the novel's narrative structure physical
intimacy. Furthermore, Shields often does this; such dramatic immediacy on the part of the all-seeing narrator, the way in which seeing everything becomes an eyewitness event, a limiting of breadth, so to speak,
creates a democratic, non-hierarchical space, a point of view, as Michel
de Certeau suggests about walking in *The Practice of Everyday Life*, from
"down below,"[15] where panoptic oversight can be evaded, where, as Tom
finds, "[g]rit blows straight into his face, in his eyes and mouth and up
his nose" (19).

In these ways, the author gives a bodily dimension to the otherwise
disembodied narrators of these two novels. Each story is frequently
localized, its angle of vision inverted, seen, as it were, from below,
beside, among. At these moments, the story moves at the speed of one or
other of the characters, issuing from inside the body; the reader is put in
the position of looking out through the character's eyes, for example, as
Tom in *The Republic of Love* is "running out the park gates now, back
down Wellington Crescent, those big dopey houses, it costs a fortune to
heat those houses, past the synagogue again, past the spiky hedges, past
the new condos. Christ, a wall of condos, you can hardly see the river
anymore. They just keep heaving them up one after another" (19). In
her book *Wanderlust: A History of Walking*, Rebecca Solnit suggests that
the "rhythm of walking generates a kind of rhythm of thinking. And the
passage through a landscape echoes or stimulates the passage through a
series of thoughts."[16] Shields often uses the rhythm of walking to construct prose that is broken up into the breathing of a walker or a runner,
short breathless segments that have an onomatopoeic verisimilitude.

At the beginning of *Larry's Party*, Larry illustrates Solnit's emphasis
on the connection between the rhythm of walking and that of thinking:
"You don't want bulk when you're walking along. He walks a lot. It's
when he does his thinking. He hums his thoughts out on the air like
music; they've got a disco beat: My name is Larry Weller. I'm a floral
designer, twenty-six years old, and I'm walking down Notre Dame Avenue, in the city of Winnipeg, in the country of Canada, in the month of

April, in the year 1977, and I'm thinking hard. About being hungry, about being late, about having sex later on tonight. About how great I feel in the other guy's Harris tweed jacket" (5–6). Exactly – the rhythm of walking, the rhythm of the prose, and how, again and again, as Solnit suggests, "walking returns the body to its original limits ... to something supple, sensitive, and vulnerable."[17] Narrative writing, Solnit argues, is "closely bound up with walking."[18] Shields recognizes and celebrates this closeness, using a flexible narrative perspective and voice to move back and forth from a distant omniscience to close physical proximity, thus acknowledging the equivalence of both public and private spaces. Everyday acts become significant and, to use de Certeau's words, thereby create "the world on the scale of our bodies":[19] "Larry was running the conversation through his head while he walked along Notre Dame Avenue in his stolen Harris tweed jacket, seeing himself in his self's silver mirror. The fabric swayed around him, shifting and reshifting on his shoulders with every step he took. It seemed like something alive. Inside him, and outside him too" (11).

Shields's sensitivity to the relationship between private and public space is nowhere more evident than in the close connection between the urban layout of cities and the mapping of the physical bodies of her characters. Often, the physical geography marks a character's movement through space and time. As Perry Nodelman suggests about *The Republic of Love*, Shields seems to use "geographical metaphors to represent a state of balance between connection and isolation."[20] While Nodelman is mainly concerned with charting the ways in which the characters of the novel work through their romantic involvement, I want to argue that the pull between connection and isolation dramatically marks the narrative perspective itself, allowing readers, characters, and narrator to pass freely between the human body and the landscape, the view from above and the eyewitness account, private physical sensations and the public spaces of the city of Winnipeg. Paying attention to geography, Tom reveals the strategic layout of the city while he also demonstrates his tactics of walking the streets:

Instead he walked along River Avenue and across the Norwood Bridge, discovering, happily, that his vast public face had been scrubbed from the billboard and replaced with a pastel invitation to take a Caribbean holiday – palm trees, blue water, muscled bodies. The start of a song twitched in his throat. He stopped at a lunch counter for a cup of coffee and – thoughtfully, taking his time – counted out the exact change, lightening his pockets of their heavy pennies. He kept on walking –

through pared suburban neatness, then around the fake rural greenness of Kingston Crescent, then over the footbridge and north towards River Heights. The sun had returned, blinding; but the next minute a light drizzle began, and he welcomed its cool fine spray on his face, on his lips." (173–4)

Nodelman describes, too, the confluence of realism and romance (one of the themes of *Republic*) among his university students, who recognized so many connections with their city that one student actually believed that she saw Tom running down one of the streets where Shields's "republic of love" paradoxically takes up its unlikely position. What seems most important to me, though, is Shields's celebration of the democratic nature of Tom's and Fay's connection with the city, a sense that partially comes through in their constant walking. Solnit says, "Walking has become one of the forces that has made the modern world – often by serving as a counterpoint to economics." It "sews together the land."[21] Yes, and the perspectives of the novel reflect this egalitarian emphasis, the democracy of the eyewitness, the refusal to allow omniscience to control the point of view and voice.

F.K. Stanzel, in his *A Theory of Narrative*, debates whether the omniscient narrator's point of view can be transferred to the "site of action," as, for example, happens when the adverb "there" switches to the adverb "here," as it does in several of the passages quoted above. Stanzel's conclusion is that "because of his lack of corporeality, an authorial third-person narrator cannot readily establish a system of orientation" that functions in an autonomous way.[22] It seems to me that Shields has developed a fictional point of view and voice that allow her external narrator an autonomy that is quite unusual, even paradoxical. By playing with some of the traditional boundaries between the narrating – the diegetic – and the experiencing – the mimetic – aspects of fiction, she creates a fictional universe that is remarkably fluid. Think of the fantasy in the short story "Collision," where the reader is told that, "like radioactive ash or like the differentiated particles of luminescence that cling to the dark side of the globe, the chambered beginnings, middles and ends of human encounters persist, including aberrations, nervous tics and malfunctions of the spirit."[23] The narrator of this whimsical story emphasizes the disruptiveness of stories, their frequent use of tactical interference in otherwise strategic plotting, their temporal discontinuities and simultaneities, and, perhaps most important, the ways in which they use the junctures between external and internal worlds to create public and private perspectives on the narrated world. Such postmodern narrative experiments blend the aesthetic and existential elements of storytelling, so that reader, narrator, and characters move through time and space together.

WHAT ONE MAN DOES IS SOMETHING DONE, IN SOME MEASURE, BY ALL MEN

Shields's experiments also affect her approach to characterization.[24] Gérard Genette suggests that contemporary writers tend to steer away from the "classical attributes of 'character' – proper name, physical and moral 'nature' ... and along with them the signs that direct grammatical (pronominal) traffic."[25] In spite of the writer's fascination with the physical bodies of her characters and, as I have tried to show, her somewhat obsessive attention to their names, neither focus locates the essence of a character. Rather, the various peculiarly located narrative perspectives problematize conventions of characterization. Indeed, as Shields has often discussed, biographers, who sometimes believe that they can tie down the whole of the characters they memorialize, are inevitably defeated. As Daisy says about autobiography in *The Stone Diaries*, "The recounting of a life is a cheat, of course; I admit the truth of this; even our own stories are obscenely distorted; it is a wonder really that we keep faith with the simple container of our existence."[26] In *The Republic of Love*, Fay suspects, as she tells us, that character is really nothing more than a "jumble of other people's impressions" (9), and personal identity unstable (154). Furthermore, what Nodelman argues is the central paradox of the novel – that human beings are, simultaneously, "completely and utterly isolated from each other" while, at the same time "completely and utterly connected with each other"[27] – also suggests the impossibility of creating narrative characters as discrete entities. Shields's characters actively participate in the abrupt shifts in narrative perspective and voice, between closeness and distance, the past and the present. In such ways, narrative point of view and voice illustrate the psychology of identity.

Again and again, both novels complicate issues pertaining to representation and specificity and, to use Genette's terms, the iterative and the singular,[28] as in what Fay's mother says in *The Republic of Love*: "'I try to visualize this book as finished,' she says to Onion or Muriel or Fay or Bibbi or whoever is about" (131). Here the message is that the separate characters of the novel often seem indistinguishable from each other, their actions repetitive and interchangeable. While such comments undercut the singularity of narrative characterization, they emphasize a sense of community that marks the narrative structure and style. Like an advertisement, Tom's massive billboard head crops up again and again in *The Republic of Love*, positioned for all the community to see, while his voice, as he conducts his late-night radio talk show, travels through the night to his motley band of listeners. Although he is a discrete character, his name asserted at the top of the Contents page, the reader is never allowed to forget his dual function as both a representative and a particular figure. As well, Fay believes her identity to be "suspended inside an image. Hanging there by a thread" (176), implying a platonic approach to character, as does the "republic" of the title. Thus, while both novels investigate the psychology of identity, they also play with the varieties of ways that a writer can construct literary characters, experimenting with isolation and community, the discrete and the generalized representation. The shifting in narrative perspective and voice advances such experiments, moving from spatial and temporal superiority to eyewitness observations and accounts. Shields treats the bodies of her characters as remarkably porous, narrator, focalizer, and reader moving in and out of them with considerable freedom.

Further, in *Larry's Party* exaggerated repetition serves sometimes to explode characterization – to open it up to every possible angle of viewing – and sometimes to flatten the central character. The reader gets repeated information about the character named "Larry," the reiteration of whose name appears in all the chapter headings. Yet, rather than increasing the singularity that a particularized description and a name might bestow, the narrator uses the device of the CAT-scan, which, because of its scientific detachment, simultaneously distances the character while it also draws the reader further into that character's private spaces. In this novel, representation and singularity peculiarly mingle, creating conflicting, sometimes opposed, approaches to narrative character.

Even the language of this novel, as well as the various discussions of language that occur within it, demonstrates the persistent superimposition of the particular on the general, or vice versa. So, in the section entitled "Larry's Words," de Saussure's linguistic structure, *langue* and *parole,* the cultural and the particular, slide back and forth as the voices of narrator and focalizer interact. The novel illustrates how the language of a culture, a sort of metaphoric "cosmic sandwich,"[29] is possessed by a particular speaker. Notably, too, the apparent singularity of the given name is debunked in the section entitled "Men Called Larry," where, we are told, "Larry could be someone else, but he's not" (249), a kind of simultaneity of identity, belonging to others, belonging to the self. Indeed, in the last sentence of this chapter, another "Larry" character comically insists, "There's a sense in which, deep down, all the men in the world are named Larry" (261).

A KNOWABLE COUNTRY

These and other techniques reveal that *The Republic of Love* and *Larry's Party* achieve maximum flexibility in terms of perspective. By using an omniscience that erratically and often almost indecipherably jumps back and forth between the "there" of external reporting and the "here" of an immediate point of view, Shields illustrates a postmodern narrative freedom that allows for the intrusion of chance into the strategies of plotting. It is a tactic particularly striking in her short stories, where, again and again, the narrative voice strips away the specific and isolated temporal and spatial configurations of plot in order to demonstrate the connectedness of the whole narrative universe. Similar dynamics occur in the construction of character. Representation and singularity get intertwined, confused, so that community interacts with individuality, illustrating the kind of experiments that Daisy in *The Stone Diaries* undertakes in terms of creating her own "character," the "pattern of her life" unfolding like "a long itinerary of revision and accommodation" (342). In "Absence," in *Dressing Up for the Carnival*, the focalizer, a writer, ponders point of view. She asks why she "had stayed so long enclosed by the tough, lonely pronoun of her body when the whole world beckoned?" (95). The joining of the personal pronoun – the singular point of view – with the "whole world" – the omniscient perspective – is what Shields tries to achieve through narrative point of view and voice.

It is not surprising, then, that some of the narrative perspective in *Larry's Party* and *The Republic of Love* is from inside the body, the sign of which is "the tough, lonely pronoun" I. If we go back to one of the first quotations I used, "the sealed body was, after all, a knowable country, with its folded hills laid open to view,"[30] it becomes clear that for this author, it is *in* the body that omniscience and limitation mingle. Towards the end of *The Stone Diaries*, Daisy announces: "I'm still here, inside the (powdery, splintery) bones, ankles, the sockets of my eyes, shoulder, hip, teeth, I'm still here" (252). By unsealing its limited point of view, by making of the body a broad "knowable country," Shields has created an embodied omniscience that, both philosophically and psychologically, asserts community. Further, as Larry thinks, "Everyone in the world walks around with a supply of meaningful words inside their heads, bundled there like kindling or like the long-fibred nerve bundles he remembers from his high school general science class" (88). It seems, then, that for Shields, language itself is physical, connecting first- and third-person pronouns and the private and public spaces of the narrative world.

NOTES

1 Shields, *Republic of Love*, 173.

2 Shields, *Larry's Party*, 137.

3 In "Autobiography as Critical Practice in *The Stone Diaries*," Wendy Roy argues that Shields, by addressing a history of narrative "gaps and misdirections" in representations of female bodies, explores both "subversion and suppression" in ways that become "political" acts (see Eden and Goertz, *Carol Shields*, 125–6). As I have tried to show, Shields is interested in both male and female bodies. What could be more surprising than the descriptions of and addresses to the penis?

4 Vauthier, "'They Say Miracles Are Past,'" 184–5.

5 Ibid., 184, 187. Revealing another kind of contradiction, "The homogeneity of heterogeneity," in her essay "'They Say Miracles Are Past,'" Simone Vauthier argues that the narrator who, in "Various Miracles," is "also the major focalizer" and is "close to being what one used to call an omniscient narrator" views "things from a distance," never participating "in what she narrates but reports events with serene detachment that somehow combines neutrality with sympathy" (192). While I do not disagree with this analysis of this short story, I believe the narrative perspectives in the novels I discuss to be more various in terms of distance and stance.

6 Talking with Ann Dowsett Johnston in an interview for *Maclean's*, Shields responds to a question: "Does she believe in God?" Her answer: "No. Human goodness is the only thing I believe in" (Johnston, "Her Time to Roar," 51).

7 Martin, "Protean and Prolific Carol Shields," 8.

8 Shields, *Various Miracles*, 34.

9 Martin, *Recent Theories of Narration*, 132.

10 Shields, *Stone Diaries*, 229.

11 Lanser, *Narrative Act*, 142.

12 In his discussion in "Discourse in the Novel," Bakhtin writes: "Every concrete utterance of a speaking subject serves as a point where centrifugal as well as centripetal forces are brought to bear. The processes of centralization and decentralization, of unification and disunification, intersect in the utterance; the

utterance not only answers the requirements of its own language as an individualized embodiment of a speech act, but it answers the requirements of heteroglossia as well; it is in fact an active participant in such speech diversity" (Bakhtin, *Dialogic Imagination*, 272). Shields is particularly conscious of such confluences of language.

13 Barthes, *S/Z*, 4.

14 Ibid., 7.

15 De Certeau, *Practice of Everyday Life*, 93.

16 Solnit, *Wanderlust*, 5–6.

17 Ibid., 29.

18 Ibid., 72.

19 De Certeau, *Practice of Everyday Life*, 256.

20 Nodelman, "Living in the Republic of Love," 121.

21 Solnit, *Wanderlust*, 167, 163.

22 Stanzel, *Theory of Narrative*, 92.

23 Shields, *The Orange Fish*, 118.

24 The quotation that introduces this section is from "The Form of the Sword" by Jorge Luis Borges (Borges, *Ficciones*, 120). Genette discusses the line: "the classical 'attributes' of character – proper name, physical and moral 'nature' – have disappeared and along with them the signs that direct grammatical (pronominal) traffic. It is undoubtedly Borges who offers us the most spectacular example of this violation – spectacular precisely because it is put down in a completely traditional narrative system, which accentuates the contrast – in the story entitled 'The Form of the Sword'" (Genette, *Narrative Discourse*, 246). Shields's narrative experiments, like those of Borges, illustrate a postmodern style, while, at the same time, Shields also uses a realism that seems at odds with her technical innovations.

25 Genette, *Narrative Discourse*, 246.

26 Shields, *Stone Diaries*, 28.

27 In Besner, *Carol Shields*, 118.

28 Genette, *Narrative Discourse*, 116.

29 Shields, *Larry's Party*, 93.

30 Ibid., 138.

WORKS CITED

Bakhtin, M.M. *The Dialogic Imagination: Four Essays*. Trans. Michael Holquist. Austin: University of Texas Press, 1981.

Barthes, Roland. *S/Z: An Essay*. Trans. Richard Miller. New York: Hill and Wang, 1970.

Besner, Neil K., ed. *Carol Shields: The Arts of a Writing Life*. Winnipeg: Prairie Fire, 2003.

Borges, Jorge Luis. *Ficciones*. New York: Grove, 1956.

de Certeau, Michel. *The Practice of Everyday Life*. Berkeley: University of California Press, 1984.

Eden, Edward, and Dee Goertz, eds. *Carol Shields, Narrative Hunger, and the Possibilities of Fiction*. Toronto: University of Toronto Press, 2003.

Genette, Gérard. *Narrative Discourse: An Essay in Method*. Trans. Jane Lewin. Ithaca: Cornell University Press, 1972.

Johnston, Ann Dowsett. "Her Time To Roar." *Maclean's*, 15 April 2002: 48–51.

Lanser, Susan. *The Narrative Act: Point of View in Prose Fiction*. Princeton: Princeton University Press, 1981.

Martin, Sandra. "The Protean and Prolific Carol Shields." *Quill and Quire*, February 1998, 1+

Martin, Wallace. *Recent Theories of Narrative*. Ithaca: Cornell University Press, 1986.

Nodelman, Perry. "Living in the Republic of Love: Carol Shields's Winnipeg." In Besner, *Carol Shields*, 105–23.

Roy, Wendy. 2003. "Autobiography as Critical Practice in *The Stone Diaries*." In Eden and Goertz, *Carol Shields*, 113–46.

Shields, Carol. *Larry's Party*. Toronto: Random House, 1989.

– *The Orange Fish*. Toronto: Random House, 1989.

– *The Republic of Love*. New York: Viking, 1992.

– *The Stone Diaries*. Toronto: Random House, 1993.

– *Various Miracles*. Toronto: Stoddart, 1985.

Solnit, Rebecca. *Wanderlust: A History of Walking*. New York: Penguin, 2000.

Stanzel, F.K. *A Theory of Narrative*. Cambridge: Cambridge University Press, 1979.

Vauthier, Simone. "'They Say Miracles Are Past' but They Are Wrong." In Besner, *Carol Shields*, 183–208.

8

Pioneering Interlaced Spaces: Shifting Perspectives and Self-Representation in *Larry's Party*

PATRICIA-LÉA PAILLOT

Man is a particle inserted into unstable and interconnected wholes.[1]

Carol Shields opens *Larry's Party* with a tweed jacket which her "futile," "uneventful, average"[2] protagonist takes by mistake and which is subsequently used in a symbolical and instrumental way to tailor Larry's psychological and social fabric. How does the repeatedly "mediocre" (113) Canadian become so extraordinary? This ordinary, "miserable adolescent" (165) would indeed remain as such without the construction of a spatialized identity, which renders the character exceptional and serves as the structural frame of *Larry's Party*. In *L'expérience intérieure*, Georges Bataille discusses the "labyrinthine construction of being," which, he argues, takes the form of a "course we follow from lure to lure."[3] His remarks are more than appropriate to the development of Larry Weller, who, until he touches the quadrants of a button found by chance in a pocket of the tweed jacket, is described as "Delustered. Textureless. Inoffensive. Impotent. Ordinary" (166). He even pushes his creator to ironically question his existence: "*Who is this guy?*" (166). Just as a child discovers the world through touch, the tactile revelation of these quadrants, which will anticipate the epiphanic discovery of the Hampton Court maze in England, definitely modifies the linear course of Larry's life and turns *Larry's Party* into a "reversible" novel that shifts at will from ordinary story to extraordinary quest. Senses and sensations will then precede abstractions, and visual configurations will pave the way for an intellectual construction and understanding of the world. Largely as a result of the presence of pictorial mazes that subtend the different chapters and engage Larry in new forms of self-representation, the novel oscillates from the individual to the universal: "there's a sense in which deep down, all the men in the world are called Larry" (261). In the same way, Carol Shields playfully depicts Larry as a "maze nut" (91), "a shrub king of the universe" (42), or "a monarch in his chosen sphere" (67), thus already diversifying the possible angles of observation.

The landscaped art in the novel transforms the "banal," unknown florist into a famous artist whose fate and dreams are fulfilled through the design of artistic mazes with which he gradually develops a quasi-organic and mystic relationship: "a maze is designed so that we get to be part of the art" (84, 219). The maze motif therefore constitutes the recurrent frame of reference and the central architecture in which each chapter is stamped with geometrical or labyrinthine figures. Art historian Daniel Arasse, in his study of details in painting, underlines that "the dialectic of dislocation, within a unified system, dissolves boundaries or 'terms.'"[4] In *Larry's Party* we suggest that the details Carol Shields focuses on, in the divided and apparently disconnected spaces, make up a harmonious whole of seventeen chapters; some are bordering on self- contained stories, and each one is engulfed in a dialectic of closure and disclosure, passing from the infinitely great, "Larry's Search for the Wonderful and Good" (chapter 11), to the infinitesimal, "Larry's Living Tissues" (chapter 14). They all form a macro- and microcosmic osmosis that blends all the thematic and generic elements: "when you add up the world and its words you get a kind of cosmic sandwich" (93). Using the maze as a structuring principle, *Larry's Party* merges the material and human constituents of the world into a sensuous blend.

As a pioneer of his own interlaced spaces, Larry mutates through a series of states, a microcosmic universe that hyphenates individuals and nations. As he leaves his marks on space, he charts the landmarks of his life, and the notion of territory is tantamount to a self-exploration. Carol Shields thus creates a typically Canadian character, "Larry Weller, of Winnipeg, Canada" (82), profoundly anchored in space. This epitome recalls what Northrop Frye observes in *The Bush Garden* on a larger scale: "civilization in Canada, as elsewhere, has advanced geometrically across the country."[5]

In an archaeology of social sciences, the French philosopher Michel Foucault states that in Western culture, representation used to be derived from mimesis and repetition, and that man is deeply akin and similar to the land he lives in. He argues that "the human body remains half the universal atlas,"[6] and in a similar vein, Carol Shields delineates a character who connives with his land, finding himself at the junction of interrogations and elucidations that are part of an animistic vision of nature, evolving in a structurally geometric text, full of vitality and energy. In resorting to recognizable maze patterns, the narratology of *Larry's Party* follows a labyrinthine course of forward and backward movements, tentative advances, some successful, others not, to reach an ever-delayed access to the centre and meaning. In this respect, Shields builds up an asymptotic novel. In other words, it approaches the truth and meaning without ever reaching them. As a matter of fact, each chapter sheds additional light on Larry's life without providing one single key element or a global vision. The purpose and function of these fragmented chapters bring the "cyclic unity of eternal return," according to an expression used by Deleuze and Guattari, who consider that the most fragmented work of art is also the most complete one.[7] This eternal return is confirmed by Larry's statement: "center demands a reversal, a new beginning" (313). To get to that centre in her geometrical progression, Carol Shields uses manifold figures, notably straight lines and diagonals, what Roland Barthes, in his miscellaneous collection of fragmentary philosophical and literary reflections, calls "the dual pattern": "This work (the dual pattern) in its continuity follows two movements: the *straight line* (development, growth, the emphasis of an idea, stance, taste or image) and the *zigzag* (opposition, counteraction, contrarity, reactive energy, denegation, the return journey, z-movement, deviant trajectory)."[8]

The first chapters are indeed dedicated to this straight line, which remains Larry's ultimate reference: placed at the cardinal points of his life, this leitmotif is part of his makeup. Each direction of his life is stamped with this straight line, which later multiplies in many ways and suffuses every single element: his spatial occupation, "walking straight" (13); the portrayal of his first love: "Megsy was a hard straight line" (102); the images of his first marriage with a woman symbolically corseted in a "suit's straight skirt" (18). Shields even plays with the figurative meaning of "straight," adding some more dimension to words and using their potential reversibility: "Larry never did get all their names straight" (25). But, to complete the straight line of this chronological novel, which zigzags while remaining true to the text, we should add the notion of deviation, which is intrinsic to the maze and the central structuring notion of time and space. The intertwined combination of these lines keeps prevailing in Larry's self-representation: "He tries to visualize his life – his life so far – and a grid rises up in his mind, neatly squared-off but oddly disassociated" (169). In many respects these bifurcations are reminiscent of "The Garden of Forking Paths," a short story by Jorge Luis Borges in which the labyrinth is but "a labyrinth of symbols" and where "*The Garden of Forking Paths* is a huge riddle, or a parable, whose subject is time," "an infinite series of time, a growing, dizzying web of divergent, convergent, and parallel times," where "time forks, perpetually, into countless futures."[9]

As in Borges's story, Larry's green "labyrinth" – he insists on the term "labyrinth" rather than the more disconcerting "maze" – flown over as well as paced up and down, glorifies space and time equally and synchronizes them by pouring time into a spatial mould. The quadrants of the button found in the pocket of the tweed jacket act as a unifying thread by resurfacing regularly to refer to time: when Larry turns forty, he makes the comment, "Four-T: Taste. Talent. Technique. Testosterone" (172).

Furthermore, Carol Shields fuses spatialization, the loss of spatial markers, and the concomitant necessity to redirect oneself with a prevailing timeless present that Maurice Blanchot describes as "momentary exaltation" which "unifies and universalizes."[10] Since this present encapsulates all future, past, and present references – "forget about the past, forget the future. The real music is spilling out now, out of here" (138) – the author insists on recapturing the fleeting and transient time. The use of this present, abolishing a temporal distance, thus creates some proximity and complicity with Larry[11] and stresses the universal dimension of this ordinary man who knows how "to cultivate his garden."

As the different spaces of the labyrinth multiply, the narrative also unfolds in many directions involving fictional spaces, and the novel insists on what Gaston Bachelard, in a work dedicated to the importance of the present moment, calls the "essential discontinuity of time,"[12] a flexibility that allows Larry to move endlessly forward and backward in the events of his life, which gradually fit together like a construction set in which the central piece is missing: "the gaping hole at the centre" (112). The alternating narratives in a metaleptic text that juggles with analepses and prolepses reflecting the quest of this central piece, partake in this broken narratology made of deviations, digressions, and fractures, albeit united in a single story. Both direct and sinuous, the text also combines spatial and diegetic displacement, thus becoming as geographical as cognitive in a maze that maps out Larry's self and soul as much as his soil, his mistakes being regarded, for instance, as "an impasse" (83). This journey and sensuous exchange between soul, soil, and body reshape and regenerate Larry's identity, constantly challenged by the awareness of new spaces. It consequently raises the question of a definite and limited identity. As a novel of both fixed spaces and passages, *Larry's Party* inscribes identity in transience in a constellation of stories embodying multiple identities.

To express himself, therefore, Larry invests the space, increasingly erasing the borders between private and public spheres, his own maze and his firm, A/Mazing Space Inc. (145). The labyrinth, which occupies all the recesses of Larry's life and leads him to self-discovery, is the completed form and his lost paradigm.

This spatial text makes identification with the maze coincide with the quest for the essential law of the labyrinth, namely, the meandering between an entrance and the single or several exits mirrored in Larry's life: "departures and arrivals: he didn't know then, but these two forces would form the twin bolts of his existence" (37). Focusing on a protagonist who keeps on seeing himself as a "squared-off grid" (169), the novel also applies the image of the maze to language that does not escape a labyrinthine prism of understanding and representation: "There are people out there who imagine they want to pass straight from language to clarity, but Larry Weller of Winnipeg, Canada, wants, all of a sudden, at age thirty-two, to hang on to words that sit all on their own, each with a little brain and a wreath of steam around its breathed-out sound: cantankerous, irrepressible, magnanimous" (83).

Like the spaces of the maze and the fictional spaces of *Larry's Party*, words are meaningful by themselves, but they expand their significance when juxtaposed and combined. The novel consequently engenders a grammar of space in which language, word creation, and derivation are built up and extended like the spaces of the labyrinth and in which words, moving forward and backward, are meaningful in all senses and directions: "maybe you were saying God when you said dog" (88). Carol Shields uses humour and physical and critical distance (Larry discovers the Hampton Court maze in a plane) as a guide and a device to perceive and handle the tenets of the reality.

The divisions of the novel invite the reader not only to regard each spatial and fictional fragment as an essential part of the whole, thanks to a system of coherent elements that go full circle, but also to follow a road of dead ends and aporia to better reach the centre. The construction of meaning, space, and species is completed through a deconstruction, a paradoxical twofold movement of validation and invalidation in which the seemingly wrong directions become the true substance of meaning. At the same time, the path of initiation both incorporates and rejects the exploration of dead ends, necessary and yet useless in the labyrinthine quest. Consequently, Larry is caught in a stochastic process of trial and error. The unfolding of the labyrinthine path is fraught with broken lines and defines itself as "classical in its suggestion and contemporary in its postmodern gestures" (152). If this path consists in "just taking the right corner at the right moment" (359), conquest lies in eliminating possibilities at intersections. From that perspective, the novel raises the question of junctions and articulations that Larry solves by ellipses. Carol Shields leaves the reader free to fill the empty spaces left by the dots between each chapter and to find "the missing wire of connection" (214); the dialectic of void ("a silky void" [3]), silences ("a series of silences" [48]), and words shift the novel into an indeterminate entity where all interpretations are both possible and relevant thanks to numerous unanswered questions and a labyrinth-character defined by the author as "a many-jointed creature" (87).

If Beth, Larry's second wife, sees him as a disoriented man, Larry, on the contrary, turns this disorientation into a positive quest of leading threads that he finally all validates, thus demonstrating the ubiquity of meaning and truth: "there can be one route or many" (153, 313). Consequently, he challenges normative conventions in terms of maze patterns: "the maze itself has a single entrance and four exits, one in each corner. Why four? Most mazes have only one exit or perhaps two" (181). When Larry promotes all paths without imposing one single layout and course, the reader is led to extend this notion of challenge to more general considerations pertaining to life and art. The novel multiplies the different perspectives to favour escapism, and Shields draws a character more eccentric than conventional. *Larry's Party* lies in a confluence of paradoxes in which the protagonist reflects classical patterns and conventions and also personal creations: being both an inheritor and an innovator, Larry combines tradition and emancipation as he explores new spatial and imaginative territories in artwork. Everything stems from this graphic art, and imagination is first inscribed in the actual drawings of mazes opening each chapter, which vary greatly in shape, from the most elementary to the most elaborate. So what first stands out is the mechanism of inspiration: as Shields says, "he's done a preliminary set of drawings, thinking as he works how happiness lurks between the hand and the eye, and between the objective design and the abstractions that bloom in his head" (180).

The porosity between emotions, sensations, and abstractions makes Larry wonder about life and art as he wanders through his mazes. As the figurative orients the thinking process that emerges through shapes, the different layouts of mazes diagram the coming chapters, in which the author associates figures and ideas and converts them into mental images to invent stories. The novel is consequently entangled in various maze configurations in which simplicity and sophistication collaborate and which announce Larry's events; this process can be exemplified by the circular maze layout of "Larry's Threads" (chapter 12) or "Larry's Living Tissues" (chapter 14), which resembles the anatomy of a brain; the square and rational maze of "Larry's Words" (chapter 5); the simple, if not simplistic, layout of "Men Called Larry" (chapter 13). "Larry's Love" (chapter 2) is the mere reproduction of the Hampton Court maze. Shields juggles with manifold configurations to symbolize outer and inner life and establish close ties between them.

As regards identity, Larry is also caught in contradictions and paradoxes. Through the symbolical construction of an open structure evocative of emancipation, he refuses his filiation and his fatherhood. He shuns the veiled and disruptive image of his father reflected in the mirror, and he does not bring up his child, Ryan. But at the end of the novel, he is reunited with his first wife. Shields abolishes some elements that shaped Larry in order to reuse them in his "refiguration." As in the labyrinth, the different spaces evocative of identity landmarks are intertwined, and contradictions coexist to shape identity; Shields creates a system of unexpected equivalence between perceptions and dimensions in which a mirror is a surface that corresponds to a depth. In these contradictions, she leads us to follow Linda Hutcheon's interrogation, in her study of postmodernism, of "both art and theory *as signifying processes.* In other words, maybe we could begin to study the implications of both our *making* and *making sense* of our culture."[13] When Larry makes mazes, he creates a new cultural frontier challenged by new spaces; he makes sense of his life through the making of elaborate mazes that bring into light shifting and contradictory identities, mostly born out of his mistakes.

These rather ubiquitous mistakes are synonymous with an erratic and nomadic creation; the novel opens up "by mistake" (3), and Larry seems to be the constant outcome of mistakes, ranging from his first job, "an accident" (3), to his first wife —"it was a sort of mistake the way they got together" (13) – to end up himself as the perfect embodiment of mistakes: "he was one bad mistake" (13). But in *Larry's Party*, nothing is coincidental. These mistakes trigger multiple discoveries through misdirections and dead ends, in so far as the process of trial and error necessarily reduces error and wrong directions and indicates the path to the centre of the labyrinth – what Gilbert Durand refers to as "the kernel of that profound intimacy."[14] Larry incidentally discovers the magic of the Hampton Court maze when he is lost and disoriented after taking the wrong directions. In fact, *Larry's Party* combines two of Umberto Eco's three types of labyrinths: it is both a maze, because in a maze "one can make mistakes," and a net where one "meanders."[15]

Wandering, akin to disorientation and leading Larry astray, turns into an inner as much as an outer initiation. For the minute observation of his life – referred to as "a privileged corner of the world" (152) – sometimes bordering on a clinical examination exemplified by the chapter on his cells, sheds an increasing light on the web of tissue, access roads with an intensified complementarity. Indeed, the novel conveys images of a fragmented life with separate narrative segments evocative of the intertwined spaces of mazes like Larry's women, who are "separate selves but part of Larry's self" (330). But in reality, these segments build coherent, embedded spaces thanks to interspersed and recurrent details used as analeptic threads. The deceptive juxtaposition of spaces turns out to be an interpenetration of elements linked by the quest of the same goal within a common structure. Shields's vision of the world is a holistic one that corresponds to Empedocles' principle, which states that the centre is everywhere and the circumference nowhere. All elements come together and are linked, like da Vinci's cross placed in a circle or a square or as in mandalas based on the same pattern of inclusion of circles within squares, which are reminiscent of a many-faceted image of the self. It seems in fact that Larry's mazes derive more from what mandalas imply: his retro/introspection through different spaces is suggestive of the multiple projection of the self in mandalas; he passes from "the *how* of mazes" to "the *why* of the subject" (138).

So geometry and shifting perspectives remain Larry's privileged prism of understanding and reproducing the world through the building of labyrinths, where the myth of Theseus surfaces more in the quest of one's own in space than in the conquest of another creature. Larry searches for the self he has become thanks to the invested place of the tweed jacket, since "a costume is supposed to change you" (10). Referred to as his geographical belonging, "Larry Weller of Winnipeg, Canada" (83), he does not only wonder about *who* he is but also *where* he is (169), identity and introspection being closely linked with territory. The answers he puts forward are constantly topographical and geometric. His first marriage shifts from "a curved space" (36) to "a cramped crawlspace" (101), and his mother is caught in "a circle of worry" (47). Only shapes and colours are meaningful to him, a revelation that comes to him when he discovers the Hampton Court maze from above during his honeymoon. Larry then modifies his synesthetic apprehension of the outer and inner world from this altered perspective, this partition that he applies to space and what Vladimir Jankélévitch calls "the irony of fragmentation" or "the disjunction of elements"[16] and which he deplores on the grounds that it prevents humanity from having a global vision of the world. The wrong directions thus taken in the maze become the corollary of an initiation process that gradually multiplies dimensions to be free of the merely horizontality and normative aesthetics which Larry first experiences when confronted with the *relief* of the quadrant. In his anatomy of dreams, Gaston Bachelard studies the relationship between space and dreams, in a chapter devoted to the dynamics of landscapes, he underlines the specificity of an engraver, saying that "he sets the world in motion, he calls upon the forces which swell shape, he stimulates the slumbering energies of a flat world."[17] Like Bachelard's engraver, Larry gives more dimensions to a flat space. This explosion also evokes the graphic artist Maurits C. Escher and his lithographs, which Hofstader, in his famous meditation on human thought and creativity, *Gödel, Escher, Bach: An Eternal Golden Braid*, defines as "islands of certainty,"[18] emphasizing the intersection between music, artwork, and mathematics. Shields resorts to this intersection and promotes the blending of arts when she says that Larry would "like that self to be more musical" (284). In Escher's drawings, like Larry's mazes, original shapes are transformed into complicated figures; each detail is symbolical of the whole and can be seen as a separate and self-contained element.[19] The labyrinthine elements of *Larry's Party* propose different codes that can all encompass truth.

Consequently, Shields challenges classical representations by endowing her "soaring" (172) protagonist with a physical dimension, a feeling of elevation and lightness coupled with the stature that he discovers simultaneously with the poetry of the inner depth of a mesmerizing maze – what Jean-Pierre Richard calls the "infinite fecundity of the abyss."[20] This topography contaminates the world and the word, and Larry's geographical uprooting rapidly becomes an intellectual stance and a critical distance: "a man on the verge of nothing at all" (181). By deconstructing a plane geometry, this geographical distance imparts aesthetic and ethical values, for this remote position becomes an ironic posture. Larry then insists on the refusal to cling to the surface of things: "I don't say it literally," he says (10). So paradoxes pervade the underlying irony of the novel, although Larry denies handling and using irony even if he continues to use indirect means. Indeed, most of the time, he acts against banal opinion or the advice of his relatives and escapes traditional limits and prescribed attitudes.

Uprooted in England and disoriented in the labyrinth, Larry learns how to lose himself and discover his true self and ecstasy: "and now, here in this garden maze, getting lost and then found seemed the whole point, that and the moment of willed abandonment, the unexpected rapture of being blindly led" (36). He then becomes the embodiment of an irregular path that invites the reader to use new angles of observation and other access roads to decipher the hidden threads leading to the labyrinth, which progressively becomes an inner maze. Shields selects diagonals and asymmetry as new means of revelation: "asymmetry brings a better focus to the conversation" (292). The concrete and symbolic indirect way of looking widens the perspectives and offers a more complete vision in which the marginal and incidental become essential: "Larry listens. This is how he is learning about the world, exactly as every one else does – from sideways comments over a lemon meringue pie, sudden bursts of comprehension or weird parallels that come curling out of the radio, out of a movie, off the pages of a newspaper, out of a joke – and his baffled self stands back and says: so this is how it works" (58).

This distorted linearity furnishes the structural frame for topographical and tropological elements. When Shields defines Larry's states of mind as "diagonal" (244), the same diagonal can be found as the paradoxical catalyst of fractured and joint lines. During his honeymoon, Larry realizes his mistake when he watches his wife sleep restlessly and slide aslant (21). Using this recurrent diagonal as a device, Shields reunites both characters at Larry's party. In the last meeting he rediscovers the same Dorrie like an abandoned Ariadne in a recodified myth, when she is seated diagonally according to a table setting devised by the author and inserted into the novel like another labyrinth. Furthermore, the meeting of all the characters introduces a circular representation of time, since the ending returns full circle to the beginning: "where you start from, there you end" (339).

Once again, the labyrinthine motif continues to be the predominant strategy and mechanism of a back-and-forth discursive movement and narratological sequence. This spatial and temporal partition, along with the broken lines, is the surface of projection of Larry's life, moulding his numerous separations and cleavages mirrored in the stories of his parents, wife, child, and, inevitably, his world. These recurring lines in his life (Larry, incidentally, notes about his grandfather that "his world had been cleft in two by calamity" [51]) finally culminate in intersections leading him to look for anchor points, "a sense of equilibrium" (172), "a tide of balance" (181), a general fixity organized around median lines.

Even if Larry is a character of symmetry and equidistance, born in 1950 (138), fascinated by the equinox (95), living in "the middle of Canada" (35), and performing acrobatics on median lines in a text fraught with the numbers 2 and 4, Shields has nevertheless designed a character of contradictions in an "unsettling and serene" labyrinth (171). Larry's identity is caught in in-betweenness, a sinuosidal move-ment between two spaces and entities, "between the old days and the new, between one continent and another" (20), always looking for a unity that finds its ultimate expression in the fusion of the final party. Larry becomes both the subject and the object of this paradoxically open structure which is his psychological extension, helping him to attain social representation.

When Shields writes that "his body is an upright labyrinth" (269) and at the same time deploys a sinuous narratology, the reader is invited to regard the novel as a circular construction in the meanders of Larry's life, reflected in the metamorphosis into circles of rectangular drawings, again recalling mandalas. Larry is described not only as a labyrinthine body with geometrical shapes – "I was a kind of maze myself, my body I mean" (175) – but also as "a spiral being"[21] who embarks on an inner odyssey, "a life's tortuous journey" (215), in which the labyrinth is the symbol of life:

What a wonder, he thinks, that the long, bitter, heart-wrenching history of the planet should allow curious breathing spaces for the likes of mere toys and riddles, he sees them everywhere. Games, glyphs, symbols, allegories, puns and anagrams, masquerades, the magician's sleight-of-hand, the clown's wink, the comic shrug, the somersault, the cryptogram in all its forms and especially, at least to Laurence J. Weller, the teasing elegance and circularity of the labyrinthine structure, a snail, a scribble, a doodle on the earth's skin with no other directed purpose but to wind its sinuous way around itself. (152)

If the labyrinthine objective consists in finding an exit, Larry's quest of the self, which climaxes in a coma, "a maze without an exit" (273), ends up in the discovery of the inaccessible and the infinite where "the choices are limitless" (149), as in the Hampton Court maze.[22] The absence of inner boundaries increases the space of physical and metaphysical life and reinforces the image of a character embodying a cogwheel and a fragment of a structure where Larry is "nevertheless plugged into a planet. He's part of the action, part of the world's work" (77). The volume of this space, which Shields amplifies with the use of the mirror in which Larry's father's image appears, is a direct link between all the spaces and times of the novel.

In this way, the various geometries converge on the final meeting of all the characters at Larry's party to build a specular novel fraught with mirror effects, where osmosis is the end touch reuniting the parallel lines of the living world and matter: "the maze will incorporate the essential lost-and-found odyssey of a conventional maze, but will allow the maze walker to forget that the shrub material is a kind of wall and think of it, rather, as an extension of an organic world, with the maze and the maze solver merging into a single organism" (289).

With the rediscovery of Dorrie, thanks to the oblique line that was once synonymous with rejection – "the journey they appear to have taken separately had really been made together" (328) – the novel confirms the circularity of its structure, the squaring of a circle and the dialectic of closure and openness: "Imprisoned within being, one must always escape. Once on the outside, one must always re-enter. Thus, being is circuitous, redirection full of diversion, discourse ... And how sinuous Man's being is! And within that spiral, how conflicting the energies! One is unaware immediately whether or not one is moving towards the center or towards the exit. ... Man's being is an unanchored one."[23] Like Robert Kroetsch, who underlines that "we write mandalas towards a cosmology that cannot be located. Towards a cosmology we do not wish to locate,"[24] Carol Shields multiplies paradoxes with Larry Weller, the son of a woman humourously called Dot by the author, the ultimate point of convergence of all contradictory and shifting perspectives between the mother figure and the image of death united in mother earth which form the entrance and exit of Larry's life. One might say, then, that the novel emphasizes a cyclical, multidimensional, and fusional nature, harmoniously absorbing all types of contradictions, much like the entanglements of the threads in the tweed jacket of the beginning or the multiple dialogues of the last chapter, which are propitious to all forms of reconciliations, and it recalls the poet's vision:

What we call the beginning is often the end
And to make an end is to make a beginning
....
In my end is my beginning.[25]

NOTES

The translations into English of French texts are mine.

1   Bataille, *L'expérience intérieure*, 100.
2   Shields, *Larry's Party*, 65, 207.
3   Bataille, *L'expérience intérieure*, 99 and 102.
4   Arasse, *Le détail*, 252.
5   Frye, *Bush Garden*, 224.
6   Foucault, *Les mots et les choses*, 37.
7   Deleuze and Guattari, *Mille plateaux*, 12.
8   Barthes, *Roland Barthes par Roland Barthes*, 87.
9   Borges, *Collected Fictions*, 124, 126, 127.
10   Blanchot, *L'écriture du désastre*, 125.
11   In *In Visible Ink*, Aritha van Herk goes further in terms of complicity born out of ordinariness. She says that "for Carol Shields, the world is that moment when we bend to that blown page, and in reading discover a page from the story of ourselves, that coalesced moment when a complete stranger surprises us through an act of intimacy" (54).
12   Bachelard, *L'intuition de l'instant*, 15.
13   Hutcheon, "Beginning to Theorize Postmodernism," 263.
14   Durand, *Les structures anthropologiques de l'imaginaire*, 178.
15   Eco, *Semiotics and the Philosophy of Language*, 81. Eco says that "there are three types of labyrinth. The first, the classical one, was linear ... The second type is called in German *Irrgärten* or *Irrweg*; a good English term for it is *maze* ... A maze does not need a Minotaur: it is its own Minotaur: in other words, *the Minotaur is the visitor's trial-and-error process* ... In a labyrinth of the third type is a net ... A net is an unlimited territory" (ibid., 80–81).
16   Jankélévitch, *L'ironie*, 22.
17   Bachelard, *Le droit de rêver*, 71.
18   Hofstader, *Gödel, Escher, Bach*, 97.
19   See the lithograph *Reptiles* (1943), showing a mosaic of reptilian figures escaping the flat page and launching into real life, or *Liberation* (1955), in which triangles are transformed into complex figures before becoming birds flying off as independent creatures.

20 Richard, *Poésie et profondeur*, 104.
21 Bachelard, *La poétique de l'espace*, 193.
22 Here again, this passage is evocative of "The Garden of Forking Paths": "In
    all fictions, each man meets diverse alternatives, he chooses one and eliminates
    the others; in the work of the virtually impossible-to-disentangle Ts'ui Pen, the
    character chooses – simultaneously – all of them" (Borges, *Collected Fictions*,
    125).
23 Bachelard, *La poétique de l'espace*, 193.
24 Quoted in Kamboureli, *On the Edge of Genre*, 106.
25 T.S. Eliot, *Four Quartets*, 58.

WORKS CITED

Arasse, Daniel. *Le détail: Pour une histoire rapprochée de la peinture*. Paris:
    Flammarion, 1996.
Bachelard, Gaston. *Le droit de rêver*. Paris: Presses universitaires de France,
    1970.
– *L'intuition de l'instant*. Paris: Stock, 1992.
– *La poétique de l'espace*. Paris: Seuil, 1994.
Barthes, Roland. *Roland Barthes par Roland Barthes*. Paris: Seuil, 1995.
Bataille, Georges. *L'expérience intérieure*. Paris: Gallimard, 1983.
Blanchot, Maurice. *L'écriture du désastre*. Paris: Seuil, 1980.
Borges, Jorge Luis. *Collected Fictions*. Trans. Andrew Hurley. New York: Penguin,
    1998.
Deleuze, Gilles, and Félix Guattari. *Mille plateaux*. Paris: Minuit, 1980.
Durand, Gilbert. *Les structures anthropologiques de l'imaginaire*. Paris: Dunod,
    1992.
Eco, Umberto. *Semiotics and the Philosophy of Language*. Bloomington: Indiana
    University Press, 1984.
Eliot, T.S. *Four Quartets*. London: Faber and Faber, 1994.
Foucault, Michel. *Les mots et les choses*. Paris: Gallimard, 1966.
Frye, Northrop. *The Bush Garden*. Toronto: Anansi, 1971.
Hofstadter, Douglas. *Gödel, Escher, Bach: An Eternal Golden Braid*. Hassocks,
    Sussex: The Harvester, 1979.
Hutcheon, Linda. "Beginning to Theorize Postmodernism." In *A Postmodern
    Reader*, ed. Joseph Natoli and Linda Hutcheon, 243–72. New York: State
    University of New York Press, 1993.
Jankélévitch, Vladimir. *L'ironie*. Paris: Flammarion, 1964.

Kamboureli, Smaro. *On the Edge of Genre*. Toronto: University of Toronto Press, 1991.

Richard, Jean-Pierre. *Poésie et profondeur*. Paris: Points, 1955.

Shields, Carol. *Larry's Party*. London: Fourth Estate, 1997.

Van Herk, Aritha. *In Visible Ink*. Edmonton: NeWest Publishers, 1991.

9

Scenes from a (Boston) Marriage: The Prosaics of Collaboration and Correspondence in *A Celibate Season*

MANINA JONES

Good marriages surely do not exclude romance, but they require prosaics.

Gary Saul Morson

In an essay in *Prairie Fire*, later included as a foreword to the 1998 reissue of the novel *A Celibate Season* (1991), Blanche Howard relates her first meeting with future collaborator Carol Shields at an Ottawa book discussion group in the early 1970s: "we soon recognized the other as a 'book person,'" writes Howard.¹ Separated by family relocations shortly thereafter, the two writers renewed their acquaintance and deepened their friendship through the "Victorian diversion" (73) of regular letter-writing: "Carol loves to get letters –" Howard reflects, "once, visiting [Carol and her family] in Paris, my husband and I were amused at the enthusiasm with which she watches for the daily mail ... She swoops down on the mailbox as if it might contain the meaning of life – and perhaps it does."² The dedication of *A Celibate Season*, "To Carol from Blanche and to Blanche from Carol, and to the letters woven into the fabric of friendship,"³ not only affirms the importance of books and correspondence in creating a rapport between these two Canadian women of letters; it also suggests a connection between the letter-writing that laid the groundwork of their largely long-distance collaboration and the letters composing *A Celibate Season*, the epistolary novel that was its product. Indeed, the letters that make up *A Celibate Season* are underwritten by the material processes of its collaborative production. As reviewer Meg Stainsby writes, "in this work, letters are the thing."[4]

A Celibate Season, like so much of Shields's work, explores alternative stories, multiple perspectives, what Janet Giltrow calls, describing *Happenstance*'s doubled chronicling of "a marriage in transition," "the boundaries of point of view."[5] But unlike *Happenstance*, the narration of *A Celibate Season* is composed on the boundaries of both characters' and authors' point of view: Howard wrote the part of wife Jocelyn, or "Jock," and Shields took on the role of husband Chas, an excursion into masculine perspective anticipated in the husband's story of *Happenstance*[6] and expanded in Shields's most celebrated exploration of masculine sensibility, *Larry's Party* (1997). *A Celibate Season* uses an alternating letter format in which the fictional couple correspond about the daily events of their lives, temporarily living apart while lawyer Jock travels to Ottawa to serve as legal counsel for a royal commission on "The Feminization of Poverty," and Chas, an unemployed architect, minds the home front in Vancouver. Like Jock and Chas, Shields and Howard "relied primarily upon the postal system to vitiate [the isolating effect of geographical distances]."[7] As Lorraine York observes, "Until the mid-to-late–1980s, when both women traded in their typewriters for computers, they would painstakingly type out drafts of letters by their characters Jock and Chas, xerox them, and send them back and forth between Vancouver, where Howard was living, and Winnipeg, Shields's home at that time."[8] In fact, there are many places in Shields and Howard's correspondence regarding the novel when proliferating references to "letters" between the two collaborating novelists and the letters within those letters exchanged both between the authors and within the diegesis of the novel-in-progress are difficult to distinguish.

For the novel's narrators, textual intercourse takes the place of physical intimacies during the "celibate season" during which husband and wife are separated. Differences in time, space, and perspective are negotiated both in and by the letters exchanged between spouses and, it might be argued, by Shields and Howard's collaboration itself, a correspondence that, in Wayne Koestenbaum's term, "shadows" each word of the text.[9] As York suggests, the "destabilizing celibacy" of Jock and Chas's marriage is "a metaphor for the novel's collaborative conditions of production by two geographically separated but mutually engaged letter-writing individuals."[10] Indeed, otherness itself is figured in this novel as temporary celibacy, as Jock takes a "leave of absence" from the conduct of both professional (12) and marital (222) routines in order to

pursue her work on the royal commission. Absence and abstinence thus
become cognates, both tied up in an economy of suppressed conjugal
desire, as in Jock's joke to Chas "about abstinence making the heart
grow fonder" (166). And while the mundane, realist surface of *A Celibate Season* is a far cry from the self-conscious exploitation of the conditions of joint production that York sees as typical of contemporary
collaborations,[11] the novel's composite epistolary narrative is suggestive
of what I would like to call a prosaics of desire generated by the collaborative act.

In this, Shields and Howard extend what Mikhail Bakhtin would call
"prosaic wisdom" or "prosaic intelligence" as a "form-shaping ideology."[12]
In their reading of Bakhtin, Gary Saul Morson and Caryl Emerson propose the term "prosaics" to designate both a theory of literature that privileges prose and, more generally, "a form of thinking that presumes the
importance of the everyday, the ordinary, the *prosaic*."[13] Bakhtin's theories
themselves build on Leo Tolstoy's observation in an essay titled "Why Do
Men Stupefy Themselves?" that real ethical decisions are made, and life is
truly lived, at everyday moments we rarely acknowledge.[14] Thus for
Tolstoy, both art and life begin "where the tiny bit begins,"[15] an argument
that implies the possibility that, as Howard put it in her comic description
of Shields's habitual swoop on the mailbox, the meaning of life might be
discovered in the daily mail.

For Bakhtin, prosaics registers a conviction that quotidian experience
is essentially messy, disorganized, characterized by surprise, openness,
and creativity, in short, what he calls "unfinalizability" (*Anezavershen-
nost*).[16] The prosaic is surely another term for what Shields refers to as
"the natural gas of the quotidian,"[17] fuel for a motor force that propels
her narratives; her confession that from the start of her writing career she
found herself attracted to "randomness and disorder, not circularity or
narrative cohesion," might as well be describing Bakhtin's "unfinalizability." Shields seems to have sought out fictional devices that would be
fitted not just to the untidiness of ordinary life but to a desire to trouble
aesthetically unified forms: "I had observed," she writes, "how the
human longing for disruption was swamped in fiction for an almost
mechanical model of aesthetic safety."[18] The narrative of *A Celibate Season* is, of course, generated by marital disruption, the physical separation
prompted by Jock's "career conflict" between (local) domestic and (long-
distance) professional roles, a move Chas characterizes at various points
in the novel as risky to the safety of their spousal relationship. It is also,
however, fundamentally predicated on a disruption of conventionally

defined singular authorship, one that, true to Shields's description, troubles traditional notions of artistic unity and jeopardizes models of "aesthetic safety" as well.[19]

"Separation had never happened to either of us in real life," Howard writes, clearly thinking of each writer's stable marriage and secure home life.[20] The composition of *A Celibate Season*, prompted by Shields's suggestion to Howard in 1983 that they "do a novel together,"[21] is, however, invested in their experience of other forms of separation and risk. It is, for example, based on the collaborative writing relationship's "split up" of the unified notion of solitary authorship, an arrangement that Howard, unintentionally echoing Chas's concerns, acknowledges is potentially "dangerous" to their friendship (71). Shields and Howard's decision to undertake a project together also prompted Howard to identify other material concerns that would unbalance any simple egalitarian sense of co-authorship. She mentions the conflict between her own "languishing" career as a novelist, as distinguished from Shields's "burgeoning" reputation at the time of the novel's inception: Shields would be spending time on a project when, in Howard's words, her labour might be "more beneficially spent elsewhere."[22] Their collaboration, then, motivated by friendship, is conditioned by differences of reputation and aesthetic value.

For Howard, the novel also stirred her consciousness of other "career conflicts": those of a writing wife, produced by a separation between traditional domestic and professional roles for women of her generation, whose yearning for work outside housekeeping and husband support "carried social disapprobation"; she identifies writing as the kind of "portable vocation" that can be accommodated to the demands of family life.[23] Yet in her essay Howard relates an anecdote in which Erma Bombeck, entering the hospital in (maternal) labour, tried to have "writer" entered on the official record as her career, only to have the nurse scratch it out in favour of "housewife."[24] Interestingly, at the time *A Celibate Season* was being written, Shields was manipulating the possibilities of a gender gap between author and authorial signature, experimenting not just with masculine point of view but with the cultural weight of masculine authorship; she comments wryly in a letter to Howard: "Other news: all is well, fall is here, Ian (my pseudonym) has had 2 acceptances! [handwritten:] Now *he* is a serious writer!" (21 October 1983).[25] Unlike Shields's masculine authorial alter ego, Bombeck, the domestic humorist to whom Howard refers, found it difficult to be taken seriously as a wife/mother and professional writer, though in the end she based her career as a popular writer on that very doubling of roles.

In both its content and composition, *A Celibate Season* hints at the renegotiation of just such homely and professional "career conflicts." The prosaic is embodied in the novel both in the sheer dailiness of "the daily mail," with its conversations about lentils, sequins, and the purchase of purple boots, and in the epistolary form of this collaborative work. The textual exchanges of the novel-of-letters seem in many ways ideally suited to convey what Shields calls a "narrative hunger" to give fictional form to the fragmentary, disjunctive stories that come from other places, other perspectives, other people.[26] Certainly, her contribution of Chas's letters is meant to use the forum of correspondence to dilate upon the relative nature of the marital roles and gendered responses of an ordinary man, to comment, in other words, on the discursive production, in the textual exchanges of the daily mail, of a daily male.

The epistolary narrative is driven, not just straightforwardly, but back and forth between two correspondents. The letters that compose *A Celibate Season* affirm the prosaic temporal and spatial perspectives, the discursive positioning of dialogue and response, in the headers that date and locate each epistle, suggesting obliquely the degree to which the correspondents interlocate each other in their reciprocal communications: "29 Sweet Cedar Drive / North Vancouver, B.C. / 5 January" (109), or "4 Old Town Lane / Ottawa, Ont., Sunday, Jan. 5" (107). Even the device of "crossed letters," often cited as an excessively mechanical element of the form (though it also happens in the correspondence between Shields and Howard), throws into relief the extent to which utterances are context-specific and dependent on their responsive role.

In addition to the dialogue between the narrative voices, the letter form also accommodates other signs of (to cite Balachandra Rajan's phrase somewhat out of context) "the form of the unfinished": spontaneous ejaculations, interruptions, parenthetical remarks, references to and quotations of external conversations and statements, numerous postscripted – and post-postscripted – afterthoughts, and what Bakhtin would call "active double-voiced discourse," a component of dialogue in which the correspondents' sensed presence of each other, their anticipation of response even at the moment of articulation, is registered: "'What is a prose poem?' I can hear you asking from Ottawa," Chas writes (129), for example, after he is assigned to compose one for a creative writing course, or Jock's "Why, you may ask (probably are), is the Commission so frantically busy all of a sudden?" (151). Letters index both material exchange and reciprocity, the degree to which authorship and readership are implicated in each other.

As York puts it, the epistolary novel is "a very concrete rendering of Benjamin's notion of the producer as reader and the reader as producer, authors of letters in epistolary novels are simultaneously readers of letters."[27] The foregrounded nature of this aspect of writing was clearly one of the joys Howard took in the collaborative act: "Well here's chapter one," she wrote to Shields in 1983, "and I can't tell you how much more fun it is to write something for someone else's eyes than just to write for the faceless mass who may or may not read it. I kept thinking, will Carol like this? and she'll laugh at that, and so on."[28] Shields and Howard's collaboration "folds in" "external" details and conflicts of current events and their own lives (they initially set the novel "this year" in 1983), such as Howard's involvement in the British Columbia political scene or the real-life daily newspaper articles she clipped and sent to Shields and which Shields then incorporated into Jock's narration (54), resulting in what archivist Catherine Hobbs cites as another instance of the novel's "playful borrowing from the circumstances surrounding the writing of the novel."[29] Shields's undated note to Howard in acknowledgment of the clippings recognizes the destabilization of authorial property and propriety the exchange and embedding of such texts represents: "I very much appreciated all the clippings and you will see that I have helped myself liberally. Are you allowed to plagiarize yourself?" Even as such shared texts are integrated as communal property, their incorporation is registered as transgressive and their ownership questionable.

Letters, finally, treat life as a prosaic text, as untidy and processual; they are, at least in part and in theory, "written forward" as life is lived,[30] a feature most strikingly conveyed in the ambiguous final phrase of the novel, Chas's exclamatory "Onward!" (226). In fact, the narrative of *A Celibate Season* is caught in an ambivalent tension between the necessity of "living forward" into messy, always yet-to-be-determined familial configurations and unstable gender roles – a situation in which, for example, Chas can be "the lady of the house" (17) or in which Jocelyn must acknowledge the possibility that she is not "a fellow woman" (24) with her female colleague – and nostalgia for an imagined past unity, a marriage where sex seemed "merely incidental to wholeness" (140) and gender roles were complementary and dependably predictable. This tension between instability and integrity is spatialized in *A Celibate Season* in the figures of an idyllic family home and varieties of ongoing "home renovations." Just as architect Chas occupies and rebuilds the family kitchen in his wife's absence, Jock effectively redesigns woman's place in the public sphere in her alternative approach to housekeeping: professional work on behalf of the House of Commons. Her 'Commonsplace' observations on the everyday events of life on the Hill – the prosaics of politics, if you will – are reflected by the commission's work, which politicizes the prosaic facts of women's poverty, suggesting the ways in which domesticity is economically underwritten by society, and deviations from its conventional marital and domestic manifestations (e.g., single working mothers such as Sue and Jean, rural widows such as the witness at the commission's Northern hearing, communal group homes such as the one where commission member Jessica Slattery resides) are economically and socially penalized. The "extraordinary" workings of politics on the national stage are, it turns out, themselves Housework, constituted as they are by the politics of less spectacular housework, the nitty-gritty details of ordinary domestic arrangements.

Nostalgia for an idealized traditional domestic arrangement is, of course, satirized in the relationship of Jock and Chas's Vancouver neighbours Marjorie and Gus, a couple whose apparently exemplary Laura Ashley home decor – the home as "a pleasing and attractive refuge" – and conventional roles in an "intact" family (121) conceal a disturbing dysfunction which the text repeatedly hints at but never names. This reticence may in part be because the genre of the domestic comic novel cannot quite accommodate *A Celibate Season*'s own satirical inference: that the traditional family's power structure, based on the infantilization of women's domestic roles, carries disturbing implications of pedophilia, as intimated by Gus's attentions to Jock and Chas's adolescent daughter.

The terms of domestic integrity, *A Celibate Season* implies, are subject to both interrogation and renegotiation. The letters that compose the novel, with their reiterated signatures of husband and wife and alternative takes on relationship conflicts and reconciliations, imply the contractual nature of marriage itself. The signature here is not presented simply as a legal guarantee, a sign of what Seán Burke would call "responsible discursive accountability."[31] It also defines the marital relationship as a cultural entity established and contested within the undertakings of people's *everyday* relationships. The letter-as-contract thus suggests the ongoing necessity of collaboratively rewriting the terms of marriage and gender roles according to changing times and situations, though, in the end, *A Celibate Season* seems ambivalent about the goals of this project. Even in – or perhaps because of – its ambivalence, the novel stages a destabilization of heterosexual marital integrity. It stages an important subversion of conventional authorship as well, especially since the "signatures" at the bottom of each of the novel's letters are doubled by the implicit and overt authorial signatures of Howard and Shields.

The first letter of *A Celibate Season* begins with a mock performance of the dislocation of desire within marriage. Newly arrived in Ottawa and temporarily lodged at the Château Laurier, Jock finds that her capacious and luxurious accommodations produce only a kind of eroticized homesickness: "I'd have felt less bereft if the room had been little, with, instead of two big double beds, one modest, cell-like single covered with chaste white cotton – why two doubles anyway? Are there people so sexually athletic that, having worn out the resilience of bed number one, they roll – not coming unstuck – onto bed number two.... I'd better get off that line of thought" (11–12). Reading this paragraph with the novel's collaborative authorship in mind, I could not help but recall the many images of sexual intimacy evoked in theoretical writing on same-sex collaboration. From the metaphorically lesbian "dynamic of desire, energy, and euphoria" evoked by Carey Kaplan and Ellen Cronan Rose,[32] to lesbian couple Susan J. Leonardi and Rebecca A. Pope's contention that their "concrete erotic connection ... [is a] literalization of the erotic always inherent in the collaborative process,"[33] to Wayne Koestenbaum's assertion that "men who collaborate engage in a metaphorical sexual intercourse,"[34] to Jeffrey Masten's reading of collaboration in Renaissance drama as a form of "textual intercourse,"[35] it has become almost a cliché of writing on collaboration that sexual intimacy "doubles" for the *double-lit* and *double-écrit* – the doubled reading and writing – of collaborative consummation. Might the doubled double beds (lits doubles) of Jock's comic fantasy express a dynamic of desire, not just between the novel's dislocated spouses, but between its displaced authors as well?

The fact that Shields and Howard were heterosexual friends and not lovers emphasizes the necessary discursive separation between the subjects of the enunciation and the subjects of the enunciated fictional narrative. So, even while it might hint at correspondences between collaborative and romantic desire, this novel insists on a slippage between its authors and its narrative voice and content. To return to Jock's sexual fantasy of the two double beds, these collaborators "come unstuck" in the transition from represented to representing couple. And yet, as Elizabeth Grosz contends, the subject of the enunciation and the subject of the enunciated cannot ever be authoritatively separated, "for the processes of the production of the utterance are always inscribed in the utterance itself."[36] Shields and Howard's novel is not autobiographical in the sense that it simply reproduces in fiction the intricacies of its authors' relationship; neither is it a "seamless" unity in which the authors simply disappear into the fabric of their narrative; nor can it, given the multiple mutual revisions that Howard and Shields undertook as part of its composition and revision, be "puritanically parsed" (in Koestenbaum's term)[37] in order to determine separate authorship.

Shields and Howard's homosocial authorial "marriage" destabilizes all of these straightforward readings. *A Celibate Season* does not "lesbianize authorship" in the sense that York applies the term to more self-referential, experimental collaborative writing. However, I cannot as categorically dismiss the novel as York does, as simply reinstating "heteronormative and other conservative positions"[38] or as corrective of "*any* tendency to assume that collaborative authorship is necessarily subversive" of gender and authorial norms.[39] *A Celibate Season*, for example, notably takes as a central pre-text Gillian Hanscombe's 1982 work *Between Friends*, an overtly lesbian epistolary novel in which fictional correspondence represents the development of erotic relationships between women.[40] Shields appears to have recommended *Between Friends* to Howard, who began to read it as she and Shields conceived of their own co-written novel.[41]

York suggests that in *A Celibate Season*, "secret extra-marital flings aside, heterosexual marriage emerges triumphant, if a trifle battered about the edges, by the end of the novel,"[42] and while this assessment may be true, I would emphasize that heterosexual marriage is genuinely "battered *about the edges*" of heterosexuality itself, threatened less by the "sexual dalliances" that constitute Chas's and Jock's brief (heterosexual) infidelities than by the narrative's hints at other ways in which desire might, but is not, in this "fairly conventional" novel, quite permitted to circulate. For example, in her early days in Ottawa, Jock's middle-class naïveté about women's poverty ("Surely no one is starving," she asserts) is met by an enigmatic stare from Jessica, Jock's radical feminist co-worker: "I've been trying to analyse that look," muses Jock, concluding that it constitutes a challenge, "as though she were testing me to see if I was a fellow woman. I don't think I am. She scares the hell out of me" (24). Jessica is in virtually every way in excess of Jock's naive bourgeois values and comfortable norms of femininity: overweight, flamboyantly flatulent, coarse in her language and demeanour, ambiguous in her sexuality, and yet clearly appealing in her candour and her insistently practical approach to helping other women, she represents, in many ways, the novel's unresolved conflicts about the nature of femininity, agency, and desire.

The challenge Jessica poses arises in part from her commitment to a *communal* domestic arrangement and *communal* values that cannot be accommodated to bourgeois familial models, a commitment that comes off as merely "common" (or vulgar) in Jock's simplistic middle-class view: the group home where Jessica lives, is, according to Jock, "Pandemonium, what with eight mothers and kids of every age, a common living room dominated by TV, common eating areas, and common God knows what else – I could never live like that. (Why not? I ask myself)" (40). The "common God knows what else" of Jessica's household, with its possibility of multivalent sexuality, is surely a more serious challenge than the brief, comic ménage à trois with his female writing instructor and housekeeper that constitutes Chas's extramarital sexual infraction. Jessica's challenge to the complacency of Jock and Chas's relationship is epitomized by the fact that she is the author of the *only* letter in *A Celibate Season* written by neither Jock nor Chas; the farewell card Jessica slips to Jock just before the latter leaves for home, reads simply, in bold print, "I LOVE YOU." That this note, writes Jock, "has shaken me more than I would like to admit" (223) gestures toward the alternative ways desire might address itself. It is a letter, significantly, Jock mentions only in a P.P.S. to her husband, and one to which she is apparently incapable of formulating a response.

I see *A Celibate Season*, in its authorship and in its narrative, troubling the conventionality that York reads as simply reinstated by the novel.[43] I would thus argue, with Holly Laird, that "even the most normative [collaborative] plots are marked by curious breaking points where sexual identity is destabilized,"[44] intentionally or not. Patently not grounded on the idealized grand passions of authorial/erotic consummation but on something much more homely in its production, the authorial alliance between Shields and Howard "shadows" *both* the Jock-Chas marriage and the unfulfilled, though not unfelt, connection between Jessica and Jock. In this, their authorial relationship might be said to bear some similarity to what in the nineteenth century was commonly known as a "Boston marriage,"[45] a frequently – though indeterminately – celibate domestic living arrangement between women partners that, among many other things, institutionalized women's loving friendships and allowed their professional aspirations to be developed within a domestic context alternative to traditional heterosexual marriage.[46] As Kate McCullough

puts it, the nineteenth-century version of the Boston marriage challenged "the split between domestic and public life encouraged by 'separate spheres' ideology."[47] It is no coincidence, then, that the Boston
marriage has long been associated with women's collaborations, since
several famous nineteenth-century writing partnerships were thus
defined.[48]

As Judith Thompson and Marjorie Stone observe of the romanticized
figuring of collaborative relationships, "quite apart from love and the
passions that survive its end, there are many other quotidian activities,
circumstances and relationships that form the matrix for the coming
together of literary couples and their making of texts."[49] In their discussion of their own co-authorship, Linda and Michael Hutcheon counter
prevalent characterizations of collaboration as an act of passionate abandonment, with the much more ordinary metaphor, not of the double
bed, but of the dinner table as a locus of spousal dialogue, a formulation
which, they readily admit, "isn't half as sexy a concept of collaboration
as some sort of erotic entanglement – but after twenty-five years of marriage, we have to admit that we find it not uncomfortable."[50] In fact, in *A
Celibate Season*, the dinner table is reconfigured as both a flashpoint for
marital conflict and a simultaneously domestic and professional site,
when Chas moves his architect's drafting table into the kitchen in his
wife's absence. The dinner table is also, similarly, the literal site of at
least one of Shields and Howard's face-to-face collaborations: Howard
remembers working "diligently all day at the dining room table [of
Shields's Winnipeg home], each reading aloud our own letters and
interrupting one another with corrections, cutting, adding, changing,
arguing over commas."[51]

In some ways, the celibacy sustained between Jock and Chas makes it
"safe" for us to consider the relationship between Carol and Blanche
without scandalizing heterosexual sensibilities. However, I want to see
prosaic celibacy as related to – indeed, productive of – an intimate
dynamic of authorial/marital reciprocal desire. This, it seems to me, is
made evident in the letters exchanged within *A Celibate Season* and their
recounting of the increasingly comic and increasingly frustrating misad-
ventures of the fictional couple's attempts to reconsummate their marriage. For example, after a disastrous Christmas reunion in Vancouver,
during which the couple's planned sexual encounter is foiled by an argument about Chas's surprise renovations, Jock, deprived of the actual
presence of her male partner in Ottawa, finds desire rekindled by
repeated reading of letters from her mail partner: "Thank God for these

letters. I have read and reread yours, and love and longing are definitely stealing back into the big space recently occupied by anger." She thus begins to reconcile herself to a reconstructed world in which her changed working circumstances are reciprocated in Chas's reimagining of their home space: "Maybe I really *will* like the solarium" (124). Chas's response comically and hyperbolically depicts the ways in which bodies and discourses transform one another, when he finds his virility reinstated by Jock's response: "Your letter has just come and I've read it three times, the third time with an erection the size of a – well, never mind" (126).

Homeliness and otherness are uncannily linked in *A Celibate Season* to produce a kind of "prosaic desire," premised on the deferred possibility of union, an impulse generated within discursive exchange that applies to both literal and collaborative "marriage." It is, in fact, such ordinary otherness that holds their marriage and their alternative perspectives together. Jock and Chas's separation – and the ordinary discourse that mediates it – thus signifies the extraordinary "otherness" at the centre of the most intimate relationships. Shields has noted that double spousal narration (with which she had also experimented in the story "Others" in *Various Miracles*) can "demonstrate what I believe to be true of long-lasting relationships, that the two individuals remain, in one sense, strangers to one another while, at the same time, knowing each other better than they know themselves."[52] It is through the exchange of the details of their ordinary lives that Chas and Jock each provoke desire – textual and erotic – in their "significant other." For example, after a difference of opinion that nearly puts their relationship at risk, Chas writes, "Keep writing, lovey, and let's try to keep this ship floating along" (113). In another letter, he writes to praise Jock for a televised interview in which he scarcely recognizes his thinner, newly professionalized – and sexually unavailable – wife: "I had to keep asking myself if that was really the woman I sleep with. (Used to sleep with)" (62). He explicitly identifies this letter as "a love letter," though the content of the interview deals with the homely/professional topic of wages for stay-at-home spouses (62).

The figure of celibacy thus becomes a signifier of sustained difference, a trope for the at least temporary deferral of romantic notions of sexual/marital/authorial unity that produces the desire which underwrites marriage, and distinguishes it from simple sexual union or a utopian merging of the souls, just as it is the differentiation between collaborative partners that underwrites collaboration, making it different from, say, channelling or a utopian merging of the souls. Eroticism and celibacy, like romantic and prosaic love, are mutually conditioning, not mutually exclusive elements. In her insightful discussion of eroticism in collaborative authorship, Linda K. Karrell argues that the erotic component of collaboration involves not just a "blurring of boundaries or a figurative 'union,' whether sexual or otherwise," but also a recognition that is much "more pragmatic, more potentially revolutionary and more profoundly threatening":

the recognition of difference that is not subsequently assimilated or suppressed ... Because collaboration is always about negotiating a relationship in some sense – a relationship between writers, between sources of influence, between prior texts and current ones, between literary conventions or expectations – collaboration inevitably encounters a relational difficulty: acknowledging the other, who is commonly the screen onto which the threat of difference is projected ... The possibility of transforming difference into a positive force, which can occur during the recognition and negotiation of difference, is one of the compelling aspects of collaboration for both writers and readers.[53]

A Celibate Season uses letter-writing and marital tension to represent this "relational difficulty," resisting simplistic tropes of sexual/marital/ authorial wholeness. Thus it recognizes the possibility of, as Karrell puts it, "difference *that is not subsequently assimilated or suppressed*." Just as it suggests that the desire provoked by separation and otherness, and not simply the accomplishment of sexual union, is at the heart of marriage, so alterity conditions collaboration.

Jock's marital infidelity, significantly, takes place in colleague Austin Grey's presumably single "narrow little bed" (211). Jock rejects the possibility of pursuing this relationship because, in contrast to Austin, an unmarried, lyric poet who "floats free" of social ties, she affirms that "I have another life, a long, solidly packed history with so many separate tentacles and chambers I could never count them all" (212). Shields and Howard thus signal a rejection of a model of authorial alienation offered by poetic modernism: Howard confirms she used modernist poet F.R. Scott as the model for Austin Grey[54] and claims to have "plagiarized" internally cited instances of Austin Grey's poetry from Scott.[55] In her sexual act with Austin, Jock feels "*known* – that strange biblical term" (211), but her correspondence with Chas confirms an ongoing process of imperfect knowing: "maybe we don't know each other as well as I thought we did" (119), she writes. Jock chooses, it might be said, a messy marriage over a neat divorce. The tentacles and chambers of her life are discursively reflected, not by the polished unity and univocality of lyric verse, but by the unruly double-voiced prose of her ongoing correspondence.

A Celibate Season ends with the prospective reunion of Jock and Chas in their Vancouver family home.[56] Its final reaffirmation of middle-class heterosexual marriage re-enacts the classical comic structure in what some might call a "mechanical model of aesthetic safety." However, the conclusion of the novel only further defers any simple comic, utopian vision of sexual reunification: "can we edge back into togetherness gradually," asks Jock in her final letter, "Give ourselves some breathing space, a chance at transition. (Would you be terribly hurt if I took over the spare room for the first few nights?)" (222). Chas replies with a proposal for the continuation of their textual correspondence that would register alterity and continue to negotiate difference in its most minute detail, even while the couple cohabit in their newly renovated Vancouver home:

You know something? Writing these letters to you all year has had a curious effect on me, letting me know, in fact, what I'm thinking. I'll miss that. Would it be idiotic to suggest that in the future we slip each other a letter now and then? I can imagine myself leaving you notes under your pillow or in the sleeve of your raincoat or under your coffee cup. I can also imagine finding letters from you pinned to the shower curtain or folded in my pants pocket, notes full of your old corny jokes, but also those surprising disclosures that you make from time to time that I've been too preoccupied in the past to notice. (224)

Shields once commented, "We want, need, the stories of others. We need, too, to place our own stories beside theirs, to compare, weigh, judge, forgive, and to find, by becoming something other than ourselves, an angle of vision that renews our image of the world."[57] Chas's proposal for life-long letter-writing suggests one modest way of incorporating a "significant otherness," what Shields might call "the mystery of personality and the unknowability of others,"[58] within the very texture of everyday married life. In *A Celibate Season* "the letters woven into the fabric of friendship" surely signal a parallel commitment to recognize, to contend with, to relate to, the significant other of collaborative partnership.

NOTES

I would like to express my gratitude to the Social Sciences and Humanities Research Council of Canada, Blanche Howard, George Brandak of the UBC Archives, Neal Ferris, Marjorie Stone and Judith Thompson, Lorraine York, and the UWO Canadianist group (Melina Baum-Singer, Barbara Bruce, Frank Davey, Kaya Fraser, Michelle Hartley, Jessica Schagerl, Karis Shearer, and Kristen Warder) for their contributions to this chapter.

1   Howard, "Collaborating with Carol," 72.
2   Ibid.
3   Shields and Howard, *A Celibate Season*, v.
4   Stainsby, Rev. of *A Celibate Season*, 133.
5   Giltrow, "Strange Attractors," 61.
6   The husband's story of *Happenstance* was first published by McGraw-Hill Ryerson in 1980; the wife's story was published two years later as *A Fairly Conventional Woman* by Macmillan. The double volume, with two "front" covers and a text that could be flipped over and read alternatively, beginning with either "the husband's story" or "the wife's story," was published as *Happenstance: Two Novels in One about a Marriage in Transition* in Great Britain by Fourth Estate in 1991 and in Canada by Vintage in 1994.
7   York, *Rethinking*, 102.
8   Ibid.
9   Koestenbaum, *Double Talk,* 2.
10 York, *Rethinking*, 105.
11 Ibid., 97.
12 Morson and Emerson, *Mikhail Bakhtin*, 15.
13 Ibid., 15.
14 Cited ibid., 23.
15 Cited ibid., 37.
16 Ibid., 36–7.
17 Shields, "Arriving Late," 247.
18 Ibid., 248.
19 As Brian Johnson points out, Shields's later novel *Swann* (1989) also raises questions of literary authority "inaugurated by Roland Barthes's 1968 eulogy for the author in which he attacks 'the image of literature to be found in contemporary culture [that] is tyrannically centered on the author'" ("Necessary Illusions," 50).
20 Howard, "Collaborating with Carol," 73.
21 Ibid., 72. *A Celibate Season*'s two central literary models are Fanny Burney's *Evelina: or, A Young Lady's Entrance into the World: in a Series of Letters* (1779)

and, as I shall indicate later, Gillian Hanscombe's *Between Friends* (1982) (See Hobbs, "Voice and Re-vision" in this volume).

22 Howard, "Collaborating with Carol," 71–2.

23 Ibid., 73.

24 Ibid.

25 Letters between Shields and Howard are cited from UBC Archives, Howard and Shields correspondence.

26 Shields, "Arriving Late," 248.

27 York, *Rethinking*, 104.

28 UBC Archives, Howard and Shields correspondence, Howard to Shields, 16 October 1983.

29 Hobbs, "Voice and Re-vision," in this volume.

30 Morson and Emerson, *Mikhail Bakhtin*, 72.

31 Burke, "The Ethics of Signature," 287.

32 Kaplan and Rose, "Strange Bedfellows," 550.

33 Leonardi and Pope, "(Co)Labored Li(v)es," 632.

34 Koestenbaum, *Double Talk*, 3.

35 Masten, *Textual Intercourse*.

36 Grosz, "Sexual Signatures," 19.

37 Koestenbaum, *Double Talk*, 1.

38 York, *Rethinking*, 97.

39 York, "Lesbianizing Authorship," 159; emphasis added.

40 Hanscombe, interestingly, would go on to publish, in collaboration with her partner Suniti Namjoshi, the lesbian love poem sequence *Flesh and Paper* (1986).

41 Cf. Hobbs, "Voice and Re-vision," in this volume.

42 York, *Rethinking*, 97.

43 Unlike York, I read a satirical edge to *A Celibate Season*'s depiction of what she calls "a Martha Stewart-like middle-class WASP domestic sanctity" (York, *Rethinking,* 97). This edge is only functional because, for example, I read with irony Jock's persistent misidentification of her own temporary, middle-class encounters with financial need with those of the working-class women who are the subjects of her governmental commission, a misidentification that remains deaf to the details of their ordinary lives, despite the formal "hearings" she attends. In a postscript to her final letter to Chas, after the conclusion of the hearings, Jock writes, "After all these months of thinking about wealth and poverty, I'm still bewildered – more so than when I ventured forth to set the world straight, back in September. Tell me, Chas, what do those words *mean?*" (223). While in theory the royal commission's report on "The Feminization of Poverty" is motivated by a wish to uncover and understand the stories of disenfranchised women, readers are left wondering to what degree it will be truly informed by the prosaic desires of those it claims to

serve. Even Jessica, the Harvard-educated committee member who lives in a group home and passes herself off as impoverished and illiterate, commits the misjudgment of sympathetically projecting her own "middle-class morality" in her attempt to aid Jean, her sexually harassed housemate (97).

44 Laird, *Women Coauthors*, 11.

45 I am grateful to Karis Shearer for bringing this term to my attention in relation to this novel. The term "Boston marriage" originates with Henry James's novel *The Bostonians* (1886), which describes a passionate relationship between two women. The expression has gained renewed currency in recent years with David Mamet's play *Boston Marriage* and is now often used to describe a lesbian relationship that is not actively sexual.

46 Abbott, *A History of Celibacy*, 387–8.

47 McCullough, "The Boston Marriage as the Future of the Nation," 69.

48 Most notably, writing partners Katherine Bradley and Edith Cooper (known as "Michael Field") and Edith Somerville and Violet Martin (known as "Somerville and Ross").

49 Stone and Thompson, "'Between the two of us,'" n.p.

50 Hutcheon and Hutcheon, "'All Concord's Born of Contraries,'" 64.

51 Howard, "Collaborating with Carol," 75.

52 Shields, "Arriving Late," 250.

53 Karrell, *Writing Together / Writing Apart*, 25.

54 UBC Archives, Howard and Shields correspondence, Howard to Shields, 14 January 1984.

55 Ibid., Howard to Shields, 10 March 1984.

56 The dynamics of collaboration and otherness within marriage are, it is worth noting in passing, referenced at the level of national politics as well. In this way, *A Celibate Season* hints that a dialogic approach might also exemplify the Canadian nation as a bicultural "marriage," even as it reveals the limitations of the conventional marital model itself. Jock's Ottawa education is perhaps epitomized in her French-immersion experience. Her education in the French language – "*parlezing français*," as Jock calls it (87) – is a central part of her Ottawa experience which manifests itself in her insertion of French phrases in her letters. While Chas at first finds her references both alienating and irritating, he gradually draws bilingual references into his own writing, signalling the "untranslatability" of concepts from one linguistic locus to another and hinting that the citation and maintenance of otherness, as opposed to its absorption, might be an approach not just to the politics of marriage but to the concept of marriage in national politics.

57 Shields, "The Same Ticking Clock," 256–7.

58 Quoted in de Roo, "A Little like Flying," 43.

WORKS CITED

University of British Columbia Archives. Blanche Howard fonds. Howard and
Shields correspondence, 1981–86.

Abbott, Elizabeth. *A History of Celibacy*. Toronto: HarperCollins, 1999.

Burke, Seán. "The Ethics of Signature." In *Authorship: from Plato to the
Postmodern*, ed. Seán Burke, 285–91. Edinburgh: Edinburgh University Press,
1995.

de Roo, Harvey. "A Little like Flying: An Interview with Carol Shields." *West
Coast Review* 23, no. 3 (1988): 38–56.

Giltrow, Janet. "Strange Attractors." *West Coast Review* 23, no. 3 (1988): 57–66.

Grosz, Elizabeth. "Sexual Signatures: Feminism after the Death of the Author." In
Space, Time, and Perversion: Essays on the Politics of Bodies, 9–23. New York:
Routledge, 1995.

Howard, Blanche. "Collaborating with Carol." *Prairie Fire* 16, no. 1 (1995):
71–78.

Hutcheon, Linda, and Michael Hutcheon. "'All Concord's Born of Contraries':
Marital Methodologies." *Tulsa Studies in Women's Literature* 14 (1995): 59–64.

Johnson, Brian. "Necessary Illusions: Foucault's Author Function in Carol
Shields's *Swann*." *Prairie Fire* 16, no. 1 (1995): 56–70.

Kaplan, Carey, and Ellen Cronan Rose. "Strange Bedfellows: Feminist
Collaboration." *Signs: Journal of Women in Culture and Society* 18, no. 3
(1993): 547–61.

Karrell, Linda K. *Writing Together / Writing Apart: Collaboration in Western
American Literature*. Lincoln and London: University of Nebraska Press, 2002.

Koestenbaum, Wayne. *Double Talk: The Erotics of Male Literary Collaboration*.
New York: Routledge, 1989.

Laird, Holly. *Women Coauthors*. Urbana and Chicago: University of Illinois Press,
2000.

Leonardi, Susan J., and Rebecca A. Pope. "(Co)Labored Li(v)es; or, Love's Labors
Queered." *Publications of the Modern Language Association* 116, no. 3 (2001):
631–7.

Masten, Jeffrey. *Textual Intercourse: Collaboration, Authorship, and Sexualities in
Renaissance Drama*. Cambridge: Cambridge University Press, 1997.

McCullough, Kate. "The Boston Marriage as the Future of the Nation: Queerly
Regional Sexuality in *Diana Victrix*." *American Literature* 69, no. 1 (1997):
67–103.

Morson, Gary Saul, and Caryl Emerson. *Mikhail Bakhtin: Creation of a Prosaics*.
Stanford: Stanford University Press, 1990.

Rajan, Balachandra. *The Form of the Unfinished: English Poetics from Spenser to Pound*. Princeton: Princeton University Press, 1985.

Shields, Carol. "Arriving Late: Starting Over." In *How Stories Mean*, ed. John Metcalf and Tim Struthers, 244–51. Erin, ON: Porcupine's Quill, 1993.

– "The Same Ticking Clock." In *Language in Her Eye: Views on Writing and Gender by Canadian Women Writing in English*, ed. Libby Scheier, Sarah Sheard, and Eleanor Wachtel, 256–9. Toronto: Coach House, 1990.

– and Blanche Howard. *A Celibate Season*. Toronto: Vintage, 1998.

Stainsby, Meg. Rev. of *A Celibate Season* by Carol Shields and Blanche Howard. *Room of One's Own*, 15, no. 2 (1992): 133–37.

Stone, Marjorie, and Judith Thompson. "'Between the two of us': A Theoretical and Historical Introduction to Literary Couplings." In "Literary Couplings and the Construction of Authorship: Writing Couples and Collaborators in Historical Context" (unpublished ms.). Courtesy of authors.

York, Lorraine. "Lesbianizing Authorship: *Flesh and Paper*." *Essays on Canadian Writing* 54 (1994): 153–67.

– *Rethinking Women's Collaborative Writing: Power, Difference, Property*. Toronto: University of Toronto Press, 2002.

10

"Artefact Out of Absence": Reflection and Convergence in the Fiction of Carol Shields

ELLEN LEVY

In *The Stone Diaries* the dying Cuyler Goodwill, as re-created in the imagination of his absent daughter, Daisy, muses on the parts of oneself that one never sees, concluding, as his life draws to a close, that one would need a "double mirror" to contemplate those remote quarters of the anatomy forever hidden from the subject's view. His thought, though focused on body parts, voices Daisy's understanding of the quest for indirect access, for the mirror that allows moments of glancing recognition through the darkness that hides us from ourselves.

Daisy's recourse to her father's imagined life (and death) constitutes a stance habitually adopted by those who populate the fiction of Carol Shields. From its earliest days her work has displayed a penchant for double structures: one thinks of the twinned novels *Small Ceremonies* and *The Box Garden* or of the combinatory processes employed in *Happenstance* and *The Republic of Love*, the first juxtaposing, the second alternating, heterodiegetic narrations focused on the complementary halves of a couple. The 1991 experiment *A Celibate Season*, written with Blanche Howard, literalized this process by locating the double voice at the authorial level, whence it was filtered into the conjugal exchange of letters that makes up the text.

In *Small Ceremonies* and *The Box Garden* Shields mirrors the first-person narrations of two sisters (whose sisterhood is underscored by their being the daughters of one of two sisters who herself was one of two sisters) and who are, furthermore, practitioners of the sister arts of biography and poetry. Though the lives as well as the literary practice of the sisters may be contrasted (Judith is happily married, stable, and productive; Charleen is divorced, troubled, and temporarily blocked), the two novels explore similarities in the context of these differences.

Judith the biographer, for example, has been tempted by the desire to commit a fiction, seeing as she does how life-writing is in any case an extrapolation from available data, an eking out of the ineffable from the unspoken and the unrecorded. But her attempts to novelize are complicated by the uncontrollable behaviour of an ambulatory plot, which makes its way from the notebooks of an unpublished author, into whose flat (and, temporarily, into whose imagination) she moves, to the pages of a best-selling author, who has himself purloined it and fixed this malleable and protean storyline in *Graven Images* – the title of his published book. When the plot of this plot is rounded out by the borrowings of its original possessor and when the author of *Graven Images* is revealed to have invented the past on which his autobiographical fiction is based, the breach between fact and fabulation is reduced to the finest of fissures.

The poet sister, Charleen, sees her literary pursuits in terms of capturing the unmediated minutiae of existence, unassisted by the mechanistically metaphorical or the spuriously symbolic, a practice not so alien, indeed, from her sister's sounding of the glazed-over planes of her biographical subject's life for telling cracks of truth. Their proclivities converge on the dismantling through art of habitual distinctions between the true and the fictitious:[1] just as Charleen sees the matter of poetry in the rendering of surfaces, in reporting "on the flower in the crannied wall, on coffee spoons and peaches, [on] a rusted key discovered in the grass,"[2] so Judith recognizes the utility of "uncovering currents of the extraordinary in even the most ordinary personalities" (109).

The crannied flower, the peach, the (nonetheless resonant) key – these are presumably elements that must be endowed with fullness of sense in the mind of a poem's reader. Similarly, the reader of biography must be incorporated into the equation of lives viewed by other lives, into the dynamic of the reflected other so necessary to the construction of the self.[3] How else can the gulf between text and world be bridged? When Judith spurns the novel whose plot has been borrowed to the third degree, her teenaged daughter shyly reminds her of how even the paltriest fictions solicit an empathy which lies at the heart of literary communication. To hear the music of another life is to combine an acceptance of its ultimate muteness with a capacity for responding to its faintest melodies.

Readerly perspective is of the essence in *Happenstance*, too, since response to this novel varies according to whether the reader begins with the husband's story or the wife's. Practical Brenda, speculative Jack: he is an historian and she a quiltmaker. They go their separate ways for a week, the itinerary of each, unbeknownst to either, echoing that of the other – following parallel roads, sometimes obscured by snowfall, to an intersection of delicately incremented wisdom. Their ostensibly divergent mindsets – Jack has a diachronic awareness of causality, Brenda a synchronic instinct for design – nonetheless meet in subtle ways. Jack, for example, is aware that the history he loves is no more objective than the partiality its chronicles may allow: most of life passes unrecorded; what we call history is the reconstruction from random evidence of a fiction about the past. "More often, it seemed to him, history was ... what *wasn't* written down. A written text only hints, suggests, outlines, speculates ... Everything had to be read backwards in a kind of mirror language."[4] Brenda, on the other hand, has an intuitive appreciation of the present; for her, the past consists of unconnected patches of dailiness made shapely by retrospection. Yet she recalls how, on a trip to Europe during a period of bereavement, these opposing viewpoints were momentarily melded by the sudden illumination, in a dark chapel in Brittany, of a medieval altar painting. The panel was decorated with scenes from daily life centred on the very church, when it was new, in which she and Jack were then standing. More than the mirrors of Versailles, which had thrown out at them a sort of reverberating hollowness, this unexpected vision made Jack's sense of continuity real, connecting it to Brenda's celebratory love of the everyday. The illumination over, Brenda found herself in a darkness pulsating with colour, a moment that seems to have initiated – although she herself would never phrase it this way – her quest for artistic self-expression.

In a private moment during his wife's absence, Jack enters her quilting room and contemplates her most recent piece. Intrigued, he thinks about how he might discuss it with her, but at the same time, he knows that he never will, that she would not understand his questions any more than he would understand her answers. This acceptance of the unspoken is a feature of Shields's couples. They know that not only are other lives essentially mysterious, but that the core of one's own may be equally out of reach. If we are strangers, as Shields's texts repeatedly demonstrate,[5] to earlier versions of ourselves or to the public persona of our present incarnation, how can communication with even those who are most intimate be unchecked and unbounded?

It often transpires that within Shields's mature couples a productive virtue is made of such necessity. (It should be parenthetically noted that although husbands and wives will be primarily discussed, what is said here may also be applied to other intimate pairings: parent and child, sibling and sibling, artist and mentor.) Judith, for instance, in *Small Ceremonies* takes secret comfort in the alterity of husband Martin. When she happens upon a number of unexplained skeins of coloured wool in one of his desk drawers, although baffled and intrigued, she clings to the enigma, both respectful of separateness and satisfied with the notion that an explanation, although not apparent, remains satisfyingly latent. Similarly, both Jack and Brenda know that there are areas of their partner's life into which they will never intrude, areas of their own that will forever be locked from view. The bipartite structure of the novel in which this couple figures invites the reader into some of these unlit nooks, while it dramatizes the exclusion from them of one or the other protagonist. An emblematic instance of this is the builder's name that Brenda once found carved on the lintel of her and Jack's bedroom door and whose existence she has kept secret, as if the inscription "Jake Parker, builder, 1923" were the Sibylline warning to stand back ("procul, ô procul este, profani"), marking the threshold between sacred regions of singularity — and which like all thresholds both separates and beckons to be crossed. It is Brenda's private wisdom to understand, along with Judith, Charleen, Daisy, Reta, and other Shieldian wives, the advantages of a "delicately gauged"[6] remove.

The measurement of such margins of otherness is repeatedly taken in Shields's fictions at moments when people are face to face at table. Often involving a couple, such scenes exist in a variety of models and sizes, including the parodic mutation. Judith and Martin, for example, celebrate a windfall at the end of *Small Ceremonies* with a meal in a revolving restaurant. Looking at Martin's wrist on the table, Judith acknowledges that his carpal joint "hums with a separate and private energy."[7] At the same time she realizes that her imperative need to examine other people's lives feeds not only her vocation as a "biografiend,"[8] but also the psyche of her more discreet spouse: he needs something "infinitely more complex" than she does, for "what he needs is [Judith's] possession of that need" (179). Her moment of recognition is heightened by the fact that at another table a party of deaf-mutes are communicating with a flurry of elegant butterfly gestures, in "a cloud of perfect, shapely silence" (178), their movements seeming to point to the passionate wonder of all the unknown destinies by which she is surrounded and yet into which her life seems fortuitously to fit, lives that commune silently in the dark world through which the restaurant is turning.

A similar scene in *Happenstance* is conjured out of the separate recollections that Brenda and Jack have of their first meal together, shared after having met, rather appropriately, in the map room of a research institution. In the course of this rather homely luncheon, each is visited by the conviction that the other will give direction to the future: Jack has a sudden intuition that something important is happening, something accompanied by "carloads of predetermination";[9] Brenda sees the illumination traverse Jack's countenance – "a consciousness as carefully mapped as a coastline"[10] – and knows that she will marry him. This thought comes to her "like a streak of lightning cutting swift stripes on sleepy darkness" (112), a description that suggests that the quilt designs she will later create, themselves abstract effulgences, are mute renderings of key moments of her life.

In *The Stone Diaries* the table scene is stolen by Clarentine Flett, who overhears at a kitchen doorway Cuyler Goodwill's profession of love to his young wife, Mercy, and huddles it away to feed her secret life, while in *The Republic of Love* the elided scene is merely suggested by a list of the groceries that constitute Tom and Fay's humble honeymoon fare after the upheavals of their courtship. In *Larry's Party* it is multi-form: now a family dinner whose arrangement suggests the labyrinthine complexity of family relations; later the party of the title amidst the boisterous confusion of which noiseless reconnections are ocularly forged. In *Unless* Shields works a comic variation on the scene, bringing together in kitchenly intimacy two strangers, Reta's mother-in-law and her visiting New York editor, the former having forgotten how to speak and the latter not yet having learned how to listen. They nonetheless – as the generic rules of the table scene require – manage to staunch their separate lonelinesses in a flow of confessional outreaching.

The table, an opaque horizontal plane inverting the qualities of the mirror, permits the insight that comes from looking outward and across. In "Hinterland" (*Various Miracles*), Meg and Roy, an American couple on holiday in Paris, contemplate on separate visits to the Musée de Cluny a gilded statue of the young Virgin Mary in whose wooden womb is fitted a hinged niche. Within it can be seen a tiny sculpted scene of the crucifixion – as though the whole procession of Christian events, in its ineluctable finality, were embedded there, in the locus of origins. When the couple find themselves together again at dinner, Roy having fled the museum after a bomb scare, their own future – envisioned collectively in an accretion of images whose apparent randomness is nonetheless finely orchestrated – seems to be contained within the relational space figured by the table:

in a space the size of this small table, waits a series of intricate compromises, impotence, rusted garden furniture, disordered dreams ... A certain amount of shadowy pathos will accrue between what they remember and what they imagine, and eventually one of them, perhaps lying limply on a tautly made-up bed, will gruesomely sentimentalise this Paris night. The memory will divide and shrink like a bodily protein, and terror, with all its freshness and redemptive power, will give way, easily, easily, to the small rosy singularity of this shaded lamp, and the arc of light that cuts their faces precisely in half.[11]

The table motif is brought into conjunction with another, the reflecting surface, in "Mirrors" (*Dressing Up for the Carnival*), a story that epitomizes the interplay of identity and distance in the intimate relationship. Here a couple (they remain for the reader a balanced and anonymous "he" and "she") have institutionalized what began as an accidental ban on mirrors at their summer cottage. The end of their first glassless season finds them face to face in a restaurant where the presence of a wall mirror suddenly casts light on their period of unselfconsciousness – the face, which the wife perceives in a moment of delayed recognition as her own, is that of inner contentment, stripped of vanity, disappointment, diffidence. Absence licenses reflection, the wife's speculations, for instance, on the nature of mirrors, combining as they do disparate substances, fusing the transparent and the opaque and suggesting in the startling simplicity of their alchemy the possibility of renewal. The husband, too, is led into mirror-inspired observations: on appearances and how they deceive, on deceptions and how they illuminate, on the way in which his wife's familiar features are both those of a stranger and the screen behind which his own identity shelters. Their cottage sits beside Circle Lake, an unsilvered mirror whose reflection of the starry firmament is the metaphorical alternative to the pocket-sized mirror of limitation; in it they can see "the sky lifting and falling and spreading out like a mesh of silver on the lake."[12] It beckons towards a knowledge that is neither seen nor spoken, but intuited in the unhasty companionship of parallel lives. Although at the beginning of their relationship each had tried to verbalize his or her secret life, "the truth had been darkened out" (74). In the rhythm of days and nights spent with only each other as reflecting surface, such fragile verities as lie within the scope of acknowledgment are given the opportunity to be observed.

The mirror has always been an ambiguous object, bringing together in intriguing combination semblance and substance, full when empty and containing nothing while seeming to contain everything.[13] Its association with illusion has often in the past made it seem an instrument of the devil, yet in its flat and undistorted version, in its use as what Umberto Eco deliciously calls a "catoptric prothesis,"[14] it also verifies what is real. Its inbuilt contradictoriness is summed up by its French historian, Sabine Melchior-Bonnet, with the double epithet of *menteur et mentor*.[15] Potentially a pathway to the ideal, it can also be an instrument of the basely solipsistic, the passive mirror of Narcissus crowding out the active one of transformation, as in the case of the self-regarding character Watson in *The Box Garden*, whose withdrawal from adult responsibility is symbolized by his final enclosure in a mirror-lined room from which the enrichment of human contact has been banished.

Shields captures the richness of the mirror motif in "Scenes" (*Various Miracles*), in which the interplay between the exploration of the self and the exploration of the world is traced in relation to a bevelled mirror that the protagonist, Frances, inherits from her grandmother: Frances, a child so young that she must climb down from her grandmother's bed to touch the ridges and hollows of the naive carving that surrounds the glass; Frances, a fourteen-year-old whose awakening sense of the complexities of identity finds expression in centring her face at the junction of glass and bevel, thus splitting the face in two; Frances, at forty-four, for whom the looking glass has been transmuted into language, from which she shapes stories of sternness and nurture, good sense and transgression, that in their complementarity mirror the perfect ovoid of life's potentialities.

The notion of language as mirror is further explored in "Absence" (*Dressing Up for the Carnival*), in which the "she" of the story loses the *i* of her keyboard, provoking a meta-linguistic crisis of representation that draws her, with Perecian verve, to outposts of metaphor and perimeters of mind. In the thriving figurative systems of this story, language becomes an architecture within which to parse the grammar of self. The text that "she" produces, "an artefact [born] of absence,"[16] generated by the convergent forces of necessity and invention, asserts the uniqueness of words, while practising their modification, and the auto-teleological nature of creativity, while suggesting its roots in the urge to surpass the

confines of personality. The subtraction of the lost letter of the individual frees "she" to reflect on how language can be "made" to "do." Like
Escher's drawing hand drawing a hand drawing, the story reflects its
own genesis in a language that embodies the paradox of the unexpected
rightness of what accident has arranged.

A similar richness of imagination is required of the artists in "Windows" (*Dressing Up for the Carnival*) when a window tax leads to the
gradual closing of domestic apertures. Left in threatening obscurity,
with no outlet to the world and no inlet of light, both vocation and relationship are called into question. Yet darkness generates sparks of inspiration, for the pair slowly re-examine matter and method and, by "that
accident we call art,"[17] paint a window into the boarded-up void. Not
only do they create the illusion of light, but their work veers into a collaboration unsought for by artists hitherto kept apart by both technique
and conceit. Through illusion and accident, but also meticulous attentiveness, the pair transform a dead surface into one rippling with life.
The finished window affords a transcendent moment when the painting
seems freed from the bounds of two-dimensionality, imitation and limitation surging into illumination. These artists make visible an idea of
light while the story doubles their feat by painting glass in words: "Glass
possesses different colours at different hours of the day. Sometimes it
pretends it's a mirror. Other times it gathers checks and streaks and bubbles of brilliance and elegant flexes of wood. Its transparency winks back
at you, yet it withholds, in certain weathers, what is on the other side,
revealing only a flash of wet garden grass, a shadow of a close-standing
hedge, or perhaps a human figure moving across its width" (123).

These metaliterary phrases echo the economy of withholding and
revealing practised by a narrator who, for example, never discloses
whether he (or she) is male or female and epitomize the linguistic qualities of her (or his) discourse, with its occasionally transparent indicative-
ness and its more often inflected figurative indetermination. Their flexes
of mood, their insistence on the instrumentality of human perspective,
their play on the interpenetration of reflexivity and opaqueness, act as a
verbal looking glass to the experience of looking. And just as darkness in
this story clears a path to the knowledge of light, so the story's lack of
clear referentiality opens its frame, splintering sense with the luminosity
of metaphor.

The Shieldsian sentence is alive with these rippling effects, breeding
circuits of suggestiveness and implication. But as in the case of other
doubling structures, in the articulation of the literal and the figurative,

connection is inherent in separation. George Eliot once wrote that "we can ... seldom declare what a thing is, except by saying it is something else."[18] It is hardly surprising that this process of approaching essence through indirection, which is so much a part of the fictionalizing impulse, should be so integral to an author whose work, whatever else it discusses, always also addresses the question of art. All of Shields's writer-characters and their avatars (weavers, quilters, painters, gardeners) are aware of what the translator-novelist Reta Winters makes explicit in *Unless*: "I am focusing on the stirrings of the writerly impulse, or the 'long littleness,' to use Frances Cornford's phrase, of a life spent affixing small words to large, empty pages. We may pretend otherwise, but to many writers this is the richest territory we can imagine."[19]

Shields favours metaphors from the "small ceremonies" of everyday life, from domains such as those of sewing, ironing, cooking, planting, and the observation of weather. These of course are isotopies close to the lives of the unsung women whom she so often commemorates. *Small Ceremonies* contains a variation on the genre whose generosity of inclusion is particularly pleasing, for it is a husband, Martin, through whom a weaving metaphor is woven into the text. Martin, a Milton specialist whose latest article has been rejected for lack of originality, decides to make a tapestry with coloured yarns representing the themes of *Paradise Lost*. The complex thematic patternings of the epic are rendered visible; indeed, to the surprise of his wife, Judith, they are transformed into an object whose aesthetic qualities are independently prized. Through Martin's handiwork, Shields incarnates a familiar figure for literary patterning, turning the relationship between the literal and the figurative on its head, suggesting the permeability of rhetorical strata.

In *Unless*, written a quarter of a century after Martin's tapestry was woven into the texture of *Small Ceremonies*, Reta considers this junction of levels, associating it with the gift of unspoiled vision and modified perspectives: "Metaphors hold their own power over us, even without their fugitive gestures. They're as real as the peony bushes we observe when we're children, lying flat on the grass and looking straight up to the undersides of leaves and petals and marveling: Oh, this is secret territory, we think, an inverted world grown-ups can't see" (40). Metaphors allow us to exist on more than one plane at once, and those who continue to nurture an interest in what the surface conceals (as the poet Charleen says of her biographer sister) see the connections that others miss, provide the links, fill in the ellipses and the silences. Many of Shields's characters direct our regard to the hinges and joints of sundered entities, to the junctions that permit what Daisy calls the "holy convergence"[20] of the heterogeneous. Kay, in "Times of Sickness and Health" (*Various Miracles*), a butterfly grazing her knee, gazes at the "tiny transparent panes" between the "windows of colour on the wings,"[21] fantasizing about what the fluttering creature makes of her and feeling that, with this ephemeral contact, almost anything imaginable becomes possible. Judith thinks of her biographical subject's life as a well-sewn leather glove into whose seams she must delve if she is to find an approximation of truth. In "Windows" the artist-narrator is pleased with the panes of glass that have been painted but especially loves their crossbars and mullions, their "shy intersections," which themselves have been created by the intersection of aesthetic visions, while Jack and Brenda's son has discarded the pennants of his childhood in order to hang on his wall an Escher print of white seagulls rising in which the dark intervals form a second, corresponding flock of birds. And Daisy Goodwill's daughter, Alice, sitting at her aged and ailing mother's bed-side, realizes that death occurs while we are still alive: "Life marches right up to the wall of that final darkness, one extreme state butting against the other. Not even a breath separates them."[22]

Both infinitesimal and infinite, such spaces are the locus of mystery, the chaotic but productive chasms from which we extract meaning and order. Their less-than-a-breath interstices are the threshold that carries us between knowledge and innocence, ephemera and substance, the hidden and the revealed, the human and the divine, the general and the particular, the transient and the immutable, pain and pleasure, humour and desperation, the inner and the outer, the poetic and the pragmatic, ideas and objects, fact and illusion, the knowable and the unknowable, the significant and the trivial, relief and shadow, the actual and the possible, the complete and the incomplete, the ordinary and the extraordinary, and even, in *The Stone Diaries*, between the organic and the inorganic.

This latter work probes the vital space between the "lifelong dia-logue"[23] within the individual mind and the "imaginative life projected onto others" (72). Even a most hermetic inner world, such as Daisy's, can only be represented by a kaleidoscope of voice and vision, by a system of outward projections sending images back to the isolated self. Subjectivity is experienced as process, accumulation, multiplication, erosion, with the self as a kind of searchlight sweeping the objective world for recognizable pattern. Like the tapestry stone – a fusion of fossil life – that Daisy's father carves, it is subject to continuing transformations. In the dialectic of metaphorical systems based on organic and inorganic forms that structures this narrative, the transient and the perpetual are made to cohabit, culminating in the sarcophagal figure Daisy imagines herself into while she is still alive.

This ultimate transformation remains unrealized, for Shields is also an accomplished artist of the incomplete. Of the many mentor figures who form, with younger woman protagonists, a variation on the couple motif (one thinks of Fay and Onion or Reta and Danielle), Dorothea Thomas, an elderly quilter whom Brenda meets at the quilters' convention in *Happenstance*, perhaps best embodies this idea. Late in life, Dorothea has begun to make story-quilts, which scandalously refuse closure. They have proved less popular than the more naive quilts she made previously, but having once understood that stories are made of both have and might have, do and might do, there is for Dorothea no turning back. As another quilter of histories says elsewhere, "we carry a double history in our heads, what is and what could be."[24]

Brenda herself is working on an unfinished quilt in which she has dared to dispense with a blocked pattern. Working under the sign of fertility in a room presided over by the vegetation of a burgeoning spider plant, she is creating a brilliant explosion of light, boiling yellows seething in a cauldron of uncontained energy, which seems to deconstruct her last completed quilt, "The Second Coming," described as a depiction of energy contained, the two quilts together evoking the formlessness and forming that in their encounter produce the work of art.

Brenda cherishes the unrestrained power of her unfinished quilt, which will remain incomplete even when ended, for its subject is the unbounded potency of what is not there. It is like the perfect sentence sought by the writer in "Absence," who acknowledges that "the thump of heartbeat was what she wanted [her sentence to have], but also the small urgent jumps between the beats."[25] Looking at his wife's new quilt in her absence, Jack sees the stitching as "purposeful and relentless, suggesting something contradictory and ironic that interested him."[26] A fine fabric stitched with irony, a dazzling tissue of interwoven degrees – Jack's insight seems to designate the texture of the text that contains him, for Shields's work infuses the sincere with the parodic, taking from this further opposition gainfully surpassed the sense that we have in reading her of a writing on the cusp, unstable but transcendent, always on the threshold of a second becoming.

I should like to conclude with the word "celery," lost and then found again – indeed, pried out of a crack in the pavement – by the little boy in "Soup du Jour" (*Dressing Up for the Carnival*). He has been sent to the corner grocery in search of this humble but essential component of the dish that gives the story its title. The soup to which the title refers may also be "the soup of common delight and simple sensation"[27] into which readers of a contemporary newspaper column have been invited to dip their daily bread in a phrase relayed by the narrator, who both mocks its hyperbolic sanctimony and echoes its underlying import. Indeed, "soup du jour," through its bilingual form, already points to the notion of conjoining. It is the heady broth that the narrator creates by peppering the earnest with the self-mocking, by adding the surreptitiously telling to the ostensibly random ingredients of the tale, teasing poignant connections out of unemphatic lives, much as the child teases an identity from the fissures in what has been paved over concerning his origins. A daily *soup*, we come to understand, if properly mixed, becomes an opus.

Begun in an upbeat journalese ("'The quotidian is where it's at'" [163]), "Soup du Jour" stirs a lyric paean to the reformulation of experience into a comic evocation of the *Zeitgeist*. This double tonality reiterates on the level of linguistic register what the characters – the little boy, his single mother, his unknown father, the father's wife – practise on an experiential plane: the transformation of experience, through acceptance or resignation, growth or entropy, anamnesis or anticipation, into the exceptionally vivid, the fervently meaningful; the evanescent captured and memorialized; the unitary permuted into the universal; the temporal spanned empathetically; pain and guilt surpassed through contentment of being.

There are owls in this story hooting wisely outside an open window where an elderly woman sits thinking of the simple French verbs she is conjugating as a house whose doors and windows allow the exploration of time. She does not know the little boy travelling to the corner shop, nor will he ever know her, but there is resonance in their blind coexistence: when she was a little girl, a flying lamb chop taught her that affliction could be rewritten into whimsy; he is about to discover that the absence of a word such as "celery" or "father" can be an invitation to self-definition rather than an irretrievable loss. Hence, when he does retrieve the name of the humdrum but all-important ingredient he is in quest of, it conjures up more than leafy stalks and pungent aroma; indeed, it gives birth to an idea that "swims and rises and overcomes the tiny confines of the ordinary everyday world to which, until this moment, he has been condemned" (171), and, like the simple words in which the lady takes delight, the word "celery" celebrates life.

NOTES

1 I am adapting a phrase of Terry Eagleton's here from a review of Nick Groom's *The Forger's Shadow*, "Maybe He Made It Up," *London Review of Books* 24, no. 11 (6 June 2002): 6.

2 Shields, *Box Garden*, 110.

3 "Narcisse dont l'histoire est si souvent interprêtée depuis Ovide a choisi le plus bas degré de la connaissance – celui de son reflet – et il est puni par Némésis pour avoir méprisé l'amour d'Echo – c'est-à-dire refusé cette médiation de l'autre dans la construction de soi" (Melchior-Bonnet, *Histoire du miroir*, 117). "Narcissus, whose story has so often been interpreted since Ovid, chose the lowest degree of knowledge – that of his own reflection – and was punished by Nemesis for having despised Echo's love – that is, for having refused the mediation of the Other in the construction of the self" (my translation).

4 Shields, *Happenstance* (HSH), 107.

5 One thinks of Cuyler Goodwill's strange transmutation in *The Stone Diaries* from inarticulate mason to garrulous entrepreneur or of Larry Weller's almost equally mysterious evolution in *Larry's Party* from small-town florist to renowned land-scape architect; one remembers Daisy Goodwill's wonder at the polite murmurings of Grandma Flett as unwelcome visitors assail her on her hospital bed.

6 Shields, *Happenstance* (HSW), 159.

7 Shields, *Small Ceremonies*, 179.

8 James Joyce, cited by Holroyd, *Works on Paper*, 15.

9 Shields, *Happenstance* (HSH), 129.

10 Shields, *Happenstance* (HSH), 111.

11 Shields, *Various Miracles*, 127.

12 Shields, *Dressing Up for the Carnival*, 73.

13 Plotinus, cited in Cousineau, *Letters and Labyrinths*, 81.

14 "We trust mirrors just as we trust spectacles and binoculars, since, like spectacles and binoculars, mirrors are protheses. In a strict sense, a prothesis is an apparatus replacing a missing organ (an artificial limb, a denture); but, in a broader sense, it is any apparatus extending the range of action of an organ" (*Eco, Semiotics and the Philosophy of Language*, 208).

15 Melchior-Bonnet, *Histoire du miroir*, 119. (*Menteur et mentor* translates literally as "liar and mentor," although "misleader and leader" perhaps captures better the play on the signifier in Melchior-Bonnet's phrase.)

16 Shields, *Dressing Up for the Carnival*, 109.

17 Ibid., 115.

18 Eliot, *Mill on the Floss*, 140.

19 Shields, *Unless*, 137.
20 Shields, *Stone Diaries*, 59.
21 Shields, *Various Miracles*, 63.
22 Shields, *Stone Diaries*, 342.
23 Shields, *Unless*, 96.
24 Ibid., 149.
25 Shields, *Dressing Up for the Carnival*, 111.
26 Shields, *Happenstance* (HSH), 182.
27 Shields, *Dressing Up for the Carnival*, 162.

WORKS CITED

Cousineau, Diane. *Letters and Labyrinths: Women Writing /Cultural Codes*.
    Newark: University of Delaware Press, 1997.
Eco, Umberto. *Semiotics and the Philosophy of Language*. London: Macmillan,
    1984.
Eliot, George. *The Mill on the Floss*. [1860]. Ed. Gordon S. Haight. Oxford
    World's Classics. Oxford: Oxford University Press, 1996.
Holroyd, Michael. *Works on Paper: The Craft of Biography and Autobiography*.
    London: Little, Brown, 2002.
Melchior-Bonnet, Sabine. *Histoire du miroir*. Paris: Hachette, 1994.
Shields, Carol. *The Box Garden*. London: Fourth Estate, 1977.
– *Dressing Up for the Carnival*. London: Quality, 2000.
– *Happenstance: The Husband's Story* (HSH). London: Flamingo, 1994.
– *Happenstance: The Wife's Story* (HSW). London: Flamingo, 1994.
– *Larry's Party*. London: Fourth Estate, 1998.
– *The Republic of Love*. London: Flamingo, 1993.
– *Small Ceremonies*. London: Fourth Estate, 1995.
– *The Stone Diaries*. London: Fourth Estate, 1994.
– *Various Miracles*. London: Fourth Estate, 1995.
– *Unless*. London: Fourth Estate, 2002.

Eros in the Eye of the Mirror: The Rewriting of Myths in Carol Shields's "Mirrors"

HÉLIANE VENTURA

The rewriting of classical mythology seems to enjoy a special place in Canadian literature, be it in the field of poetry, the novel, drama, or the short story. Anne Carson's *Autobiography of Red* (1998) is one of the most recent and outstanding examples of such palimpsestic practice in verse. Robert Kroetsch's Demeter, the male eponymous hero of *The Studhorse Man* (1970), might be regarded as best emblematizing the recontextualization of myths in Canadian fiction. "Let's murder Clytemnestra according to the principles of Marshall McLuhan" (1969) by the playwright Wilfred Watson also embodies the hybridized form of the classic rewrite in the field of drama. As early as the sixties, Sheila Watson transposed the myths of Oedipus, Daedalus, and Antigone, which were published in a single collection, *Five Stories*, some twenty years later. Equally in the domain of the short story, Margaret Atwood reiterated the myth of Isis and Osiris in the story entitled "Isis in Darkness," in the collection *Wilderness Tips* (1991). In 1998 Alice Munro revisited the myth of Orpheus and Eurydice in the story "The Children Stay," in *The Love of a Good Woman*.

In 2000, in the collection *Dressing Up for the Carnival*, Carol Shields presents a revision of several myths linked with the presence of a mirror in the story precisely entitled "Mirrors." Jean-Pierre Vernant, in *L'individu, la mort, l'amour*, reminds us of the particular place that mirrors occupy in antiquity: "In the field delineated by the ambiguous relationship between the visible and the invisible, life and death, the image and the real, beauty and horror, seduction and repulsion, this object of everyday use occupies a key position, of strategic importance: in so far as it seems susceptible to conjoining these normally opposed terms, it lends itself more than any other object to the problematization of the question of seeing and being seen."[1]

Shields's treatment of the motif of the mirror is ambiguous: she explicitly includes a reference to the myth of Narcissus in the narrative, yet a number of major divergences in the development of the plot invite us to reconsider the story and contemplate it as a possible anti-Narcissus myth. Relying on the power of reversibility that mirrors are endowed with, Shields metamorphoses the original myth into its contrary at the same time as she incorporates and modifies other implicit references to the Platonic Eros, to propose in the end her own philosophy of love, based on a celebration of the mischievous god. Thus her story achieves a euphoric dimension since her protagonists have enjoyed thirty-five years of marital bliss. The key to their abiding conjugal felicity seems to lie in an act of deprivation. During the holidays, in their log cabin by the lake, they have purposefully renounced all mirrors and elected "an annual season of non-reflectiveness."[2] This act of renunciation leads us to investigate the power that the absence of a mirror acquires in Carol Shields's story and consequently to locate the extraordinary, neither in a logic of baroque supplement nor in a technique of lean depletion, but rather in a paradoxical and playful strategy of specular inversion.

In Carol Shields's text, mirrors have apparently been eradicated from narrated space: they seem to exist only in the act of narration through the reference to their elimination, which is diversely presented as "a sacrifice," "an abjuration," a form of "ascetism," or a "deprivation." From the start, a religious semanticism pervades the text, which inscribes the protagonists' act of renunciation in the metaphoric category of spiritual exercise and redemption, while the possession of a mirror is implicitly considered synonymous with damnation, through a relationship of reciprocal presupposition. The protagonists are consequently perceived as the happy few, the elect: through their voluntary forswearing of mirrors, they have found the original innocence of the Garden of Eden. The suppression of the mirror has brought about the impression of authenticity.

A similar paradoxical inscription of transcendence can be found in the overall construction of the tale. As Agnès Minazzoli remarks, from the Middle Ages to the Renaissance, there developed throughout the Christian world a specific type of literature which, under the name *speculum perfectionis* or mirror of the soul, mirror of the world, of wisdom, of virtue, or of perfection, set for itself the task of "reflecting the light and glory of the creator in order to make them shine through."[3] In a first stage of this argument, Carol Shields's short story can be regarded as a recontextualization in contemporary western Canada of the *speculum perfectionis* from the Middle Ages. The pristine environment represented by the log cabin by the side of Big Circle Lake and the virtuous life led by the married protagonists, whose names are suppressed from the narrative, reinforce their emblematic status in a pastoral myth that appears diametrically opposed to Narcissus's.

The protagonists' tastes are also in keeping with their status as biblical characters. To celebrate their thirty-five years of marital bliss, they are to go to New York to attend a play described as "serious drama": "They stay away from the big musicals as a rule, preferring, for want of a better word, serious drama. Nothing experimental, no drugged *angst* or scalding discourse, but plays that coolly examine the psychological positioning of men and women in our century. This torn perplexing century. Men and women who resemble themselves" (68). The resemblance evoked here in the context of "serious drama" refers us equally to Christian theology and to the creation of man "in the semblance of God." The off-Broadway play also falls into the category of the contemporary, recontextualized *speculum perfectionis* because it represents "the quest for original unity, the search for God through his signs, the deciphering of enigmatic and mirrored images to find back resemblance."[4]

During the first summer spent at the lake, the husband sets about rehabilitating the log cabin, and for three weeks he works, together with his wife, from morning to dusk, with hardly any interruption. When he inwardly gives thanks to his wife for the happiness he experiences, he also invokes resemblance: "He felt a longing to turn to her and say: 'This is what I've dreamt of all my life, being this tired, this used up, and having someone like you, exactly like you, waking up at my side'" (74). This marital relationship based on loyalty and stability mirrors the love of Christ. It provides a vision of Christian fellowship and of heroic endeavour, which belongs in the refoundation of the world deprived of evil. It falls into the category of Christian love as *agape*, the love defined by Paul in these terms: "Love is patient; love is kind and envies no one. Love is never boastful, nor conceited, nor rude; never selfish, not quick to take offence. Love keeps no score of wrongs; does not gloat over other men's sins, but delights in the truth. There is nothing love cannot face; there is no limit to its faith, its hope, and its endurance."[5] This Pauline version of a "pure love", based on selflessness, altruism, and oblation, suffuses the relationship between husband and wife and clearly inscribes their story in the biblical vein as an anti-Narcissus and anti-erotic love story, should we first envisage the term "erotic" in its common usage of denoting carnal passion.

However, this first approach, valid as it may appear, needs correcting. For one thing, the story, which represents the pious eradication of mirrors, is precisely entitled "Mirrors," and more paradoxical still, it takes great pains to describe the state of mirrorlessness that the protagonists seem to have embarked on, the better to conceal the presence of a substitute, the lake by the side of which their log cabin has been erected. Its name, Big Circle Lake, overdetermines its function: while the couple are represented in a state of mirrorlessness, they are made to inhabit a house next to a circular watery surface, the reflection of which is deliberately suppressed from utterance. It might be legitimate under the circumstances to posit the hypothesis that the eviction of mirrors from the narrated world is but a subterfuge destined to take in the reader and that, with the presence of Big Circle Lake, the text secretly installs the mirror that it claims to evict.

Moreover, Big Circle Lake is not the only clandestine substitute for the mirror in the text. The theatre stage also prolongs reflection beyond the boundaries of Big Circle Lake, all the way to Broadway. Mirrorlessness does secretly accommodate mirroring. Consequently, even in the description of the first stage of their relationship, we cannot remain content with the pristine vision of the faultless couple by the side of the lake of original perfection. In the short story "Mirrors," right from the beginning, the protagonists belong in the age of experience, and contrary to what the narrative attempts to make us believe, the state of mirrorlessness cannot be equated with selflessness and opposed to self-seeking to enhance the protagonists' virtue. During the first summer by the lake, before the house is rehabilitated, the husband is presented as washing rather rapidly in the lake, and for several days his wife noticed a three-cornered smudge of dirt on his forehead. The smudge, of which she is particularly fond and which she refrains from mentioning to him, acquires symbolic significance. As demonstrated by the future vagaries of his sexual conduct, the husband is not *sine macula*, and the wife, although presented as the exact opposite of a vain woman, is nevertheless indirectly depicted as capable of rash and impulsive behaviour. It is said of her, "Even though she was not in those days an impulsive woman" (72), which by reciprocal presupposition suggests that she will become in the future a different sort of person. As the story reveals more information about the characters, the original purity of the pastoral myth, linked with the forswearing of mirrors, seems to cloud over: the annual season of non-reflectiveness allows for the simultaneous presence of selflessness and self-seeking in the psychological build-up of the characters, just as it accommodates several kinds of duplicitous mirrorings in narrated space and the space of utterance.

Because the story encapsulates so many paradoxes and contradictions, it invites us to reconsider our premise. As Sophie Marret remarks,[6] such reading, which proposes to regard modern myths (or the rewriting of the myths of antiquity) as the mere resurgence of a primitive cosmogony, leaves us somehow unsatisfied. It is maybe necessary to try to locate the significance of the myth elsewhere. According to Lacan, myth is the privileged site where a truth linked with the unconscious is allowed to surface through the principle of the half-said: "The half-said is the internal law of all utterance of truth, and what embodies it best is myth."[7] The mirror in Shields's story should not be considered simply the latent motif of her story. It must be contemplated as the instrument and the model of this literary construction, which represents the state of mirrorlessness only to emphasize through specular inversion its all-pervading presence, its effects, and its functions as stemming from the unconscious and finding an expression in the text through contradiction and denegation.

The most striking instances of the duplicitous presence of the mirror come from the metaphoric use of the word "surface," which recurrs throughout the story. About their first summer in the log cabin by the lake, the narratorial voice says that "the truth had been darkened out. Now it erupted, came to the surface" (74). This statement reinforces the idea that Big Circle Lake is not simply a *speculum perfectionis*, but also an *Innenwelt* and *Umwelt*, a double mirror, interior and exterior, in the landscape and the inner recesses of the soul, through which the truths that had been repressed so far are allowed to return. The word "surface" can also be found in other expressions that testify to the inescapable presence of a mirror in the text or at least of an effect-of-the-mirror: "these inviting surfaces slip from remembrance the minute you turn your back" (69). Such is the way the log cabin is described, which does not fail to suggest specular evanescence.

Some propositions destined to define the characters are also overdetermined, as far as their specularity is concerned: "Their political views tend to fall in the middle of the spectrum" (69). As Barthes notes, the word "spectrum" finds its roots in *specere*, which means "to look at," but it also adds "this rather terrible thing," which he calls "the return of the dead."[8] One might recognize in this spectral allusion the mirror of vanities, the one that appears under the shape of an anamorphosis at the feet of Holbein's *The Ambassadors* and reappears here in Carol Shields's "Mirrors" all the more powerfully as it disguises itself under the insignificant garb of a political affiliation. The topos that is indirectly and secretly suggested here, as in *The Ambassadors*, is the memento mori.

Whatever the narrative says, the looking glass is not evicted from representation. It surreptitiously infiltrates the text through metaphors, polysemy, and anamorphosis, and it also openly makes its presence felt through explicit visual indexation. In the restaurant where the protagonists decide to dine out at the end of their first summer by the lake, they are surprised to discover the reflection of their faces in the mirror hanging on the wall. This recognition scene closely resembles an anagnorisis, as defined by Aristotle in his *Poetics*: "It is a turning point in a drama at which a character recognizes the true state of affairs, having previously been in error or ignorance."[9] Unlike Oedipus, Carol Shields's husband and wife do not become aware of the identity of their father or spouse. But this moment of awareness of their new identity is the culminating point of their first summer by the lake. It is marked by the opening up of a new space in the text, something akin to a gap, a blank space, a distance from the immediacy of reflection, which makes room for critical reflection and enables one to grasp one of the values of specularity: "To mimic what actually happens, to duplicate actualization with a counteractualization, identification with distance, like the authentic actor or dancer, this is to give the truth of the event the opportunity not to be mistaken for its inevitable actualization."[10]

Because of the distance that is created between the characters and the moment they recognize each other, the mirror hanging on the restaurant wall acquires the status of an emblem of truth. It is as if, in this season of non-reflectiveness, their identity had been set aside. The gap that opens up between themselves and the moment they recognize their faces in the mirror is what guarantees the recapturing of the self through simultaneous empathy and distance. It prevents the type of superficial adherence that a more immediate acknowledgment would have fostered.

It also makes room for a revision of the status of the mirror in the ideological scheme of the characters. They continue to deny themselves the comfort of mirrors during their summers at the lake, but the wife, for instance, cannot help remembering the little mirrors that used to be found in brand new ladies' handbags. This memory is a positive one, and these mirrors of the past are also lent the status of an emblem of truth: "They were crude, roughly made mirrors, and she wasn't sure that people actually used them. They were like charms, good-luck charms. Or like compasses; you could look in them and take your bearings. Locate yourself in the world" (76). The allusion to these little rectangles reintroduces the presence of mirrors in the text explicitly though analeptically. It also leads to a praise of mirrors from the wife's point of view: "The simplicity of glass. The preciousness of silver. Only these two elements were needed for the miracle of reflection to take place" (78). This eulogy is not limited to a particular moment or a particular place: it functions through generalization thanks to nominal sentences. Relying on Émile Benvéniste's path-breaking analysis, Louis Marin sets down the characteristics of the nominal sentence: "a complete essence, an absolute truth, a permanent value, timeless, placeless, outside the pale of a relationship with the enunciator-descriptor or the narrator; a definite assertion, an authoritative argument."[11] Commenting on Benvéniste's description of the nominal sentence, he emphasizes the paradox of its apparent inscription outside discourse and of its real presence in a particular subjectivity: "In effect the nominal assertion, the characteristic of which is to posit the utterance outside temporal or modal localization and outside the enunciator's subjectivity, is always linked with discourse; it presupposes dialogue; it is introduced to act and convince, not to provide information."[12]

Its use to characterize a mirror immediately lends it a transcendent and extraordinary aura. Through the subjective praise that the wife embarks on, the mirror is installed in its true value. It is installed in the text, whether it is perceived *in absentia* or *in praesentia*, through its effects and its functions. Nevertheless, it should not be understood as being statically established there. It might be better construed as being forever in the making, a moving constellation of singular facts: maybe it is the incarnation of a Deleuzian event in so far as "one can only speak about events as the deployment of singularities in a problematic field near which solutions are found."[13] To clarify this apparently confusing definition of the Deleuzian event, we must first apprehend its opposite. To put it briefly, a Deleuzian event is not a single occurrence happening in a single place at a given time in the epiphanic mode. It is a rhizomatic arrangement that needs to be understood as a multi-stable deployment.

The deployment of the mirror event in the text may be grasped more easily through the metaphor used to describe the children drifting through the walls of the log cabin at the time when it is being further renovated and enlarged: "The children drifted through the half completed partitions like ghosts, claiming their own territory" (75–6). The image suggested here is that of a passage through the other side of the mirror. The half-completed partitions render possible the metaphoric replacement of a wall with a looking glass. Like Alice, the children go through the mirror, bearing witness to its presence in the space of utterance. In narrated space, mirrors have been eliminated, but their presence, which is necessarily an absence, makes itself felt through the representation of the place in discourse, which consecrates the extraordinary dimension of the log cabin by the lake as subtending the possibility of the inversion of signification.

The renovation of the log cabin has momentarily perturbed the prevailing harmony. The metaphor used to describe the perturbation clearly suggests the shattering of glass: "Workmen came every morning, and the sound of their power tools shattered the accustomed summertime peace" (75). The feeling of tranquility recaptured after the workers have left is evoked through a synesthesia that suggests the fulfillment brought about by the communion of the individual with his or her surroundings: "She found herself living all day for the moment they would be gone, the sudden late afternoon stillness and the delicious green smell of cut lumber rising around them" (75). The green smell is a supplementary clue as to the functioning of specularity in narrated space and the space of utterance. The fusion of the visual and of the olfactory illustrates and announces the commingling of the individual and the world in a landscape invested with meaning once it is recomposed after a perturbation. Like Andrew Marvell's protagonist in "The Garden," the individual seems to be one with the world and to become "a green thought in a green shade."[14] Instead of being taken in by the deceptive reflection of the fountain, the female protagonist reverses Narcissus' trajectory and achieves an epiphanic anabasis, an upward movement towards the surface, which brings about her identification with nature. This process of union or identification is also contradictory and specular, that is to say, inverted, since she achieves a feeling of recomposition of the self thanks to the smell of cut lumber around her, in the regained circle of original perfection.

The working of specularity in the short story can also be apprehended through the husband's portrayal. At the beginning of the story, husband and wife are depicted as involved in a marital relationship that Christian heritage has marked as mirroring the love of Christ. Towards the end of the story, the husband has moved away from this initial position in an exactly symmetrical and inverted fashion. In his late forties, he falls in love with a vain woman whose beauty "had to be checked and affirmed almost continually" (77). This extramarital affair is a double betrayal, since, for one thing, the husband is not true to his wife and for another he also forswears the vow of mirrorlessness by accepting his mistress's dependency on mirrors. He eventually manages to bring this affair to a termination without his wife becoming aware of his faithlessness, but because of the extramarital affair that almost destroyed his marriage, he no longer feels rejuvenated by his communion with nature. When he comes back to the log cabin for his annual holiday, he is alienated, denied the comfort of wooden surfaces, estranged from the original transparency of the fountain: "A wave of darkness had rolled in between what he used to be and what he'd become, and he longed to put his head down on the smooth pine surface of the kitchen table and confess everything" (77).

The metaphor of the wave of darkness perfectly illustrates the textual duplicity of the treatment of the mirror motif in Carol Shields's short story, which simultaneously denies the presence of mirrors and ceaselessly reintroduces them explicitly or implicitly in the protagonists' ordinary existence. The smooth surface of the pine table in the kitchen of the log cabin metaphorically substitutes for Narcissus' mirror, and the husband cannot see his reflection anymore because the secret betrayals he has indulged in have tainted the purity of the surface. The husband seems to long for a restoration of his self-image on the smooth mirror of the pine table. His mirror substitute is made of wood, and the simplicity of wood echoes the simplicity of glass. What the husband aspires to is the rehabilitation of his self in the rehabilitated cabin. It is for this reason that, on the particular summer when he brings his extramarital affair to its termination, he sets about building a cedar deck. By becoming a carpenter again, he resumes the biblical status of Joseph, he participates again in the refoundation of the world deprived of evil, and he endeavours to achieve his redemption. But his redemption can also be construed as extremely ambiguous, since it seems to be primarily aimed at falling in love again with his own rehabilitated image on the wooden surface of the newly built summer deck.

The story provides us with two further instances of specular reversibility, which might be understood as the final key to the mythological enigma Shields sets up. Through free indirect discourse, the husband first expresses doubts as to the validity of their gesture of forswearing mirrors: "He longs sometimes to tell them that what they see is not the whole of it. Living without mirrors is cumbersome and inconvenient, if the truth were known, and moreover, he has developed a distaste in recent years for acts of abnegation, finding something theatrical and childish about cultivated denial, something stubbornly wilful and self-cherishing" (79). At the end of his lifelong quest for authenticity, he seems to think that the refusal of artifice is more artificial than artifice itself, and he suggests that the only possibility of reaching some kind of truth lies in the abjuration of abjuration. Authenticity cannot be brought about by renouncing mirrors; it is engendered by renouncing renunciation, which paradoxically consecrates innocence and hyper-consciousness.

This duplicitous philosophy is confirmed through the last anecdote given to us about the couple's marital life. In the middle of the night, the husband wakes up and contemplates his wife sitting up next to him and reading a book. He locks eyes with her for a few seconds, and the solution to the enigma of their extraordinary marital felicity suddenly dawns upon the reader: they have ensured the continuance of their union for thirty-five years by replacing the artificial mirrors with the natural one. In each other's pupils they have learned to mirror each other secretly. While pretending they had done away with mirrors, they were in fact deceiving everybody without letting them know about their subterfuge.

The final revelation of their trick simultaneously cancels and reinforces the claim to authenticity since the artifice they have used is the more natural one. They have clandestinely replaced the mirror with the pupil, which is the smaller circle of the eye, at the same time as they have surreptitiously found another substitute in the lake by the side of their log cabin, which is called Big Circle and provides another natural extension upon which to mirror the I. In between the acknowledged pupil and the unacknowledged lake, the emblematic and anonymous couple of Shields's story have reinvented the original myth of Narcissus by inaugurating the reversibility of a death-dealing, self-seeking narcissism into a life-giving one. They have learned to reach out to each other and commune with each other through the exchange of the gaze instead of finding the deadly embrace their predecessor encountered when he discovered in the water of the fountain that he was only looking at himself.

In the mirror of the eye, what emerges for the husband and the wife is the perfection of circularity, the fulfillment of unity, the fusion of the self and the world. Shields transmutes the lethal power of the Narcissus myth into a source of life, an enabling and empowering force that renders possible the coincidence of one's own centre with a universal centre.

This coincidence is presented as sacred and transcendent, but it is also shown as mundane, located at the intersection of the profane and the sacred, in the interface of asceticism and subterfuge. In the encounter with the other, Shields introduces the element of disguise and playfulness, as demonstrated by the last lines of the story: "And then she had turned and glanced his way. Their eyes held caught on the thread of a shared joke: the two of them at this moment had become each other, at home behind the screen of each other's face. It was several seconds before he was able to look away" (80). The transmutation of a death-dealing narcissism into a life-giving narcissism operates through the metaphor of the thread conjoining the amused protagonists. In Greek mythology the thread is associated with two main episodes: the episode of the labyrinth in which Theseus was guided thanks to Ariadne's thread and that of the Fates, who bring people's existence to an end by cutting the thread of their life. The gaze that is exchanged between the protagonists at the end of the story provides direction for both of them at the same time as it keeps the Fates at bay. It consecrates the victory of love over death, that is to say, of Eros over Thanatos.

In common usage, Eros is generally associated with the passion of erotic and erratic love. It is most often indexed to a visual representation of the god as a blind and winged archer, the whimsical and chubby son of the goddess Aphrodite, ready to pierce hearts at random. In her rewriting of Greek mythology by the side of Big Circle Lake, Shields incorporates the commonly represented mischievousness of the young Eros, but she does not rely upon any other aspects pertaining to this late development of the existing versions of the god of love. Rather, she invites us to return to the Platonic Eros as expounded in *Alcibiades*. We could even go as far as saying that she playfully and secretly reflects one of Plato's dialogues in her short story, the better to illustrate the secret of specularity. Plato's text is worth quoting as the original source, the fountain of her inspiration:

– When we look into the eye of someone who is opposite, our face is reflected in what is called the pupil of the eye as if in a mirror. The one who looks into it sees himself.
– This is true.
– Thus when the eye considers the other eye, when it stares into that part of the eye that is the best, the one that sees, it is itself that which it sees.[15]

In an article entitled "One Two Three Eros," Jean-Pierre Vernant proposes the exegesis of this passage, highlighting in a very striking manner the formula that Plato expresses – $1 + 1 = 3$ – a formula that he shows to be valid on the two levels upon which Eros operates. On the level of physical life or the heteroerotic level, love consists for two beings to engender a third one, different from each of them and yet prolonging them. Eroticism according to the body consists in producing a substitute for immortality in the midst of transience. On the level of spiritual life or homoeroticism, what one sees in the eyes of the beloved is not the human face of a human being but the mask of the god that possesses one, which carries one away in a state of divine madness. It is a face illuminated with a radiance that comes from elsewhere, from another world: it is the figure of Beauty as a transcendent essence. The fusion of the self with God can only be achieved through the intermediary of the other: through the love of the other, one reaches the divine otherness from which every source of unlimited beauty is derived.[16] Such is the philosophical lesson of the Platonic Eros. Such is the philosophical lesson reflected and recontextualized in the extraordinary mirror of Shields's short story. This philosophical lesson has also been reiterated in the twentieth century by Deleuze: "to become imperceptible, to have undone love to be capable of loving. To have undone the self to be alone at last and meet the true double at the other end of the line. A stowaway in a still journey."[17]

The secret of the extraordinary duration of the union of Shields's emblematic couple might well be inscribed on what Deleuze also calls "a secret line of deterritorialization,"[18] on this thread of reciprocated love, which simultaneously encapsulates the possibility of erotic transcendence according to Plato and accommodates self distance and self derision. Before Carol Shields, E.T.A. Hoffmann provided a similarly playful recontextualization of the Greek myths linked with the presence of the mirror: in the story inside the story of "Princess Brambilla," King Ophioch and Queen Liris, leaning over the magic Lake of Urdar, discover their inverted image and burst out laughing as they exchange a loving gaze. Like them, Shields's protagonists seem to be saved by the duplication of their reflection and by laughter. They seem to have been rescued from what Lacan calls "the endless quadrature of the mending of the self"[19] because they have managed to make the circle of the *Innenwelt* coincide with the circle of the *Umwelt*. By looking at each other as if through a mirror, they do not need to go from the inside to the outside. They can remain fixated in the identification with each other, "in the joyful assumption of their mirrored image"[20] in a double mirror stage, in the reciprocity with each other, inside Big Circle Lake and the smaller circle of the eye.

In the short story entitled "Mirrors," Shields has made us witness the lovers' progress from the forswearing of mirrors as an emblem of vanity to the secret accommodation of mirrors as an emblem of truth, which reaches its final climax in the acknowledgment of the beloved's pupil as the natural looking glass reflecting the divine essence of love. This progress is quite literally extra-ordinary since it moves away from an ordinary, vain, and self-seeking conception of love to embrace a transcendent, philosophical, and Platonic conception of Eros.

The extra-ordinary dimension of this progress should also be recognized in the fact that it is specular instead of linear. Shields's couple have found the secret of an abiding conjugal love because, instead of moving along the thread of entropy, they have embarked on the reflexivity of requited love. They have found in the principle of reciprocal reflection, upon which their love is predicated, the means of knowing themselves and each other, of distancing themselves from each other while remaining in the reciprocity of seeing and being seen. They have learned to accommodate the otherness of the same and the sameness of the other, while mirroring each other in the pupils of their eyes.

With this abiding and playful reflection, which simultaneously reverses the fatal course of Narcissus' life and the short-lived vagaries inspired by the young Eros, Shields does not simply provide us with her own *ars amatoria*; she provides us with an *ars poetica*, a lesson in aesthetics, which could very well be derived from what Baudelaire suggests in "The Essence of Laughter": "The artist is an artist only if he manages to be double and if he ignores nothing of the phenomena of his double nature."[21]

Shields's duplicitous treatment of the mirror motif simultaneously enhances her innocence and her hyperconsciousness. She revises the myths of antiquity to destabilize their established version and break up their hard segmentarity. On the surface of the fountain, Narcissus "arrested forms and forces"; he arrested his image in what Carl Einstein terms "a conceited naturalism."[22] On the thread of each other's eyes, Shields's protagonists do not "substantify reality"; they create a reciprocal flux that can be called a "flowing, moving naturalism."[23] In her revised version, the ordeal of being face to face, the peril of the eyes, is metamorphosed into a current of exchange, which, "like in an initiation rite, removes you from the world of matter, from the world of becoming, and transports you elsewhere, to give you back your real self, in the semblance of God, through the exchange with others."[24]

When depicting the exchange with the other, Carol Shields makes her protagonists find, deep within themselves, that better part which Plato refers us to; her extraordinary gift may consist in making the divine stranger surface in each of the lovers she depicts in her short stories and her novels. Whether they are called Tom, Eugene, Chas, or Larry, or whether they have no names at all, they will long continue to beckon to us from Big Circle Lake, like the mermaid on the cover of Fay's book in *The Republic of Love*, with one of their hands uplifted, symbolizing "a hunger for the food of love."[25]

It is this essential hunger that characterizes all of Shields's characters: it is this hunger that makes them extra-ordinary.

NOTES

Quotations from French-language sources have been translated by the author.

1 Vernant, *L'individu, la mort, l'amour*, 120 : "Dans le champ que dessinent les rapports ambigus du visible et de l'invisible, de la vie et de la mort, de l'image et du réel, de la beauté et de l'horreur, de la séduction et de la répulsion, cet objet d'usage quotidien occupe une position clef d'importance stratégique: dans la mesure même où il apparaît susceptible de conjoindre ces termes normalement opposés, il se prête, plus qu'un autre, à la problématisation de tout le domaine du voir et de l'être vu."

2 Shields, *Dressing Up for the Carnival*, 70.

3 Minazzoli, *La première ombre*, 13: "reflète, pour faire briller à travers lui, la lumière et la gloire du créateur du monde."

4 Ibid., 113: "déchiffrage des images en énigme et en miroir pour retrouver la ressemblance."

5 1 Corinthians 13.

6 Marret, "L'inconscient aux sources du mythe moderne," 299.

7 Lacan, *L'envers de la psychanalyse*, 127: "le mi-dire est la loi interne de toute espèce d'énonciation de la vérité, et ce qui l'incarne le mieux c'est le mythe."

8 Barthes, *La chambre claire*, 23.

9 Baldick, *Concise Oxford Dictionary of Literary Terms*, 8.

10 Deleuze, *Logique du sens*, 188: "être le mime de ce qui arrive effectivement, doubler l'effectuation d'une contre-effectuation, l'identification d'une distance, tel l'acteur véritable ou le danseur, c'est donner à la vérité de l'événement la chance unique de ne pas se confondre avec son inévitable effectuation."

11 Marin, *Le récit est un piège*, 75: "une essence complète, une vérité absolue, une valeur permanente, hors temps, hors lieu, hors toute relation avec le locuteur descripteur ou narrateur: assertion définitive, argument d'autorité."

12 Ibid., 75–6: "En effet, l'assertion nominale, dont la caractéristique est de poser l'énoncé hors de toute localisation temporelle et modale et hors de la subjectivité du locuteur est toujours liée au discours; elle suppose le dialogue; elle est introduite pour agir et convaincre, non pour informer."

13 Deleuze, *Logique du sens*, 72: "on ne peut parler des événements que comme des singularités qui se déploient dans un champ problématique, et au voisinage desquelles s'organisent les solutions."

14 Marvell, *Complete Poems*, 101:
      Meanwhile the mind, from pleasure less,
      Withdraws into its happiness
      The mind, that ocean where each kind
      Does straight its own resemblance find,
      Yet it creates, transcending these,
      Far other worlds, and other seas,
      Annihilating all that's made
      To a green thought in a green shade.

15 Plato, *Alcibiade*, 132e–133a: "Quand nous regardons l'œil de quelqu'un qui est en face de nous, notre visage se réfléchit dans ce qu'on appelle la pupille comme dans un miroir; celui qui y regarde y voit son image.– C'est exact. – Ainsi, quand l'œil considère un autre œil, quand il fixe son regard sur la partie de cet œil qui est la meilleure, celle qui voit, c'est lui-même qu'il y voit."

16 Vernant, *L'individu, la mort, l'amour*, 164.

17 Deleuze and Guattari, *Capitalisme et schizophrénie*, 241–2: "Devenir soi-même imperceptible, avoir défait l'amour pour devenir capable d'aimer. Avoir défait son propre moi pour être enfin seul, et rencontrer le vrai double à l'autre bout de la ligne. Passager clandestin d'un voyage immobile."

18 Ibid., 240.

19 Lacan, *Écrits*, 97: "la quadrature inépuisable des recollements du moi."

20 Ibid.: "dans l'assomption jubilatoire de leur image spéculaire."

21 Baudelaire, *Œuvres complètes*, 2: 542: "L'artiste n'est artiste qu'à la condition d'être double et de n'ignorer aucun des phénomènes de sa double nature."

22 Einstein, *George Bracque*, 57.

23 Ibid., 57.

24 Vernant, *Figures, idoles, masques*, 131: "comme au cours d'une initiation, vous arrachent au monde sensible, au devenir, vous transportent ailleurs et rendent votre vraie personne, dans et par le commerce avec l'autre, semblable au divin."

25 Shields, *The Republic of Love*, 310.

WORKS CITED

Atwood, Margaret. *Wilderness Tips*. Toronto: McClelland and Stewart, 1991.

Baldick, Chris. *The Concise Oxford Dictionary of Literary Terms*. Oxford: Oxford University Press, 1990.

Baudelaire, Charles. *Oeuvres complètes*. Vol. 2 Bibliothèque de la Pléiade. Paris: Gallimard, 1976.

Barthes, Roland. *La chambre claire: Note sur la photographie*. Paris: Gallimard, 1980.

Carson, Anne. *Autobiography of Red*. New York: Knopf, 1998.

Deleuze, Gilles. *Logique du sens*. Paris: Minuit, 1969.

– and Felix Guattari. *Capitalisme et schizophrénie: mille plateaux*. Paris: Minuit, 1980.

Einstein, Carl. *George Bracque* (1931–1932). Trad. E. Zipruth. Paris: Editions des Chroniques du jour, 1934.

Hoffmann, E.T.A. *The Golden Pot, and Other Tales*. [1821]. Trans. Ritchie Robertson. Oxford: Oxford University Press, 2000.

Kroetsch, Robert. *The Studhorse Man*. Toronto: Macmillan, 1969.

Lacan, Jacques. *Écrits*. Paris: Le Seuil, 1966.

– *L'envers de la psychanalyse* (1969–1970). Paris: Le Seuil, 1991.

Marret, Sophie. "L'inconscient aux sources du mythe moderne." *Études anglaises* 55, no. 3 (2002): 298–307.

Marin, Louis. *Le récit est un piège*. Paris: Minuit, 1978.

Marvell, Andrew. *The Complete Poems*. Harmondsworth: Penguin, 1972.

Munro, Alice. 1997. "The Children Stay." New Yorker, Double Fiction Issue, 22, 29 December 1997, 91–103.

Minazzoli, Agnès. *La première ombre: Réflexion sur le miroir et la pensée*. Paris: Minuit, 1990.

The New English Bible. Oxford: Oxford University Press, 1970.

Plato. *Alcibiade*. Trad. Chantal Marboeuf and J.F. Pradeau. Paris: Garnier Flammarion, 2000.

Shields, Carol. *Dressing Up for the Carnival*. London: Fourth Estate, 2000.

– *The Republic of Love*. Toronto: Fawcett Crest, 1992.

Vernant, Jean-Pierre. *Figures, idoles, masques*. Paris: Julliard, 1990.

– *L'individu, la mort, l'amour*. Paris: Gallimard, 1989.

Watson, Sheila. *Five Stories*. Toronto: Coach House, 1984.

PART THREE

Extra-Ordinary Performances:

Production and Reception

12

Disappearance and "the Vision Multiplied": Writing as Performance

MARTA DVOŘÁK

This essay sets out to throw light on the work of a highly erudite, franco-phile Canadian writer by placing it within the larger cultural context of certain aesthetic currents such as modernism and postmodernism, in particular their subsidiary tendencies in European and especially French postmodern writing. The discussion will focus first of all on a story from the collection *Dressing Up for the Carnival*, "Absence," situating it within the continuum of experimental writers such as Raymond Queneau and Georges Perec, whose landmark works – whether they be direct influ-ences or not – can serve a useful exegetical function. This involves the exploration of the writer's craft as a combination of workmanship and play, notably shedding light on Shields's recurrent recourse to self-imposed formal constraints. These constraints, applied in a metatextual manner, are apparently designed to emphasize the agonistic dimension of writing as performance. I shall demonstrate the diverse strategies that Shields deploys to call attention to the dexterity, even virtuosity, with which writers can employ the building material available to them. The value consequently placed on complexification and the surmounting of difficulty is interestingly ambivalent, and my discussion will then attempt to elucidate to what extent Shields's postmodern stance con-tains, moreover, a phenomenological quest grounded in modernist prac-tices which are rooted in turn in the language theories of Bertrand Russell, Frege, and Wittgenstein. Such a quest to grasp reality coexists with a tendency that Shields, like Jane Urquhart, Margaret Atwood, Anne Michaels, and Timothy Findley, to name but a few, has inherited from the modernists: slipping beyond the spheres of subjectivity and perception into the mythopoeic, marvellous, or extraordinary, to suspend the referential functions of language and proffer epiphanic disclosures. Subtending the ludic preoccupation with language and the mechanisms of the creative process is perhaps a drive to set up a state of contemplation that is ultimately Romantic.

Such a ludic preoccupation can be exemplified by international modernist figures ranging from Nabokov and Virginia Woolf to Raymond Queneau. The latter especially experimented with surrealism, privileged language over plot, and challenged an entrenched post-Romantic mindset by debunking the notion of inspiration in favour of composition. Metatextual writings such as *Exercices de style* (1947), seeking to explode the boundaries of language as system, placed poetics firmly back within its etymological roots, the Greek *poieîn*, which signifies to make or to fashion. The movement, school, or rather writing *work*shop that he co-founded in 1960, OuLiPo,[1] attracted members from the national and international scene, from Italo Calvino to Harry Mathews and Georges Perec. To trigger innovation, they rehabilitated the notion of formal constraint in literary creation and reinjected into their texts self-imposed restraints such as mathematical structures, rhetorical devices – particularly those based on the resemblance of form or sound – and even lipograms: texts written with one hand tied metaphorically behind one's back, since the writers voluntarily deprive themselves of the use of one letter. Perec notably became notorious for the longest lipogram in the history of French literature: *La Disparition* (1969), ostensibly a detective story about the "disappearance" of two protagonists, but actually a 315-page metatextual novel written without one single letter *e*, the most common vowel in the French language.[2] Called the acrobat of contemporary literature,[3] Perec clearly set out to identify writing as performance.

One can argue that it is just such a performance that Shields offers us in her story "Absence." Playfully, as is her wont, our woman writer stages a woman writer protagonist writing about a woman writer writing. The triplication is already in accordance with a postmodern predilection for the specular fiction identified by Lucien Dällenbach as embedding, doubling back, and feeding on itself with imitations, variations, and inversions. The strategy is even more remarkable in Shields's subsequent novel *Unless*, which self-reflexively constructs a similar *mise en abyme* through the rhetoric of denial: "I would become a woman writing about a woman writing about women writing, and that would lead straight to an echo chamber of infinite regress in company with the little Dutch girl, the girl on the bathroom cleanser, the vision multiplied, but in receding perspective. No."[4]

The aporetic collision of augmentation and diminution (*regress/receding* versus *multiplied*) is highlighted when the narrator suggests that the significance of event for an individual is *reduced* in direct proportion to the "slow, steady *accumulation* of *incremental* knowledge"[5] of the species. The specular parallelisms are reminiscent of the endless series of possibilities Atwood metaphorises in *The Handmaid's Tale* as "the reflections in two mirrors set facing one another, stretching on, replica after replica, to the vanishing point."[6] They serve to call attention to the fabricated nature of the text, which is further foregrounded in *Unless* through the intratextual duplication or recycling of the story "A Scarf," in the manner of a David Hockney collage with all its slippages, each image feeding on the preceding one.

The recourse to specularity signals a ludic desire to play with form and system, which escalates to OuLiPo proportions when the omniscient narrator's writer-protagonist is confronted with a broken typewriter key and embarks on a lipogram, deciding to "work *around* the faulty letter."[7] The explicit, "material" fictional obstacle consisting in the jammed key is mirrored in the framing lipogram by an implicit, gratuitous, self-imposed constraint or deprivation: writing without the vowel *i* the story of a writer writing a story without the vowel *i*. Like Perec, Shields chooses to position writing as an agonistic craft. *Agon*, or combat, the category of play that generates the pleasure of surmounting obstacles, according to theorists of play such as Johan Huizinga and Roger Caillois, is regulated by elaborate codes – whether it be chess, bridge, or concertizing – involving cognitive strategies, method, and a taste for the difficult. As opposed to other categories of play such as *alea* (chance) or *ilinx* (vertigo), which belong to the pole of *paidia*, grounded in primary desires and sensuality and involving impulse, *agon* belongs to the pole of *ludus*, involving knowledge, discipline, and constraint: the site of play that is arguably responsible for the development of culture within civilization.

When Shields banishes the vowel all the more central to English speech since it is "the very letter that attaches to the hungry self" (108), with the exclusive power to signify the subject, she engages in a process of contraction. The lexical restriction is metaphorised in spatial terms: "Vocabulary, her well-loved garden, as broad and taken-for-granted as

an acre of goldenrod, had shrunk to a square rod" (105). The lexicon
hitherto out of bounds entails a grammatical constriction: the first-person subject pronoun has disappeared along with various third-person
subject and object pronouns, while other parts of speech such as prepo-
sitions,[8] the present participle, and "the flabby but dependable gerund"
have also "dropped through language's trapdoor" (111). With such
recourse to concretization and personification – among her trademarks
– Shields highlights the loss of building material by drawing attention to
the weight and mass of language, as well as to the kinetic function of the
words that have vanished: "whole parcels of grammar ... seemed all at
once out of reach, and so were those bulky doorstop words that connect
and announce and allow a sentence to pause for a moment and take on
fresh loads of oxygen" (111).

   Yet the agonistic bending of language is twofold. Accompanying the
self-imposed centripetal movement of scissions and omissions is a centrifugal impetus, a stretching outwards categorized by a quest for
exhaustivity and totality. Excision and mutilation generate invention, an
innovative exploration of the less-charted potentials of language, an
exploration that is characterized by profusion, accumulation, and saturation. Among the sundry figures obeying such an incremental logic we
can identify enumeration, seriation, polysyndeton, metabole, analogy,
metaphor, metaplasm, paronomasia, and even parenthesis, all functioning within the dynamics of replication and augmentation. Shields is
particularly skilful with enumeration, which linguists such as Roman
Jakobson see as the exposure of the paradigm, outside the function of
communication, noteworthy for its capacity to display in a small space.
As with Perec's texts, readers cannot fail to remark Shields's recurrent
inventories aspiring to exhaustivity, carrying out an amplifying metonymic function, serving to connect the abstract and the concrete, the
general and the particular, producing and foregrounding relationships
of inclusion. One significant example is the opening list of "Absence"
announcing that the writer-protagonist wishes to "create[9] a story that
possessed a granddaughter, a Boston fern, a golden apple, and a small
blue cradle" (108).

   The amplifying device of enumeration, by definition open-ended,
generates the retardatory device of suspension, all the while suggesting
that there is always something left to be said or disclosed. Yet even
Shields's recurrent recourse to chaotic enumerations such as this of
terms that are not of the same nature, a writerly device usually deployed
to undermine connections, often implicitly seek an ordering principle

capturing an underlying unity or perspective. The preoccupation with connections and correspondences is expressed most clearly in metatextual terms: "Some hand must move the pen along or press the keys and steer, somehow, the granddaughter towards the Boston fern or place the golden apple at the foot of the blue cradle" (111). The items denoted as narrative ingredients are revelatory of a fascination with what we could call the *infra*-ordinary, the small, homely objects that are the components of domestic experience, as well as an aporetic tendency to expand outwards and fuse the infra-ordinary with the extra-ordinary of storytelling and cosmic legend.

The plotless story "Absence," most explicitly perhaps among the ones included in *Dressing Up for the Carnival*, is self-conscious writing belonging to the mode that Linda Hutcheon has identified as "narcissistic narrative," shifting the focus "from the 'fiction' to the 'narration'" and making the narration "into the very substance" of the content.[10] The fundamentally metatextual dimension of the story about the double struggle to write a story is nonetheless replicated in disguised forms in other stories that ostensibly address events revolving around domesticity and commodification. The story "Invention" notably begins by recounting how the narrator's grandmother invented that infra-ordinary pedestrian object, the steering-wheel muff, and built a commercial empire that destroyed her marriage as it grew. Albeit less rapidly than "Absence," the story slides imperceptibly from narrative to narration as the focus glides from the world of commodities to the world of language. In an appropriately random, digressive fashion, the narrator challenges the notion of perfectibility along with that of scientific or technological progress by proclaiming that "invention is random and accidental."[11] The text deflates the mythical overtones that have been culturally constructed around certain products or theories, by resorting to playful seriation, periphrastic parallelisms, and juxtapositions that engender unusual equivalences between, for instance, gunpowder and the hoola hoop or chairs and Darwinism: "For instance, someone discovered one idle afternoon that a loop of plastic tubing will defy gravity if gyrated rapidly around the human body. Someone else, in another slot of time, noticed that a mixture of potassium nitrate, charcoal, and sulphur will create a new substance which is highly explosive ... Other people – through carelessness or luck or distraction or necessity – invented keys, chairs, wheels, thermometers, and the theory of evolution" (178).

Simultaneously, the narrator celebrates other inventions that pertain to the world of writing and that remain unacknowledged and unsung:

the banal word-space, the full stop or period, the comma, and the hyphen. Through a litotic analogy with the apparently insignificant yet ground-breaking zero, the narratorial voice lauds the blank, praises the oxymoronic weight of emptiness, and celebrates the silence that "distinguishes speech from speech and thought from thought" (176). Playfully attributing the scriptoral invention of the comma to a slip of the pen of another absurdly precise, yet historically vague member of the family ("one Brother Alphonse, a very distant cousin on my paternal grandfather's side" [177]), the narcissistic narrator's voice, overlapping with Brother Alphonse's, metalinguistically dubs it "a curled worm of ambiguity" and describes it in temporal and spatial terms as the very site of creation in process: "a sacred pause, a resting place during which time he might breathe out his thanks to God for the richness of his blessings, and prepare his next imprecation" (177).

Mixing fantasy and self-reflexivity, the narrator attributes the invention of the hyphen to a sixteenth-century cooper-cum-grammarian ancestor. The extravagant logic according to which a barrel-maker is best qualified to be a wordsmith is presented by an analogy between the hyphen and a barrel, which is so extra/ordinary that it verges on the conceit. The barrel is held together by an iron hoop, which "connects what is unconnectable," for as the personification makes clear, the barrel-maker's bent staves "long to spring apart" (177). With the implied authorial voice overlapping, the narrator argues that the hyphen "takes on the same function. A diacritical mark of great simplicity, it joins what is similar and also what is disjunctive. Two words may be read as one, a case of compounding meaning and doubling force, but this horizontal bar, requiring only a sweet, single stroke of the pen, divides as well as marries" (178). The metalanguage sets up a parallel between the page and the land, between art and craft, between the building materials of a text – signs of its object/ivity – and those of a farm: "Aesthetically, the hyphen is superior to the slash, you will agree, and it makes a set of parentheses look like crude homemade fencing" (178). The resonances with the stance of utilitarianism, which links the beautiful and the good with the concept of the useful, making them convertible and indissociable, are made explicit in the affirmation that "successful inventions are both functional and elegant" (178).

As in the story "Invention," the concern with connectability in general and the functional in particular subtends the story "Absence," albeit in a more discreet fashion, emerging notably when the writer-protagonist, discouraged by the formidable task she has set herself and by an apparently losing battle, muses that "to make a pot of bean soup would produce more pleasure. To vacuum the hall rug would be of more use" (111). Battling neither hunger nor domestic entropy, the story being crafted seems to derive its significance from the exquisite difficulty of the performance. The agonistic dimension of Shields's framing writerly task is foregrounded in the embedded writerly activity: we learn of the writer struggling to adapt to her new confines that "[h]er head-bone ached; her arm-bones froze," and that she "suffered too over the *sounds* that evaded her" (110, Shields's emphasis) The deviations of circumlocutions and synonyms are acknowledged to be inadequate, the signifieds, the "levels of sense and shades of deference" of words being "untransferable" (109), and in addition, the writer has to make do with imperfect acoustic images: she is "forced to settle for those other, less seemly vowels whose open mouths and unsubtle throats yawned and groaned and showed altogether too much teeth" (110). Calling attention to the embedded writer's struggle with "the melody of her prose" (110) adds value to the feats of the framing writer with respect to sound and rhythm. On the same page alone, we can detect the devices of polysyndeton, consonance, assonance, and highly alliterative binary structures (teased/taunted, pause/pry, stutters/starts, to name but a few), as well as onomatopoeic lexemes or phonetic intensives whose sound, to some degree, suggests their meaning (yawn/groan).

The duple framing and framed combat focuses attention on language as system, a system composed of both acoustic and visual elements, which are concretized on a double plane. As in "Invention," words and letters, the building blocks of language, are defamiliarized and object/ified when the implied authorial voice depicts the banished letter as, first and foremost, a figure, a shape on the page, a "slender, one- legged vowel, erect but humble" with its accompanying "dot of amazement" (110). With the accent placed on the manu/facturing process (in its original etymological connotation of careful crafting by hand), the figures are wrought or reconfigured into assembled objects with mass and sentience: "she wanted only to *make*, as she had done before, sentences that melted at the centre and branched at the ends, that threatened to grow unruly and run away, but that clause for clause adhered to one another as though stuck down by Velcro tabs" (110, emphasis added).

The sentience produced by the device of concretization is, as we have already seen with the toothy, yawning vowel mouths, once more reinforced by intensive recourse to personification and metaphor. The metaphors are at times so startling that they verge on conceit: "Memory barks, and context, that absolute old cow, glowers and chews up what's less than acceptable" (109–10). The spectacular gap between context and cow exemplifies the source of power of the metaphor, which the surrealists identified as residing in the radical alterity of the worlds that it paradigmatically superimposes. Like the members of OuLiPo before her, Shields recognizes the analogous force of the lipogram, which resides in the spectacular gap between the suppression of one simple little letter and the magnified consequences that the act entails. The lipogram is in effect a sort of clinamen, the infinitesimal deviation of the trajectory of primitive atoms from which everything becomes possible. Inventing formal mechanisms to exploit the capacities of minuscule variations produces the fusion of apparently parallel realities – those of the word and the world, the text and the self: "the broken key seemed to demand of her a parallel surrender, a correspondence of economy subtracted from the alphabet of her very self" (111).

Such interconnections are rooted in the conception of thought based on atomic theories proffered by Bertrand Russell, Wittgenstein, and Frege, which influenced modernists such as Virginia Woolf. The logicians' concept of a natural language or grammar based on the structure of thought, as well as a preoccupation with the small and a fascination with the interconnections between the particles making up the universal state of things, can be detected in Woolf's essay "Modern Novels," published in 1919. The modernist manifesto eschews verisimilitude and, with just such an atomic analogy, calls for the representation of the myriad impressions that fall upon the mind in the ordinary course of life: "From all sides they come, an incessant shower of innumerable atoms, composing in their sum what we might call life itself."[12] Woolf extends and emphasizes the analogy through reiterated artistic injunctions: "Let us record the atoms as they fall upon the mind in the order in which they fall, let us trace the pattern, however disconnected and incoherent in appearance, which each sight or incident scores upon the consciousness. Let us not take it for granted that life exists more in what is commonly thought big than in what is commonly thought small."[13] Her fascination with the subjective perception of the small is what animates the atomized impressionistic descriptions of flowers, droplets, and light in her short story "Kew Gardens" or the world seen from below through the Lilliputian eye of a snail.[14]

Shields's pointillist manner of writing, based on specular accumulation, tenuous storylines, and complex minute perceptions of infra-ordinary, normally unnoticed or unrecorded incidents, is reminiscent of what amounts to an unofficial but prophetic modernist manifesto in

Woolf's first published short story, "The Mark on the Wall": "As we face each other in omnibuses and underground railways we are looking into the mirror ... And the novelists in future will realize more and more the importance of these reflections, for of course there is not one reflection but an infinite number; those are the depths they will explore, those the phantoms they will pursue, leaving the description of reality more and more out of their stories, taking a knowledge of it for granted" (6).

These are the reflections with neoplatonic overtones with which Shields constructs a story such as "Soup du Jour." Sent on an errand, the focalizer, a small boy named Simon, is so intent on counting the sidewalk sections and avoiding the cracks that he forgets which single soup ingredient he has been sent to buy. Cringing from the shame of having to admit failure to his mother or the shopkeeper, he calls up the vivid mental image of the Monday evening bowls of soup, eliminating one by one from his usual shopping list the coloured vegetables he envisions floating in the broth. There follows an epiphanic disclosure ("the word celery arrives, fully-shaped"), the loveliness of which is generated on two levels. First, in the fresh approach substituting the signifier – "the *word* celery" – for the conventional visual image of epiphany; secondly, in the homeliness of the referent, which is inversely proportionate to the boy's "thunderous gratitude."[15] Resembling what Woolf in her essay names "the semi-transparent envelope, or luminous halo,"[16] which she calls on writers to refigure, Shields's celery, transformed from pedestrian referent to ontological sign, explodes everyday reality and transports the reader, along with little Simon, into a numinous supra-reality: "He says it out loud, *celery*, transforming the word into a brilliantly coloured balloon that swims and rises and overcomes the tiny confines of the ordinary everyday world to which, until this moment, he has been condemned" (171).

Shields does so through the sensorial dynamics of the metaphorical process, generating the pleasure of the text and setting up a state of contemplation through an act of memory that blurs the two Husserlian modes of primary memory and secondary memory. Little Simon's epiphanic recollection blurs the presentative mode of primary memory or retention, which is a form of "perceiving" the past, and the representative mode of secondary memory or recollection, in which the imagination recreates and reconfigures. By giving the secondary memory the qualities of the primary memory, Shields confers upon the imagination the attributes of the senses and takes us back to the origins. The gap between presentation and representation is filled in, and the ex-static quality of "now" restored, for the reader, along with the focalizer, is transported into what Paul Ricoeur terms "l'ek-stase de l'être-là" – the ek-stasy of the being there.[17]

In a parallel fashion, within the cultural continuum which, from Joyce and Mansfield to Faulkner or Buckler, emerged from a resurgence of interest in Renaissance studies and suggested a supra-reality beyond the senses, Shields has set up a unifying, combinatory metatextual, metaphorical, and metaphysical network reminiscent of Ricoeur's observation that whether we ponder the metaphorical nature of metaphysics or the metaphysical nature of the metaphor, we are in the presence of one same movement that carries words or things somewhere beyond, or *meta*.[18] Through figurations of nature and culture, she transforms objects into signs in a quest for the essence behind thing and thought. The writer-protagonist of "Absence" wonders if the table objects to the weight of her arm, if the lamp is tired, the floorboards cheerful, or the door numb with lack of movement, and she suggests a sentient correspondence between the constriction of language and the parallel constriction of self: "was the broken letter on her keyboard appeased at last by her cast-off self?" (111). Calling up the manner in which the flowered wallpaper comes alive in Katherine Mansfield's story "Prelude," in turn rooted in the pantheistic reverberations of the Romantics and the Emersonian Oversoul, Shields's writer's thoughts "flowed through every object and every corner of the room, and a moment later she *became* the walls and also the clear roof overhead and the powerful black sky" (111–12).

Clearly discernible is Emerson's well-known transcendental manifesto positing a neoplatonic eternal One, "to which every part and particle is equally related," causing "the seer and the spectacle, the subject and the object"[19] (138) to be one. Equally discernible is Emerson's debt to the idealism of Schopenhauer, who declared the artist to be "a clear mirror of the essence of the world."[20] Shields's stance is clearly aligned with Schopenhauer's call to fill one's consciousness with the visible contemplation of a natural object to the point where the pure subject exists only as "the clear mirror of the object" and "can no longer separate the perceiver from the perception, but the two have become one."[21] The framed writer in "Absence" effaces the self as she effaces the *I*, and significantly, the erasure is a transcendental liberation: "Why, she wondered aloud, had she stayed enclosed so long by the tough, lonely pronoun of her body when the whole world beckoned?" (112).

Unlike Perec's postmodern scission and omission grounded in the ludic display of arbitrary artistic control and deriving power from its very gratuitousness, Shields's decision to efface the vowel *I* is an ontological statement. Her writer-cum-wall/roof/sky is anchored in the Schopenhauerian consciousness "taken up with one single sensuous picture,"[22] which is no longer the individual thing as such but "the Idea, the eternal form."[23] Seeking to construct a vision that pierces *eikos* (appearance or perceptible reality) is inherently a Romantic stance, reminiscent of Shelley's call to the poet to lift "the veil from the hidden beauty of the world,"[24] which the postmodernists have inherited indirectly through their modernist counterparts. Shields's preoccupation with natural objects, the emphasis on subjectivity, the belief in revelation and quest for transcendence, is clearly a Romantic heritage, interestingly at odds with her more cerebral, postmodern manner of denying inspiration and displaying craftsmanship. Unlike the pure formal play of the French postmodern current I have briefly considered, which also instrumentalized constraint, Shields's metaphorical writing seeks to generate meaning through form. Yet, in addition to the undeniable textual overlapping of the metaphorical and the metaphysical, it can be noted that her apparently idealist metaphysical current dovetails with a strong metatextual dimension that centripetally draws the focus back from the world to the word, from the cosmos to the page. The final paragraphs of "Absence" provide one final specular confrontation of the embedded writerly figures, which proves to be fundamentally aporetic:

> But the words she actually set down came from the dark eye of her eye, the stubborn self that refused at the last moment to let go. "A woman sat down –"
> Everyone knew who the woman was. Even when she put a red hat on her head or changed her name or turned the clock back a thousand years or resorted to wobbly fables about granddaughters and Boston ferns, everyone knew the woman had been there from the start, seated at a table, object and subject sternly fused. No one, not even the very young, pretends that the person who brought forth words was any other than the arabesque of the unfolded self. (112)

Under the mask of the Romantic metaphysical layer of meaning, the seriation reinforced by polysyndeton marks a self-reflexivity that is resolutely postmodern. The voice of the framing narrator and the point of view of the focalizer overlap with the authorial voice in what amounts to a questioning of critical notions of literary analysis, in particular a blurring of the rather taxonomical categorizations involving the perlocutionary network or relationships among author, implied author, omniscient narrator, narrator as external observer, narrator as protagonist, and, ultimately, receptor. We are in the presence of metafiction usurping the role of the critical text, drawing attention to the cultural conventions that define narrative, as well as to the received notions of the subject. The representational self-consciousness of the piece makes it exemplary of the hybrid genre of metatextual, metacritical, or theoretical fiction that critics have identified with respect to writers such as Nicole Brossard, Daphne Marlatt, and Margaret Atwood, notably.[25] Interestingly, Shields's metanarrative encroaches on and dovetails with the hybrid genre of fiction theory or ficto-criticism, as exemplified by Aritha van Herk's piece "A Ghost Narrative: A Haunting" – also marked by seriation and polysyndeton – in which van Herk challenges the neat categorizations of critical schools of literary analysis, from "Russian formalist theories: or Bakhtinian (dialogical) theories: or New Critical theories: or structuralist, semiotic, and tropological theories" to "reader response theories, or poststructuralist or deconstructionist theories: of narrative that is, narrative and what it is supposed to narrate."[26]

The specular closure of Shields's "Absence," like van Herk's piece, interrogates the nomenclature and taxonomical classifications that narratologists have set up in a systemic attempt to map universal paradigms. It suggests that such attempts are ultimately reductive and strain to define the undefinable. The hand that "must move the pen along or press the keys and steer"[27] the receptor from one narrative sequence to another is not so easily labelled omniscient narrator, homodiegetic narrator, intradiegetic narrator, implied author, or writer. Complicating the ordering principles and blurring them in a fashion that is characteristic of postmodern suspicion with respect to categorical truths, Shields seems to suggest that the writerly mouthpieces, the carefully architectured time frames and meticulously sensuous descriptions of objective correlatives, are mirror images of Shields herself. Wearing a mask or not, under a different name or not, appearing under the first- or the third-person pronoun, with or without a hat, the locutor is always the self, the writer herself, like the little Dutch girl, in infinite regress. Once more, Shields's postmodernism proves to be infused with Romanticism and its penchant for subjectivity and self-revelation. Yet, in a specular, postmodern twist, the writer-cum-little Dutch girl in infinite regress also – in an empathetic, arabesque fashion – reflects back to the reader the vision multiplied, but in receding perspective, of his or her own unfolded self.

NOTES

1 The acronym is short for L'Ouvroir de Littérature Potentielle, or Workshop for
   Potential Literature.
2 The only published English translation of the book, *A Void* by Gilbert Adair,
   stunned English-language critics equally. There are to date two other manuscripts,
   both of them unpublished: *Vanish'd!* by John Lee and *A Vanishing* by Ian Monk.
3 Having deprived himself of one word out of three in the dictionary, Perec went
   on to repeat his feat with *Les Revenentes* (1972), this time banishing the
   vowel *a*.
4 Shields, *Unless*, 269.
5 Ibid., 269, emphases added.
6 Atwood, *The Handmaid's Tale*, 165.
7 Shields, *Dressing Up for the Carnival*, 108.
8 Shields makes a deliberate exception by inserting one occurrence of the preposi-
   tion "with," as if to foreground her choice of restraint and its subtending issues of
   writerly will and power.
9 The substitution of "create" for the expected word "write" is a preparatory component allowing the reader to anticipate the second, macro level of the framing
   lipogram.
10 Hutcheon, *Narcissistic Narrative*, 28.
11 Shields, *Dressing Up for the Carnival*, 178.
12 Woolf, *Essays*, 3: 30.
13 Ibid.
14 Woolf, *The Mark on the Wall*, 13.
15 *Dressing Up for the Carnival*, 171.
16 Woolf, *Essays*, 3: 37.
17 Ricoeur, *Temps et récit*, 139.
18 Ricoeur, *La métaphore vive*, 366.
19 Emerson, *Essays and English Traits*, 138.
20 Schopenhauer, *The World as Will and Idea*, 109.
21 Ibid.
22 Ibid., 109.
23 Ibid., 102.
24 Shelley, *A Defence of Poetry*, 1076.
25 See the works by Barbara Godard, Sharon Wilson, Christl Verduyn, and Marta
   Dvořák listed below.

26 Van Herk, *In Visible Ink*, 102.
27 Shields, *Dressing Up for the Carnival*, 111.

WORKS CITED

Atwood, Margaret. *The Handmaid's Tale*. Toronto: McClelland and Stewart, 1985.

Caillois, Roger. *Les jeux et les hommes, le masque et le vertige*. Paris: Gallimard, 1958.

Dällenbach, Lucien. *Le récit spéculaire: Essai sur la myse en abyme*. Paris: Seuil, 1977.

Dupriez, Bernard. *Gradus, A-Z: A Dictionary of Literary Devices*. Trans. and adapted by Halsall. Toronto: University of Toronto Press, 1991.

Dvořák, Marta. "Metafiction and Ficto-criticism in Canadian Postmodern Writing: The Ultimate Subversions of Genre?" *Essays on Canadian Writing* 84 (Winter 2005).

Emerson, Ralph Waldo. *Essays and English Traits by R.W. Emerson*. Ed. Charles W. Eliot. Harvard Classics. New York: P.F. Collier and Son, 1909.

Godard, Barbara, ed. *Collaboration in the Feminine: Writings on Women and Culture from Tessera*. Toronto: Second Story, 1994.

Huizinga, Johan. *Homo ludens: Essai sur la function sociale du jeu*. Trans. C. Seresia. Paris: Gallimard, 1951.

Hutcheon, Linda. *Narcissistic Narrative: The Metafictional Paradox*. New York: Methuen, 1988.

Jakobson, Roman. *Essais de linguistique générale*. Paris: Editions de minuit, 1963.

Mansfield, Katherine. *Selected Stories*. Ed. D.M. Davin. Oxford: Oxford University Press, 1981.

Perec, Georges. *Georges Perec: Romans et récits*. Éd. établie et présentée par Bernard Magné. Paris: La Pocothèque, 2002.

Ricoeur, Paul. *La métaphore vive*. Paris: Seuil, 1975.

– *Temps et récit*. Vol. 3, *Le temps raconté*. Paris: Seuil, 1985.

Schopenhauer, Arthur. *The World as Will and Idea*. Ed. David Berman. Trans. Jill Berman. London: J.M. Dent, 1997.

Shelley, Percy Bysshe. *A Defence of Poetry*. In *English Romantic Writers*. Ed. David Perkins, 1072–87. New York: Harcourt, Brace and World, 1967.

Shields, Carol. *Dressing Up for the Carnival*. London: Fourth Estate, 2000.

– *Unless*. Toronto: Random House Canada, 2002.

– *Various Miracles*. Toronto: Stoddart, General, 1989.

Van Herk, Aritha. *In Visible Ink: Crypto-fictions*. Edmonton: NeWestPress, 1991.

Verduyn, Christl. "*Murder in the Dark*: Fiction/Theory by Margaret Atwood." *Canadian Fiction Magazine/Tessera* 57 (1998): 124–31.

Wilson, Sharon. "Fiction Flashes: Genre and Intertexts in *Good Bones*." In *Margaret Atwood's Textual Assassinations: Recent Poetry and Fiction*, ed. Sharon Wilson, 18–41. Columbus OH: Ohio State University Press, 2002.

Woolf, Virginia. *The Essays of Virginia Woolf*. Ed. Andrew McNeillie. 6 vols. London: Hogarth, 1986.

– *The Mark on the Wall and Other Short Fiction*. Ed. David Bradshaw. Oxford: Oxford University Press, 2001.

13

Large Ceremonies: The Literary Celebrity of Carol Shields

LORRAINE YORK

An interviewer for the prestigious *Atlantic* magazine, interviewing Carol Shields after her Pulitzer prize win, must have thought she was on fairly safe ground when she asked Shields about her legendary ability to chronicle the "ordinary life." Instead, she quickly found the conversational ground crumbling beneath her: "I don't think I quite believe in the concept [of the ordinary]," Shields insisted. "I don't quite know what the contrary of ordinary people would be. Heroic people? I'm not interested in writing about heroic people or powerful people or rich people or movie stars, although I believe those people probably have quite ordinary moments in their lives."[1] Shields's spirited rebuff no doubt grew out of her frustration with being labelled, once again, the poet of the prosaic, the bard of the banal; as she once rather testily responded to the *National Post*'s Carl Honoré, who also tried this line of questioning with her, "I'm so tired of that description; it's such a cliché, and it can undermine the intelligence behind the work. Who do they think is not ordinary?"[2] What interests me is Carol Shields's canny analysis of the curiously paradoxical, unstable nature of the very categories of "ordinary" and "celebrity": "Either we're all ordinary," as she put it, "or else none of us is ordinary."[3]

I want to ponder exactly these instabilities of celebrity discourse in media representations of Shields herself, that avowedly "ordinary" literary celebrity. There can be little doubt about the applicability of the term "celebrity" to Shields, even though we are little accustomed to applying this label to writers. When she died in July of 2003, she was mourned as a major international literary star. *The Globe and Mail* devoted most of its front page to her passing, as well as three full inside pages. Shields's photograph graced the front page of its Review section, and her publishers placed a full-page memorial tribute to her in the weekend edition's Books section. Clearly, this was the passing of no "ordinary" citizen. And yet a constant thread running through these tributes is their marvelling at how "ordinary" Shields was; as James Adams wrote in the *Globe*'s lead article, about Shields's publishing successes, the translations into many languages, and her many awards, "these extraordinary triumphs, achieved in just the last 10 years of her life, didn't result in an out-of-the-ordinary lifestyle or a radical shift in sensibility."[4]

This sort of commentary was common in media coverage of Shields during those last ten years; much was made of her status as an ordinary-seeming, "fairly conventional woman," and yet there was a major transformation in her professional narrative when *The Stone Diaries* was published: the clichéd "sudden rise to fame" that one often finds in celebrity texts. One would expect to see that transformation mirrored in media representations of Shields's career in newspapers, magazines, and Web sites during those years after 1993. And, in part, it is. When Shields came to Toronto in the winter of 2001 to attend the opening of the musical version of her novel *Larry's Party*, the media hailed her as a visiting celebrity; as Sandra Martin wrote in the *Globe and Mail*, "It was almost as if she were a Hollywood movie star rather than a Canadian writer."[5] But this standard celebrity discourse of the "rise to fame" had by no means eclipsed the earlier discourse about her modest ordinariness. Rather, it was grafted onto the earlier discourse of conventionality, the better to produce that most powerful celebrity paradox: the "ordinary" I'm-just-like-you celebrity.

This hybrid discourse was so pervasive in media texts dealing with Shields during that decade – 1993 to 2003 – that even the rhetoric sounds eerily cloned, recycled. As Andris Taskans, editor of *Prairie Fire*, was quoted in the *Globe and Mail* in 1997, "She's that rare thing – someone who has achieved the pinnacle of fame, at least in this country, but it hasn't gone to her head."[6] Note the double discourse: Shields is both a rarity and like everybody else. In a profile in *Chatelaine* one year earlier, Lesley Hughes employed the very same rhetoric; her article promises to reveal to readers "why even a Pulitzer Prize hasn't gone to her head."[7] In an analysis of this *Chatelaine* profile that highlights the role of gender in literary celebrity, Helen Buss explains that "the sense that a woman writer must also be 'average,' that her achievements must appear incidental, that no amount of fame or money can possibly go to the heads of us wifely grandmothers is absolutely *de rigueur* in the discourse of *Chatelaine*."[8] But it is more than that; it is *de rigueur* in the discourse of celebrity in general.

In the realm of popular culture, this image of the "average" celebrity is so powerful – and lucrative – a cultural commodity that many entertainment stars are hiring public relations handlers who will help to manufacture their "ordinariness." Witness Jennifer Lopez's recent album *This Is Me ... Then*, which *Globe and Mail* journalist Simon Houpt calls "a wholesale attempt to tell her original fans that she's still the girl from the Bronx (just like them!) who just happens to like wearing diamonds."[9] (The relevant lyrics from the song "Jenny from the Block" run: "Don't be fooled by the rocks that I got / I'm still, I'm still Jenny from the Block / Used to have a little, now I got a lot / But no matter where I go I know where I came from.")[10] This is a very powerful message, but it is also unstable and risky. If audiences see this attempt to garner ordinariness as itself contrived, then they feel doubly betrayed; not only is the celebrity *not* like us; she or he is also guilty of the further inauthenticity of attempting to disguise the fact. (As a character on Canada's MUCHMusic television channel, a cynical puppet named Ed the Sock, was heard to respond to J Lo's lyrics, "Whaddya mean 'Jenny from the Block?' It's more like Jenny *owns* the block!") Noted cultural critic Neal Gabler, author of *Life: The Movie: How Entertainment Conquered Reality*, comments on the risks involved in this form of media management: "If J Lo is a complete bitch, if J Lo's not 'Jenny from the Block,' then we won't have any interest in her. She has got to create vicariousness, otherwise we won't buy into the narrative of her life. Almost always, a performer's career tanks when we feel we don't have any connection to them any more, and then we must bring them back to Earth."[11]

The world of Canadian novelists might seem light years away from J Lo and the workings of public relations advisers to the stars, but I argue that the appeal of the ordinary celebrity is transferable to other cultural productions. As an initial, representative example, I will use two one-page magazine profiles of Shields: one that appeared before *The Stone Diaries*, the other after. The first, "A Fairly Unconventional Writer," by Gillian Welsh-Vickar, appeared in *Canadian Author and Bookman* in 1988, just after Shields published *Swann*. The piece draws a portrait of Shields as a relatively minor footnote in the nation's literature, a writer whose sales have been "somewhat uneven." Welsh-Vickar reports that Shields would "like to improve" these figures, but she is "still unsure how to do so." However, this market problem gets transformed into a positive quality by the end of the article; Shields is, according to Welsh-Vickar, unsure as to how to attract a large audience because, in part, she "believes in writing what she feels, and will not be dictated to by trends or markets."[12] So, paradoxically, this lack of success becomes a marker of true devotion to "Art." As Shields later commented to a journalist about these years, "I was writing exactly what I wanted to write, not what would sell ... Writing wasn't a career. It was just what I did."[13] This is exactly the cultural dynamic described by sociologist Pierre Bourdieu in his writings about cultural production. Artists gain access to high art status and respect in the form of "cultural" (rather than economic) capital when they shun the workings of the marketplace and careerism in favour of small(er) production. Mass production, on the other hand, often tends to signal a sellout to the market, less aesthetic seriousness.[14] All in all, this anti-careerism seems an odd position for a trade journal called *Canadian Author and Bookman* to espouse, but, as Bourdieu amply demonstrates, the field of cultural production is replete with ironies and doublethink.

In addition to the dynamics of culture and markets that Bourdieu describes, this piece complicates the negotiations between writer and markets in terms of gender. The article presents small production as particularly well suited to the domestic needs of women who have children; Shields becomes a "busy, amiable woman and mother of five children, who stole moments during their formative years to pursue her writing." The rhetoric is revealing; time to write is "stolen" time, stolen away from those all-important "formative" years that presumably should be the primary focus of a mother's life. The article reinforces this set of priorities by consistently placing Shields's writing career within a private, domestic narrative frame; witness this sentence: "As her family grew and became more independent, she turned to the task of novel writing." I am hard pressed to recall an instance of parenthood setting the agenda for the career narrative of a male author in quite the same way. At one point, Welsh-Vickar asks the old chestnut of a question that has often been put to women writers: "What does her family think of her success?"[15] (Read: have they been neglected for Art?) Basically, then, this brief profile presents Shields as a modest small producer whose low-scale production suits both the demands of high art and her private, domestic priorities as a wife and mother.

By comparison, the second article, Diane Turbide's "A Prairie Pulitzer," in *Maclean's* 1 May 1995 issue, transports us to another universe:
Shields's post-Pulitzer world. Instead of regretful glances at her uneven,
modest sales, we have a full-blown statistics orgy. The senior editor at
Viking Penguin describes plans for second and third printings of *The
Stone Diaries*, totaling 80,000 copies, to make a final sum of 110,000
paperback copies in print. Turbide also reports on the status of various
movie options, not only for *The Stone Diaries* but also for *Swann* and
The Republic of Love. As well, the article makes some major claims for
canonical status, since the Pulitzer now "puts Shields in the company of
such previous literature winners as John Cheever, William Faulkner,
John Updike and last year's laureate, E. Annie Proulx."[16] All of these
items – impressive sales figures, movie rights, canonical comparisons –
are criteria that are frequently assembled to confirm the status of a literary celebrity.

One would expect, therefore, to see a clean break with the media discourses of Shields's "middle seller" past. Instead, there is less evidence
than one might expect of the sort of before-and-after narrative that
celebrity discourse so delights in. (Think, for instance, of those frequent
magazine features that show celebrities inhabiting that mysterious time
before fame, gazing out from high school yearbook photographs.) The
discourse of ordinariness that marked the earlier accounts of Shields
remains; it is just grafted onto, redeployed in the service of, another narrative – the narrative of literary fame. Those features that dominate
Shields's earlier media image – domesticity, family, the quotidian – are
still here; in fact, the article opens with another well-worn celebrity narrative gambit: the testimony of a celebrity's family member. "Anne
Giardini of Kamloops, BC, almost drove into the back of a wood-chip
truck when she heard the news on her car radio last week. An announcer
had just revealed that her mother, Winnipeg-based novelist Carol
Shields, had won the prestigious Pulitzer Prize for her novel, *The Stone
Diaries*."[17] Now, though, this grown child is not part of a backdrop of
five anonymous, needy offspring, as they were in Welsh-Vickar's article,
but a named subject. She is, to use film theorist James Monaco's term, a
"paracelebrity," one who, however briefly, derives celebrity from one's
association with a celebrity.[18] (Think Ivana Trump, think Billy Carter.)
The paracelebrity marks the intersection of those forces in celebrity
power that vie for balance and complementarity within most celebrities:
ordinariness and special status. Since the paracelebrity is only remarkable because of his or her association with a celebrity and not because of

anything she or he has personally achieved, he or she ironically achieves what celebrities can only hope for: to be both ordinary and special, both a celebrity *and* a non-celebrity.

As Helen Buss has observed, magazine profiles of Shields tend to bounce back and forth between these poles of professional accomplishment and details of domestic life[19] (or, as I would say, between celebrity and non-celebrity), and this piece from *Maclean's* is no exception. Still, it is remarkable to see how intertwined the two discourses of professionalism and privacy have become; witness, for instance, the closing paragraph: "Shields's professional accomplishments as a celebrated novelist far outstrip those of her protagonist, Daisy Goodwill. But her domestic life has followed many of the same rituals and marked the same passages of marriage and motherhood ... Carol Shields's superb evocation of those longings has won her the kind of recognition that Daisy Goodwill could only dream of."[20] Celebrity is clearly preferable to obscurity, but celebrity forgets the ordinary at its own peril; ordinariness paradoxically becomes the proving ground for celebrity.

In what I have written so far, it sounds as though I have been very hard on celebrity, seeing it as a repository for all things manufactured, contrived, marked by bad faith. Since that is not the way in which I theoretically approach the phenomenon of celebrity, I want to provide a context for the way in which I understand the celebrity of Carol Shields. My study of Shields from which this paper derives is part of a larger project on literary celebrity in Canada. I acknowledge that this is by no means a recent phenomenon, as some cultural critics such as Neal Gabler or Neil Postman, who are unfailingly suspicious of celebrity and its trappings, might imply; they suggest that everything was fine in cultural production – art works were more sincere, more "authentic," somehow – before the evil, mass-media-driven celebrity machine came along. Such is not my assumption. Lucy Maud Montgomery, Pauline Johnson, Stephen Leacock, Mazo De la Roche: these are four of the most prominent of earlier Canadian literary celebrities, and I find that the tensions and challenges that they found in their celebrity are not necessarily so very different from what writers such as Shields, Atwood, and Ondaatje have faced in our own day of mass-media coverage.

Shields, Atwood, and Ondaatje are, in fact, my three main case studies, and it is remarkable how often their names are linked in roll calls of our national literary celebrities. When a group of Canada's literati met in April of 2002 to honour a by then very ill Carol Shields, the *Globe and Mail* reported that a "large part of the pantheon of Canadian writers,

including Margaret Atwood and Michael Ondaatje, was on hand to read
from Shields's work and recollect their encounters with her."[21] Literary
and other celebrities tend to confirm each other's membership in the
select group; through the power of the list, they hold each other's status
in place. When Shields died, these fellow luminaries resurfaced once again
to reaffirm her celebrity; the *Globe* republished excerpts from a speech
that Ondaatje gave at that April 2002 event, and its lead article noted
that only "Margaret Atwood, Alice Munro and perhaps Michael Ondaatje
matched or exceeded her clout beyond Canada's borders."[22] In my work
on literary celebrity in Canada, I will give an epilogue's closing glance at
the *Globe*'s addition to the celebrity trio, Alice Munro, because hers is
the fascinating case of the celebrity who shuns celebrity. Munro's celebrity is no negation of terms, however; she is all the more powerful a literary celebrity for her shunning of the limelight; you might think of this as
the Greta Garbo effect. As far as my main literary trio is concerned, however, Shields is crucial to my study because she provides the example of a
writer who has experienced the most dramatic celebrity "conversion"
scenario. Atwood and Ondaatje received attention relatively early in
their careers; both, of course, had apprenticeships, but both received
major awards such as Governor General's Awards for early publications.
Shields's celebrity narrative, by contrast, is the story of the lonely, unacknowledged journeywoman of her art, toiling away out of the light of
recognition and support, until one day she receives her "reward" for her
patient toil. As my opening comparison of the two magazine profiles
suggests, however, this conversion narrative is belied by the continuity
and evolution of such discourses about her, leading me to ponder the
curiously adaptable nature of such discourse, the way it winds itself
around available, extant discourses about writers and consumes and
redeploys them.

My theoretical framework is derived from cultural theories of celebrity, theories that have much to contribute to an understanding of how
Shields and others have been constructed as "ordinary" literary celebrities. The tension between the ordinary and the special has been at the
heart of celebrity theory for some decades. Film theorist Richard Dyer,
who wrote the pioneering book on the subject, *Stars*, refers to the
"extreme ambiguity/contradiction ... concerning the stars-as-ordinary
and the stars as special," which he understands in ideological terms.
That is, the fact that stars are often represented as "ordinary" people living extraordinary lives legitimates the assumption that "human attributes exist independently of material circumstances."[23] A more recent

theorist of celebrity, P. David Marshall, takes Dyer's argument further in his book *Celebrity and Power*; for him, the meeting of ordinariness and special status in the figure of the star embodies, in his words, "the ambiguity of the public forms of subjectivity under capitalism," because the supposed ordinariness of the star, who is "distant but attainable," "invokes the message of the possibility of a democratic age." In this way, the star manages the contradictions between the allure of democratic populism and the privilege of social elites. Because of this ambiguity, the power of the celebrity is always unstable; for instance, celebrities are seen both as powerful because people listen to what they have to say, even on topics totally unrelated to the cause of their renown, and as insignificant because they are "viewed in the most antipathetic manner" as representing "success without ... work." They become the vehicles for important debates about, in Marshall's words, "authentic and false cultural value."[24] This is certainly the case in literary production; as much as literary celebrities such as Margaret Atwood command attention and respect (or "clout" in the *Globe and Mail*'s term), they also become targets for challenges to their cultural hegemony, their right to be listened to and taken seriously on a host of issues. Other writers or literary people step up to critique their privileged position in the pantheon of literary greats, thus allowing a valuable discussion about cultural labour and value to take place.

In the case of media representations of Carol Shields, I think that this theoretical argument about stardom's management of ideological contradictions and debates needs to be read in a gendered register. Helen Buss suggests as much when she critiques popular media profiles of Shields. In an article on *Swann*, she draws upon William Epstein's concept of biographical "abduction," a "complex process by which biographers, while seeking to represent their subjects must, by necessity, exclude and/or revise portions of the subject so that she can be 'recognized' by current commodification standards."[25] Buss specifically studies the capacity of biographers and academics in Shields's novel to "abduct" the poet Mary Swann, that is, to bend her narrative to their own ends. She goes on to suggest that Shields herself may have been similarly "abducted" as a woman author. Buss sharply criticizes the continual reversion of magazine accounts of Shields to the details of her domestic, personal life, arguing that this revival of the classic "double bind" runs the "danger of placing the literary accomplishment in the discursive category of hobby or pastime."[26] This is the same complaint that Shields lodged against her habitual labelling as the poet of the prosaic; it "can

undermine the intelligence behind the work." Buss ascribes a great deal
of tactical awareness to Shields, however. Rather than being the victim
of the narrative plots of "erotics" and professional "ambition," Shields
"tactically steers the representation of her subjectivity between the two
in an attempt to avoid abduction by either."[27]

That is an intriguing notion. My own analysis of Shields's media representations as a successful author, however, do not distinguish quite as
neatly between the public, professional celebrity and the private person.
Like Shields, wondering about who is not ordinary, I hardly know
which is which anymore, or, at least, which of these categories – the
ordinary and the public – any of us could ever have some kind of
"authentic" access to. For me, celebrity and domesticity are not necessarily antagonistic, competitive realms; both are actively operating in the
discourse that has constructed "Carol Shields."

Early accounts of Shields, like my opening example of Gillian Welsh-
Vickar's, characterize her as a "small producer," almost a cottage-indus-
try producer of literature. Another of these, a 1982 article in the *Toronto
Star*, is entitled "A Small Audience Suits Author." In that article, Beverly
Slopen notes that Shields "has not yet achieved the wide readership her
fans and publishers expected," and she quotes Shields to the effect that
"I don't feel pushed to have a commercial success."[28] This piece participates in the mixed apology/defence mode of Welsh-Vickar's, in its
attempt to recast Shields's weakness as a strength. But when Shields got
the larger audience that the *Toronto Star* somehow thought she did not
want, a new narrative arose: that of the ordinary person who fell into,
almost tripped over, success. "Ordinary" people, especially when they
are women, cannot be seen to pursue success too avidly. It would be
unseemly somehow. Unfeminine. The *Winnipeg Free Press* did some
interesting editorializing along these lines when it took up a quotation
from an interview it did with Shields, in which she talks about how she
negotiated the life paths she chose, marriage and motherhood along
with writing: "I must have made compromises, but it wasn't conscious.
I just drifted along." In its headline the *Free Press* recontextualizes this
comment, grafting it onto a road-to-celebrity narrative: "You Get
Braver: Novelist, Poet, Prof and Mom Carol Shields 'Just Drifted
Along' to Success."[29] According to this logic, her attaining of success is
not seen as essentially transformative. In the 1986 profile of Shields in
Chatelaine that Helen Buss neatly eviscerates, journalist Lesley Hughes
makes exactly this connection: "It dawns on me that Carol Shields is
utterly unaffected by her success at least in part because it took her so

long."[30] There may be a fair measure of truth in that comment, but still, the narrative of a cottage-producer's "drift" into a success that she did not particularly want enables this production of an authentic, unspoiled literary celebrity.

This narrative of professional drift is not the only one associated with Carol Shields, and with her, as with all star images, we need to be aware that there are multiple narratives in operation simultaneously, not just at discrete moments in any star's career. Running alongside the narrative of the slow drift to success is the story of the tumultuous cataclysmic arrival of celebrity. This story is more than amply represented in media discourses about Shields too. Here is a short list of verbs that describe this arrival of Shields's literary celebrity that I have culled from daily newspapers across Canada and from Web sites devoted to or mentioning her: catapulted, propelled, boosted, put squarely on the literary map, put into an elite circle, soared. This sort of language has been applied to every writer who has won a major prize, of course, and many, like Shields, feel understandably moved to lower the rhetorical register. As she once mused when reading an over-the-top *New York Times* blurb about *The Stone Diaries*, "They're just reaching for phrases."[31]

Domesticity functions for Shields as one means of resisting the over-the-top conversion narrative of success. In the days following her Pulitzer prize win and Booker nomination for *The Stone Diaries*, there were many instances of Shields fending off inquiries about her fame by strategically deploying the details of domestic life. She told the *Winnipeg Free Press*, for instance, that "domestic chores can help calm the excitement. 'Yesterday I vacuumed. I found it just the right thing to do ... Today I ironed.'"[32] The *Vancouver Sun* reported that even a Pulitzer prizewinner still, in Shields's words, "stirs the porridge in the mornings."[33] How much more homely and unglitzy an image could you possibly reach for? Journalists have been eager to follow Shields's lead and have frequently recreated her in the image of the Author as Domestic Goddess, balancing composition with cooking; as Jan Moir of the *Daily Telegraph* mused, "Carol potters around the kitchen chatting with the welcoming disposition of one who might drop everything at any minute to whisk up a batch of hot scones."[34] Carl Honoré of the *National Post*, though he alters the nationality of the cuisine, offers a similar, unsettling observation: "With her grey cardigan and mild manner, you can imagine her slipping on an apron to bake cookies."[35] To linger with food imagery for a moment, when her British publisher phoned to tell her that she had been shortlisted for the Booker, she replied, "We were just about to go out and buy some yogurt." As the *Winnipeg Free Press* rather dazedly reported, "After the call, Shields and her husband simply continued out to buy their yogurt."[36] Shields's comments are disarming tactics, meant to derail the sort of narrative of success that I have just described. In this respect, I entirely agree with Helen Buss that Shields is a skilled rhetorical tactician, a balancer of discourses. The danger in this sort of tactic, however, is that it can be taken up by others, as it has been by journalists Moir and Honoré, and used to confirm gendered stereotypes: the woman writer who is really a homebody at heart and not too unfemininely ambitious.

Shields's self-deprecating references to her personal appearance are other sorts of disarming tactics that betray an ideological double edge. She consistently undercuts her appearance as a literary celebrity, declaring that, in that department, she sells her audiences short at readings and book signings: "I'm too ordinary, middle-aged, no eccentric clothing or wild hair."[37] Shields is drawing here on the stereotypical performance of literary celebrity, the dramatic clothing and hair that have become so recognizable as to be ready objects of parody. Take, for instance, Margaret Atwood's character from *Lady Oracle*, Joan Foster, a literary celebrity who, for a time, plays the role to the hilt. Joan takes account of journalistic treatments of her image very much in the way that I have been analyzing the media construction of Carol Shields, and in those accounts wild hair and clothes are *de rigueur*:

I decided I'd have to do something about my hair. It was evidence, the length and color had been a sort of trademark. Every newspaper clipping, friendly or hostile, had mentioned it, in fact a lot of space had been devoted to it ... *Joan Foster, celebrated author of Lady Oracle, looking like a lush Rossetti portrait, radiating intensity, hypnotized the audience with her unearthly ...* (The Toronto Star). *Prose-poetess Joan Foster looked impressively Junoesque in her flowing red hair and green robe; unfortunately she was largely inaudible ...* (The Globe and Mail).[38]

Not surprisingly, it was Atwood who picked up on media representations of Shields's appearance and concluded that Shields tends not to be taken seriously as a writer of weighty, serious fictions "because she's cute, short and a blond. If she were tall, brunette, with a pointy nose, nobody would have missed it." Ever self-reflexive, the author of *Lady Oracle* continued, "I'm a blend. I'm short, dark and with a pointy nose, so I can swing either way."[39] As Atwood cannily sensed, the woman writer faces a double bind about her personal appearance, personality, and deportment; as Helen Buss explained it, with reference to Shields and Atwood as the polar opposites involved, either a woman writer is seen as setting domesticity above work, as Shields was, so that the value or seriousness of the work is undervalued, or "if a woman is seen as having chosen the ambitious side of the double-bind, she is taken seriously enough to be harassed by critics and reviewers for writing without a female heart. Margaret Atwood is a case in point."[40] Even if the writer herself has given reviewers a head start in making these sorts of assumptions, as Shields has in clearly placing value on her domestic, private life, on the activities of cooking and cleaning, the result is the same: the celebrity success narrative is resisted, but at the price of reinforcing certain stereotypes about women's proper sphere.

To argue a counter-case, Shields's determined injection of this sort of realistic detail into literary celebrity may simply provide evidence of her abiding realism about the working life of a writer. As she once commented, "My kind of writer doesn't get famous. We just get more mail, more phone calls, more requests to do things."[41] There is some truth in this view. And yet I feel as though it is not the entire story. Shields, like Alice Munro, has said on several occasions that when she was growing up, being a writer seemed utterly impossible, out of reach: "I very early formed the notion of being a writer, all the while knowing that this was impossible. Writers were like movie stars. Writers were men."[42] This is a not unreasonable conclusion for a young girl from Oak Park, Illinois, to form; Oak Park was, after all, the first home of Ernest Hemingway, the writer who, more than any other I can think of, became a literary celebrity and, furthermore, a globalized brand name. In my research on literary celebrity, he is one of the few authors who are studied in this regard; Nina M. Ray, for instance, has written about the many ways in which the Hemingway name figures in celebrity endorsement of commercial products, even today, more than forty years after his death.[43] So Shields's disarming comment "My kind of writer doesn't get famous" needs to be read in terms of gender and in terms of the gendered notions of literary celebrity that she absorbed as a young woman growing up in Hemingway land. If the Hemingway myth was the example par excellence of the literary star set before her, then clearly Shields would never have imagined herself qualifying as a tiger-hunting, hairy chested literary logo.

On the surface, Carol Shields would seem to be right in her suspicion that her celebrity does not reach the commercialized heights of the Hemingway myth. After his death, Hemingway's name was invoked to sell liquor, restaurants, cars (his son and granddaughter appeared in

Oldsmobile Bravada endorsements), holiday destinations, and, most ominously, a line of firearms called the Hemingway Double Shotgun (a mar-
keting move of dubious ethics, given the events of 1961 in Ketchum,
Idaho). During his lifetime, Hemingway actually appeared in commercial
advertisements for consumer products such as Ballantine Ale (a no doubt
manly drink), Pan American Airlines (émigré authors could claim expertise here), and the Parker pen (a logical choice, but full of psychoanalytical
implications). Shields, I believe, playfully criticized this logo-land of literary celebrity in the novel that, more than any other, satirized the workings
of literary fame, *Swann*. When she has the rather oily biographer Morton
Jimroy swipe Mary Swann's beloved Parker 51, the implication is clear. In
the Hemingway land of big-time literary celebrity and its endorsements,
women need not apply; the pen is appropriately stolen by a male biographer who suffers Hemingwayesque bouts of alternating self-important
bravado and crippling self-doubt about his masculinity.

For all of Shields's characteristic self-deprecation in the face of global
literary celebrity, I would like to question and complicate her assumption that she inhabits a different realm of literary fame from the likes of
Papa Hemingway. Shields became a celebrity name too, one that wielded
a considerable amount of clout, most obviously in the literary realm but
in others too. In the literary realm, editing has become one way in which
high-profile authors can extend their literary selling power; as *Quill and
Quire* reported a couple of years ago, Vintage Canada's anthology
Dropped Threads, edited by Shields and Marjorie Anderson, featured
"Shields's name prominently on the cover," and she also promoted a
recent novel by Blanche Howard, with whom she previously collabo-
rated on *A Celibate Season*, though *Quill and Quire* notes that Shields's
involvement with that project was more "implicit"; her blurb appears on
the back cover of this novel, *Penelope's Way*, and her name is mentioned
in the publisher's catalogue.[44] Although *Quill and Quire* identifies this
practice of having a high-profile literary celebrity introduce another less-
known work or writer as a recent one, the practice is an old one. As
sociologist Pierre Bourdieu noted, "the fundamental stake in literary
struggles is the monopoly of literary legitimacy, ie, *inter alia*, the monopoly of the power to say with authority who are authorized to call themselves writers ... the consecrated writer is the one who has the power to
consecrate and to win assent when he or she consecrates an author or a
work – with a preface, a favourable review, a prize."[45]

In addition to editing and these other forms of consecration that
Bourdieu mentions, the celebrity author may have, in some instances,

some genuine, tangible power within publishing institutions: the power of determining what gets published. When Shields and Anderson were working together on *Dropped Threads*, Shields approached her publisher, Random House, with the proposition that it take on the anthology under its Vintage paperback imprint. Random House agreed – proof, as *Quill and Quire* put it, that "when a writer is conspicuous enough they can command attention, and get a publishing contract, even as an editor."[46]

To move to the intersection of literary industries with other cultural productions, the power of a celebrity author's trademark name can be quite valuable when a movie producer attempts to raise funds for a film adapted from a novel. As the producer of the film version of Shields's *The Republic of Love* recalled, Shields's winning of the Pulitzer prize certainly made the process of financing the movie easier for him: "When we started we didn't exactly get a thrilled reaction when we'd say it's a love story set in Winnipeg by a Canadian writer ... But now, when we say it's a love story by Carol Shields, people are interested."[47] The celebrity name provides brand recognizability, in the language of advertising; it opens doors because it holds out the promise of a fruitful cross-marketing of a proven literary brand name and a product in another medium.

Like Hemingway, though not to the same extent, Shields's name has also managed to signify in areas that are further removed from the literary than is adaptation filmmaking. For instance, when she was still living in Winnipeg, the "Where Winnipeg" Web site ran a feature in which Shields listed her favourite Winnipeg restaurants, food shops, and bookstores, complete with the addresses and telephone numbers of these establishments.[48] This sort of promotion builds upon a link to the recognizable qualities associated with her name – food, dining, reading, and writing – but the industries deriving benefit from the association with her name are varied. Another cultural industry, in this case Calgary's Glenbow Museum, has also found that the Shields name is powerful cultural capital that can potentially translate into greater economic gain for the museum. In 2002 the Glenbow organized a show called *Face Forward: Six Canadians Face the Millenium*. Organizers asked six Canadian cultural celebrities, all with a tie of some sort to the West, to choose items from the museum's collections and offer their comments on them. As Aida Edemariam commented in the *National Post*, some museums find that mounting blockbuster art shows brings in the bread and butter that they need in order to finance their operations (especially in this time of government cutbacks to museum funding), but others "go for

living, breathing celebrity, as the Glenbow Museum in Calgary has
done." Again, this promotion builds upon a generalized connection
between Shields and the larger realm of "culture," but it also trades upon
specific key concepts that are associated with her works and her celebrity
image; Shields chose articles that represented ideas of home, "privacy,"
and she also chose "a remarkable diary" (a glance, doubtless, at her most
celebrated novel). "The whole exhibit," she notes, "is displayed in a sort
of house-like enclosure."[49]

Sadly, the power to control the uses of Carol Shields's name now
passes into the hands of her family and executors. However varied the
uses of her name were during her lifetime, it is much to Shields's credit
that she used her star power both wisely and generously. As an instance
of that generosity, I offer, in closing, a reminiscence of Carol Shields by
Nino Ricci, a Canadian author who I think has not been particularly
well served by the star-making pressures of the literary world. He recalls
that when he was giving a reading in Winnipeg in 1990, as a fairly
unknown author before the narrative of sudden fame overtook him with
Lives of the Saints, he was scheduled to read the same night as "a writer
much more famous than I was." The other, unnamed star attracted
three hundred listeners; Ricci attracted six. But among them were Sandra Birdsell and Carol Shields. Shields seemed entirely oblivious,
unapologetic about what many would see as an embarrassing situation.
She was there to hear a reading; what else could possibly matter? So
although Ricci says he began the evening feeling mightily sorry for himself, he ended it feeling "sorry for the poor sod across town who hadn't
managed to pull in Birdsell and Shields."[50] I think of Carol Shields sitting there, attentive, rapt, waiting to hear the words of a writer she
thought very fine, let three hundred others make whatever judgment
they wish, and I think that as a literary celebrity she inhabits both those
rooms: the crowded one, packed to the rafters with her many admirers,
the crowded room of literary celebrity, and the almost empty room of
words.

NOTES

1 Bolick, "A Likely Story."
2 Honoré, "The Enormous Pleasure of Making Something."
3 Bolick, "A Likely Story."
4 Adams, "Shields's Talents Gained World Acclaim," A1.

5   Martin, "After the Party," R1.

6   Renzetti, "Convention Becomes Carol Shields."

7   Hughes, "The Shields Diaries," 110.

8   Buss, "Abducting Mary and Carol," 437.

9   Houpt, "Welcome to the Faux Reality Show of the Stars."

10 Lopez, *This Is Me ... Then.*

11 Houpt, "Welcome to the Faux Reality Show of the Stars."

12 Welsh-Vickar, "A Fairly Unconventional Writer."

13 Hughes, "The Shields Diaries," 115.

14 Bourdieu, *The Field of Cultural Production*, 39–40.

15 Welsh-Vickar, "A Fairly Unconventional Writer."

16 Turbide, "A Prairie Pulitzer," 76–7.

17 Ibid., 76.

18 Monaco, *Celebrity*, 4.

19 Buss, "Abducting Mary and Carol," 435–6.

20 Turbide, "A Prairie Pulitzer," 77.

21 Conlogue, "Canada's Gentle 'Literary Lioness.'"

22 Adams, "Shields's Talents Gained World Acclaim," A1.

23 Dyer, *Stars*, 43.

24 Marshall, *Celebrity and Culture*, 4, xi.

25 Buss, "Abducting Mary and Carol," 428.

26 Ibid., 437.

27 Ibid., 436.

28 Slopen, "A Small Audience Suits Author."

29 Quattrin, "'You Get Braver.'"

30 Hughes, "The Shields Diaries," 115.

31 D'Souza, "On Becoming a Writer," 16.

32 Rosborough, "She's One of Ours."

33 Andrews, "Pulitzer Prize Hasn't Changed Carol Shields' Life, She Says," C1.

34 Moir, "Shields Masters Culture Clash."

35 Honoré, "The Enormous Pleasure of Making Something."

36 Lyons, "Shields Takes Nomination in Stride."

37 Forbes, "More Spice than Nice," D2.

38 Atwood, *Lady Oracle*, 9–10.

39 Heer, "Literary Gathering Intended to Be a Celebration of Carol Shields."

40 Buss, "Abducting Mary and Carol," 438.

41 Hughes, "The Shields Diaries," 138.

42 Thomas, "'Writing Must Come Out of What Passionately Interests Us,'" 123.

43 Ray, "The Endorsement Potential Also Rises."

44 Crawley, "High-Profile Writers Pick Up the Red Pen."

45 Bourdieu, *The Field of Cultural Production*, 42.
46 Crawley, "High-Profile Writers Pick Up the Red Pen."
47 Turbide, "The Masculine Maze," 82.
48 "Where Winnipeg."
49 Edemariam, "True West," B11.
50 Ricci, "A Tribute to Carol Shields," 170.

WORKS CITED

Adams, James. "Shields's Talents Gained World Acclaim." *Globe and Mail*, 18 July 2003, A1, A6.

Andrews, Marke. "Pulitzer Prize Hasn't Changed Carol Shields's Life, She Says." *Vancouver Sun*, 20 October 1995, C1, C7.

Atwood, Margaret. *Lady Oracle*. Toronto: McClelland and Stewart – Bantam, 1981.

Bolick,Katie. "A Likely Story." *The Atlantic Online*. www.theatlantic.com/unbound/factfict/ff9901.htm. Accessed 3 April 2003.

Bourdieu, Pierre. *The Field of Cultural Production*. New York: Columbia University Press, 1993.

Buss, Helen. "Abducting Mary and Carol: Reading Carol Shields's *Swann* and the Representation of the Writer through Theories of Biographical Recognition." *English Studies in Canada* 23, no. 4 (1997): 427–41.

Conlogue, Ray. "Canada's Gentle 'Literary Lioness.'" *Globe and Mail*, 8 April 2002, R2.

Crawley, Devin. "High-Profile Writers Pick up the Red Pen." *Quill and Quire* 66, no. 9 (2000): 14.

D'Souza, Irene. "On Becoming a Writer." *Herizons* 15, no. 3 (2002): 15–17.

Dyer, Richard. *Stars*. 2nd ed. London: British Film Institute, 1998.

Edemariam, Aida. "True West." *National Post*, 21 January 2000, B10–11.

Forbes, Leslie. "More Spice than Nice." *Globe and Mail*, 26 February 2000, D2, D3.

Heer, Jeff. "Literary Gathering Intended to be a Celebration of Carol Shields." *National Post*, 5 April 2002, B6.

Honoré, Carl. "The Enormous Pleasure of Making Something." *National Post*, 31 January 2000, D12.

Houpt, Simon. "Welcome to the Faux Reality Show of the Stars." *Globe and Mail*, 15 February 2003, R7.

Hughes, Lesley. "The Shields Diaries." *Chatelaine* 69, no. 4 (1996): 110–15+.

Lopez, Jennifer. *This Is Me ... Then*. Sony EK 86231. 2002.

Lyons, John. "Shields Takes Nomination in Stride." *Winnipeg Free Press*, 25 September 1993, B3.

Marshall, P. David. *Celebrity and Culture: Fame in Contemporary Culture.* Minneapolis: University of Minnesota Press, 2001.

Martin, Sandra. "After the Party." *Globe and Mail*, 15 January 2001, R1, R5.

Moir, Jan. "Shields Masters Culture Clash." *Calgary Herald*, 29 January 2000, E2.

Monaco, James. *Celebrity: The Media as Image Makers.* New York: Delta, 1978.

Quattrin, Linda. "'You Get Braver'." *Winnipeg Free Press*, 29 February 1992, C25.

Ray, Nina M. "The Endorsement Potential Always Rises: The Merchandising of Ernest Hemingway." *Hemingway Review* 13, no. 2 (1994): 74–86.

Renzetti, Elizabeth. "Convention Becomes Carol Shields." *Globe and Mail*, 18 September 1997, D1.

Ricci, Nino. "A Tribute to Carol Shields." *Brick* 69 (2002): 170–5.

Rosborough, Linda. "She's One of Ours." *Winnipeg Free Press*, 23 April 1995, D8.

Slopen, Beverly. "A Small Audience Suits Author." *Toronto Star*, 22 August 1982, C9.

Thomas, Joan. "'Writing Must Come Out of What Passionately Interests Us; Nothing Else Will Do.'" *Prairie Fire* 16, no. 1 (1995): 121–30.

Turbide, Diane. "The Masculine Maze." *Maclean's* 110, no. 39 (1997): 82, 85.

– "A Prairie Pulitzer." *Maclean's* 108, no. 18 (1995): 76–7.

Welsh-Vickar, Gillian. "A Fairly Unconventional Writer." *Canadian Author and Bookman* 63, no. 2 (1988): 7.

"Where Winnipeg" Web site. www.bestmarketing.com/eddisk/celeb.htm. Accessed 30 July 1999.

14

Mischiefs, Misfits, and Miracles

ARITHA VAN HERK

To perform any ficto-critical homage to the work of Carol Shields proposes beginning with an epigraph, a pithy frame, modest rather than
forward, introductory in intent but with the gentle exertion of a raised
eyebrow, an awning hiding a venerable umbrella shop or sheltering two
characters walking arm in arm, enmeshed in a conversation so intense as
to ripple with sedulous waves. The effect of Shields's style and voice, her
fictions generous as gestures and intricate as spiderwebs, is to arouse an
ardour that can only culminate in another story, the *langue d'oïl* of a
glow-worm tale. A gesture of gratitude then, this ficto-critical mischief,
clumsy epitasis to the climax of Shields's oeuvre, mere *estribillo* to the
grace of her collected words, their emphatic refusal to elegize or mourn,
their gentle determination to celebrate – why, life, of course. Life, in all
its messy details, corollary to biography, that tricky hoard of facts. "This
is biography. Nothing matters except for the harvest, the gathering in,
the adding up, the bringing together, the whole story, the way it happens and happens and goes on happening,"[1] says one narrator, miming
Shields's own envoi, too early, leaving too many unwritten stories
bereaved of her incandescent imagination.

So what better epigraph than the enigmatic Dickinson, whose business, like Shields's, was nothing more or less than circumference, the
anatomy of the mundane.

One need not be a Chamber – to be Haunted –
One need not be a House –
The brain has Corridors – surpassing
Material Place –
    Emily Dickinson, "One Need Not Be a Chamber"

Dickinson's recognition of haunting's domesticity gestures towards Derrida's spectres but shuns mourning and melancholia. Shields's characters, too, follow and enunciate corridors that seem utterly quotidian, but perform a delicate minuet of post-mortal transcendence, haunted by the small details of meaning, or perforce the meaning of small details. These invigorated domestic components are freed, then, from their function, which shifts the reader's attention toward the inescapably seductive aspects of the quotidian, the commonplace made comely. But even that "material place" paves an insufficient path to walk up to the door of Carol Shields's ineffable ability to make stories mean more than they might.

Narrative is, according to Louis Mink, a way of knowing. Certain patterns of experience do not lend themselves to arrangement in logical categories or generalizations; they can only be apprehended as parts of a story, a story more than often surprising in its shifts or paralysis. These unpredictable patterns are the misfits of my title, what less adroit writers than Carol Shields might consider misfits, but which in Shields's case gesture toward ineluctable miracles, themselves mischiefs in a world that reads miracles as recusant. Bachelard weighs in by proposing the oxymoron of "intimate immensity,"[2] which is so germane to Shields, her observance of unconfined details betrothed to larger matters of grief and celebration. And ultimately, the question of "worthless secrets,"[3] the oblique, accidental, and ironic economies that sieve experience so that it is different for every woman and man, despite facts and actualities, stubborn and undeniable concretions.

Roland Barthes in "The Death of the Author" maintains that texts are reinscribed on readers during the reading process. He writes that "a text's unity lies not in its origin but in its destination ... [the reader] someone who holds together in a single field all the traces by which the written text is constituted."[4] And this summing-up, a travel metaphor for readers, suggests a way to absorb the curving route of Shields's own journey, her intense intimacy with the smallest and least of words, which take on incantatory power, "spell and counter-spell," and resonate with "expanded meaning":[5] "Milk bread beer ice. Ice bread milk beer. This marks the real death of words, thinks Barbara, these homely products reduced to husks, their true sense drained purely away. Ice beer bread milk. Rumblings in the throats, syllables strung on an old clothesline, electronic buzzing" (199). Syllables strung on an old clothesline. But meaning beyond "the submerged pattern of communication" (199), a whole new set of elements. Carol Shields invents her own reader, proposes a reader who must be able to play with coincidence and carnival, a reader who will be particular with the accidental glories of blisterlilies and clothespins, hyphens and radishes. And as a reading writer who must bargain with an invented but certainly extra-ordinary reader of Carol Shields, I have been introduced to Grit Savon.

Her name is Grit Savon, this reader of Carol Shields's writing. Grit deploys her name with fierce definition, and no, she repeats, innumerable times, "Grit is not short for Gertrude," while she will admit that Savon is indeed related to soap, that perfectly utilitarian, perfectly useful substance that froths water to clean clothes. Grit Savon is aware of the many contestations that take place within her acutely ordinary, even mundane days, the unvarying rasp of habits of being that are so unoriginally present in her life that she fails to notice them, fails to pay them the proper attention and homage, until they – and here is her prize for hesitation – suddenly shift and an oblique moment, peripheral and ghostly, stops her breath. This sudden epiphany (she names it unselfconsciously, without irony), this brief interval – which throbs just long enough to make her aware of the pure, shallow contingency of oxygen, the calm bellows of her lungs, with their pink tributaries of veins keeping the body working, refreshing itself, a cleansing – occurs most often when Grit Savon reads Carol Shields. In fact – and it is surely facts that Carol Shields's readers seek to embrace and evade – Grit hunts through Carol Shields's writing looking for practical advice. How to get a wine stain out of a damask tablecloth. One of Shields's characters is certain to know this useful trick and will convey it to Grit, she is certain, if she reads carefully enough.

Grit finds plenty of substance in her reading. She meets characters fearful of aging, but happy in their discomfort. They can visualize "the substance and colour" of pain, transfer that pain "to a point outside the body,"[6] but fail to ignore it completely, and live thus with a contented pragmatism. Grit knows only too well that "there are certain necessary tasks that coarsen the quality of everyday life" (4). How to navigate those necessary tasks preoccupies her rather more than it ought to. Perhaps that is the legacy of her name, its indisputable liaison with dirt. Transcending the ordinary is the task and the not-task, Grit believes, that Shields's fiction gets done, now at a time spectrally preoccupied with authenticity, with age and history and the provenance of objects that used to be innocent, merely useful. So that "biological classification, its authenticity" (5), is too relevant, too overbearing, an archive breathing down our necks and demanding answers to and definitions for the questions raised by symbol and reality, analysis and test results.

As a pragmatic reader, Grit sniffs out how impossible it is for contemporary writing to escape the dread complexities of irony, double entendre, the tense wheel of meaning and its imbrications, artistic merit's heavy hand. Even language is doubtful, not to be trusted. And Grit prefers her fictions to be trustworthy accidents, forgivably plausible and satisfying for that reason. She has this discussion about fiction's aims and results with her sister, who reads and rereads Munro's *Love of a Good Woman*, looking for answers to both love and goodness and frustrated that she finds neither. "You're in the wrong book," says Grit. "I'll give you *Dressing Up for the Carnival* when it comes out in paperback." She's unashamedly pragmatic.

So, what exactly, for this slightly abrasive reader, is the shared and attractive element of appeal in Carol Shields's characters? Were she to be asked that question in exactly the right tone, Grit would propose, not lightly but with serious intent, that they are all patrons of a laundromat. Not a cheap, rather smelly place where the machines are never disinfected, but an imaginary laundromat that encompasses both literary and literal laundromats, a warm room painted bronze and surrounded with banks of stainless steel machines, their vibration suggesting that they will live up to their expected mechanical precision in the cleansing of clothing, that cotton underwear will not emerge tattered and shapeless, but glossy with renewal, that it will emit that shine of having just been unpackaged. In fact, this imaginary site might be Heather Hotchkiss's laundry, she who is the owner/manager of a laundromat in Montreal's Les Ormes de Bois, she who "finds after the long working day, Mondays in particular, that there is nothing so soothing, so cheering, as the chopping, stirring, seasoning, and tasting that are part of the art of soup making."[7] Soup du jour and laundry, that is what Grit reads for.

And Grit Savon always and inevitably discovers, neatly tucked between the pages and the paragraphs and the words that crowd Carol Shields's books, references to her favourite preoccupation, laundry. Grit is unsurprised at the substantive experience that Mary Swann converted into art. "Chickens, outhouses, wash-day, woodpiles, porch, husband, work-boots, overalls, bedstead, filth. That's the stuff this woman had to work with,"[8] declares Sarah Maloney, but it's "wash-day" that Grit zeroes in on. She knows the transfigurative power of a line of drying clothes, despite the labour of hauling water and heating water and scrubbing and rinsing and the weary cast of arms having pinned a week's worth of heavy sheets to a line.

And even when this work is not explicit, Grit Savon will decipher laundry. She knows, for example, that Mr Scribano – that's Rita Winters's publisher in *Unless* – is secretly delighted by the large wicker hamper hunched in a corner of his and his wife's ensuite. This laundry hamper resembles a hope chest, but with an open weave, airy, even deliberately innocent, unvarnished. Raw wicker conveys that effect, and for all his age and dignity, Mr Scribano lifts the hinged lid and tosses in his socks and boxer shorts with a boyishly underhanded pitch, a basket he's made, and feels the same "incalculable reward of self-possession"[9] that Frances knew after throwing twenty-seven perfect free-throw baskets in the dewy dawn. And Mr Scribano fails to be surprised, every two or three days, when the laundry basket is nakedly empty, inviting as a newly dug flower bed or an open window. This Grit is certain of, although neither "A Scarf" nor *Unless* declares that bald taking for granted, that masculine expectation that laundry will vanish and reappear.

Grit feels utterly vindicated when she reads that "the night [her husband] died Hazel came home from the hospital and sat propped up in bed till four in the morning, reading a trashy, fast-moving New York novel about wives who lived in spacious duplexes overlooking Central Park, too alienated to carry on properly with their lives. They made salads with rare kinds of lettuce and sent their apparel to the dry cleaners, but they were bitter and helpless."[10] This gesture of repudiation is exactly right, Grit knows, and the detail about bitter women sending everything, even socks and pantyhose, to the dry cleaners resonates with deliciously unwholesome pathos. That Hazel finds happiness wearing a white smock, "which is a smooth permapress blend with grommets down the front and Kitchen Kult in red script across the pocket" (41), surprises Grit not at all. The grommets are powerfully convincing, although Grit does wonder what happens to the company smock between Hazel's demonstrations? Does it go away with Peter Lemmon, who helps Hazel to set up every day? Or does she take it home and put it through the easy-care cycle? No, Grit reads with relish, "By five-thirty

[Hazel] was too tired to do anything more than drive home, make a sandwich, read the paper, rinse out her Kitchen Kult smock and hang it over the shower rail, then get into bed with a thick paperback" (45). Grit rereads this sentence several times; she has an inkling that Hazel will begin to love rinsing out her smock (51), and when she comes to the part where Hazel realizes that "this was what other people did [an actual job], tucking in around the edges those little routines – laundry, meals, errands – that had made up her whole existence" (47), Grit literally laughs aloud. Everything, she believes, is accidentally predestined, and accidents can be arranged or pre-arranged with less than benign intent.

When she gets to "Block Out," Grit is jubilant. Meershank and Maybelle visit Porto and are insulted by how the city is underrated by the *Michelin Guide* telling them to pay attention to the "gaily colored laundry flapping overhead." Maybelle's outrage dances off the page.

"Laundry! I ask you. Never mind this incredible architecture all around us, we're asked to gape at mended tablecloths and old underpants."

Meershank looked upward. Was it the word underpants that caught his attention? Or Maybelle's brightly injured North American scorn, her admirable readiness to admire, and to deplore the kingly judgments of rubber tire merchants. So what does this uncultivated bunch know from anything? Back in Canada, she told Meershank, the least of these little Portuguese churches would have caused a major fussing over. A plastic dome built to protect the gold leaf and blue tiles. Tickets sold, conducted tours given, voices hushed toward a proper reverence. But here amid the riches of Portugal, tourists were asked to gaze at laundry! The condescension, the perversity! And what did the owners of the laundry have to say about it? Were they consulted about their contribution to the city's ambience? Adjured in the name of folklore to keep their colorful laundry flying? Don't you bet your sweet heart on it.

Socks, sheets, aprons, brassieres. Meershank took them in, groping for a portion of his wife's contempt. He respected cleanliness, that was the problem. He liked the thought of clothes whipped by soapy water and then bright air. Work pants, blankets – and were those diapers? Ah, diapers, yes, half a dozen in a neat row, holding hands as it were. Seeing them he felt, finally, a throat swell – wah! – of delectable sentiment.[11]

See? Grit would like to pluck a fellow reader's sleeve, there on the Light Rapid Transit train, the grey city speeding by the windows, and say, "See! What have I been saying all along? Everything is related to laundry!" Not a sophisticated reader-response theory, but sufficient for Grit.

Grit knows, for example, what Gwen in "A Scarf" does not know –
that her navel/novel smells off because of her desperate avoidance of a
beginning, a middle, and an end, and that avoidance is a reaction on
Gwen's part to the precise structure of her mother's Monday washday.
This chore comprised the material of necessity rather than liturgy. If
Gwen would only remember how her mother had to start at four in the
morning to heat water, then put the clothes to soak, and then proceed
through an arduous week of soil, white sheets and shirts and underwear,
then towels, then coloureds, and then the dark of workpants and jeans
and thick-knitted socks, until at the end of the day the water in the
wringer tub was grey and scummy, almost syrupy with the detritus of
skin and wear, the actual trace of dirt, real dirt, soil, not the vague pollu-
tion of air and body, but the earth, manure, even blood marking the
overalls that Gwen's father wore. Dark blue, the bib riding up over his
chest. On the line, they seemed from a distance to resemble doll cut-
outs, but without arms, fronting invisible bodies waiting to pull them
toward shape as if there were no boundary between body and elements.
Those stiffened overalls, which wore unevenly, addressed Gwen's
father's work with absolute attention, fading from blue to paler blue to
almost white in the seat and the knees, the thighs a colourless leaking
upwards too, like a tide rimming over a beach. Poor Gwen. Grit would
like to comfort her, suggest a cold rinse.

Or steer her toward Cheryl Spence, the regular at the Harbour
Heights Laundromat, who is cheerful and pragmatic rather than tor-
tured about laundry. She is the one who dumps "in her blouses, her full
cotton skirts and sundresses, her socks and underwear, her pillowcase
and duvet cover" all at one time, knowing that they need not be sorted
into a beginning, a middle, and an end, but can survive the intimacy of
washing if she is orderly and careful. "She turns all these items inside out
when she launders them, giving them a hard shake as her mother had
done, as her grandmother once did, and then she examines the pockets
for stray tissues and paper clips. Buttons are buttoned and zippers
zipped. She checks the temperature setting, measures the detergent in
the little Styrofoam cup provided by the management."[12] Cheryl is the
character who always has extra change, who is not modest about sharing
her hoard of quarters with the other patrons, and who knows when it is
time to throw "the unsorted detritus of economy and mystery" away
(98). Cheryl, Grit is convinced, would be good medicine for Gwen's
heartache, Cheryl who finds the key to life in the echoing drum of a
laundromat dryer.

Not that Grit believes that laundry is always a beacon of hope. She knows damn well why Dick Wentworth's wife, yes, that "R.S. Wentworth, teacher/scholar/critic,"[13] he of the ilkish references who wears nevertheless a "boyishly courageous" (57) blue and red tie – Grit knows *why* Dick Wentworth's "wife hanged herself. From a water pipe. In the basement of their house. In Ithaca, New York" (57). Grit wants to shout this detail aloud to Lucy Porter, who seems oblivious to Ilk's relationship to kill, such an easy confusion, and dangerous. Grit is convinced that Dick Wentworth's wife hanged herself from the pipes in the basement because of the laundry. The laundry, yes, the damn laundry, piling up in muffled and ill-kempt heaps, endlessly repetitious, the loose arms of shirts flapping limply rather than offering embrace. This woman had to steel herself to face washday, the long and awful repetition of its tedium, but the basement is what ultimately did her in, the twilight of the house's lower floor, the tomb of foundation emitting the perpetual grey chill of concrete. Dick Wentworth's wife read that underground floor as being possessed of a dread, prison-like contagion despite their having "finished" the basement – at least most of it, good Berber covering the floor and the walls plastered and painted, lined with pine shelves on which they've stacked books, although not in alphabetical order, simply arranged by the inconvenient overflow of volumes from the shelves upstairs. But the laundry room is utterly bleak, was worse than bleak to Dick's wife, the washer and dryer relegated to a corner, where they crouched malevolently on a dank patch of concrete, white enamel but gritty rather than gleaming, their lids and doors gaping and final, as if to underline her inadequacy. She might have been Dick Wentworth's wife, but she felt worthless. The laundry, piles of damp towels, twisted sheets, ended up heaped and scattered over the floor, tawdry somehow, reeking of neglect; for she never quite finished before she fled the basement for the upstairs, emerging from the stairwell panting with a heart-hammering claustrophobia. She caught herself looking upward after she had sorted and tossed a load of darks into the tub – up to the pipes that ran across the unfinished ceiling, below the floor above, a mysterious criss-cross of the house's veins and arteries. Ithaca, New York, outside the front door, but Dick's wife's basement was a prison, a horrifically unfinished story, and not full of "infinite possibilities" at all (59).

Why, wonders Grit, can't laundry rooms be sunny, upstairs on the same level as the bedrooms, so that the linens don't have to be bundled into heaps and lugged up and down endless steps? When did they become a metaphor, those sheets transforming themselves to grotesquely knotted methods of escape? She cannot be sure of the answer, but it is only too easy for Dick's vanished wife – and Grit shakes her head knowingly – to leave a note with the single word love, or kill, written in shaky letters, and to tug the solid terry cloth belt of her bathrobe from its loops, to knot it carefully, fingers against the knot of her own throat, and then to stand on a stool and snag the other end over the very solid water pipe that lurks ominously above this allotted space where she was supposed to dissolve the dirt of Ithaca, New York, and make clothes fresh and sparkling clean, as if "the narrational heart" (59) were always happy. Impossible, of course. Grit knows this. No matter how many warnings a reader might utter.

Grit gains more satisfaction from Elizabeth – Elizabeth who, prepared to die for love, pulls the plastic dry cleaner's bag over her face, the "bag that only yesterday enclosed a heavy grey overcoat, her husband's, and was carried home by Elizabeth herself from the dry cleaner's in a nearby shopping mall and put away in a cedar chest until next winter"[14] That dry cleaner's, where Elizabeth has been taking overcoats and dress pants and her husband's silk ties for years, is run by a family of would-be circus clowns who know the terrible dimensions of dry-cleaning chemicals, but know also that somebody's got to do the job, despite how troublesome those fumes are, day after day scorching tender nostril hairs and even, so the mother, coincidentally named Liz, has noticed, seeming to sear the very hairs from her skin, so that her arms have a pale and ghostly sheen, like the face of a man who has just shaved off a five years' beard. Too white, that's what those chemicals do, bleach everything down by a layer so that the skin tingles with nakedness. But someone must turn the knobs of the big industrial machines, pull out the clothes after their cleansing tumble, and align them on the wire hangers of conscience, such dreadfully unaesthetic triangles, those wire hangers, at the best places adorned with a clerical collar of cardboard, as if to stiffen the resolve of the dry-cleaned clothing.

The presser hisses and sets down on the creased fronts of dress pants with a heavy hand, the collar shaper imagines a neck inside every shirt, some smooth and strong, some weathered by those fine rivulets that trouble the middle-aged, flesh softened and trembling with knowledge. Why do collars even exist, Liz wonders, her hands shaping with practised ease the points of this artful address on virtually every shirt. Even collarless shirts have collars, just rounded rather than the folded envelope of emulated wings – and in her life, were Liz to do the math, she has laundered and hung something like two hundred thousand shirts in the twenty years that she has been running Glade's Dry Cleaner's. They get an average of thirty shirts a day, and subtracting fifty-two days because they still, with tender and old-fashioned habit, close on Sundays, that makes for nine thousand, three hundred, and ninety shirts each year, multiplied by twenty, which comes to one hundred and eighty-seven thousand, eight hundred shirts – might as well be rounded up to two hundred thousand, a number that has worn itself into the nubs of Liz's fingers, all those collars and twice as many cuffs. Yet she has never lost that pleasing second of pride when she twist-ties – always a white tag – three or four dress shirts on their hangers together and snaps a clingy plastic film over their squared shoulders, their severely placketed chests. "Clean," she wants to say. "Clean!" And Grit feels like cheering.

And like Grit, Liz would be horrified beyond measure to imagine Elizabeth lying on her bed with one of Liz's bags drawn up over her face, as if to warm her skin with her own breath. Liz knows that the bags are dangerous for children, has thousands of times said, "Please don't let your children play with these bags," had had printed on the clear plastic in dense red characters, "Keep away from children!" But she has not imagined an adult sucking that plastic wrap against her mouth, testing immortality, and all because of the crepey skin of Elizabeth's neck and how she has shaken hands with the knowledge that she has lost "the power to stir ardour" (49). Love is not so easy to furnish as a neatly turned collar, and while Elizabeth plans to rely on comfort and ritual, she ought not to discount her attractiveness completely.

Grit knows that if Elizabeth only knew the extent to which she does inspire ardour, she would be astonished. For at the flower shop next door to the dry cleaner's, that moist, earthy greenhouse of fragrance and ferns, works a young woman – Eileen, her name is, in homage to a distant Irish aunt. Eileen's breath catches every time Elizabeth pushes through the door, which she does at least once a week, a woman who does not need to hoard the occasional luxury of cut flowers, but who can buy them often. She steps into the shop almost shyly, still uneasy with this permission she has taken, fresh flowers are not only for special occasions, they can become a habit as necessary as dry cleaning itself, a "handrail" (51) of narrative for her errands, and Eileen looks up when the bell tinkles and Elizabeth's beige raincoat drifts inside. Eileen looks up and has to stop herself from flinging her arms wide in a most inappropriate greeting. Instead, she takes refuge in her stock, delphiniums and shasta daisies, suggests tea roses and birds of paradise, those violently spiked parrot-headed flowers exorbitant as plastic. At first, Elizabeth bought modest bundles, Spring Mix or Blooming Specials, $14.95, and mostly carnations, those marathon flowers that travel so far so well, but Eileen has taken to ordering exotic blooms just for Elizabeth, and together in the bunched and jungly glassed-in cooler, she points them out, saying, "Look at these phlox, and these lily-of-the-valley, they're delicate as bells." "The white of your wrists," she is reciting silently, "the extraordinary periwinkle of your eyes. Please look at me." But Elizabeth regards the flowers, bends toward them shyly, as if making their acquaintance, and it is all Eileen can do not to bend toward Elizabeth at the same time and brush her pear-skinned cheek with her fingertips.

Elizabeth is wasted on her mercilessly oblivious husband. Eileen has made a point of discovering his identity. He comes in occasionally, brushing carelessly against the plants with his heavy grey overcoat and pointing, without thought, to a bunch of roses, virulently dyed roses with defensive thorns, orange or pink, although once Eileen persuaded him to choose petals so thickly creamy that they shaded toward the vaguest hint of green, and he grunted, "All right," with such impatience that Eileen added her own little card for Elizabeth, saying, "We've missed you. Hope to see you soon." Ah, if Elizabeth could only see how she is adored, could be stroked and kissed with the tenderest hands, hands that wouldn't bruise a petal.

This Grit has read, and reads.

Just as she reads that next door to the flower shop, the cash and counter girl at the dry-cleaning establishment, whose name is Salsa, receives the heaps of clothing that people dump on her counter, and after counting the items and passing the always-hurried customer (it must be the chemical smell that makes people rush) a receipt, she takes their clothes into the back to be tagged. There she sorts them and searches through their pockets. Pockets, what brilliant contrivances they are, changes of character, that double sack of cloth within cloth, a handy envelope for hands or coins, scraps of paper or neat sticks of gum, kleenex, lint, condoms, tampax, pens, keys, yes, keys.[15] Salsa discovers the strangest items in pockets, pure madness. Forgotten bills, of course, money – fives and tens – astonishing how people who have enough so readily forget the value of ten dollars. What a prize it is, and Salsa, if Liz is not looking, will occasionally pocket this windfall herself, sliding the usually softened bill into her own wondrous cloth envelope of saving, where it emits a patch of heat the whole day. If Liz happens to be watching, she exclaims loudly and passes the money to her along with the customer's name, and Liz, being scrupulous Liz, puts it in an envelope and presents it to the customer with a sardonic gesture, as though they are accomplices in forgetfulness. Her honesty ensures her customers' loyalty; she knows well the value of that currency.

But Salsa, well, just as Grit suspects, Salsa is less invested. She works at the dry cleaner's as a stop gap, and her rifling of pockets is protection against outrageous material in the machines, ballpoint pens that scrawl across white clothes, wrapped mints, kleenex made durable by use, nail clippers. Salsa has found a computer diskette in a back pocket, and even once the remains of a slice of what must have been cake wrapped in a paper napkin. How pathetic, she thinks, to put cake in your pocket, a piece of solid yellow pound cake, and then to forget it. Lipstick she finds too, or lip balm, and business cards and various torn scraps of paper with phone numbers. These she tucks into a small wooden box that she keeps under the cash register. Why? Have they not been forgotten, neglected, relegated to the vague promise of "Call me sometime"? George, 238–7771. A lucky number, thinks Salsa, but George may still be waiting for a call. Or "Tuesday, Geneva," in pencil on the back of a folded-over Post-it note. Does the note refer to a person or the Swiss city? Such enigmatic threads of connection in the many pockets that she checks. The strips of cheer that break from the crisp moons of Chinese fortune cookies. She can imagine people tucking their oracular suggestions away. "You are doomed to a happy marriage," one of them reads, and Salsa chuckles. Is that a curse or a blessing, that shaded conundrum, that unexpected "aptitude for monogamy"[16] that the owner must wonder at possessing.

And there is the handkerchief man, tall, with almost Slavic brown eyes tilted so that he looks slightly dangerous, although he is neat rather than untrustworthy. He brings in his chinos – pants that are not quite dress pants, closer to casual, cotton and polyester blend rather than wool. He obviously wants them pressed and his wife will not iron, or she doesn't do the job right, or he has no wife. Salsa has checked his hand and it's ringless, bare, a clean, square hand without the roughened glaze of labour, no thick knuckles or uneven nails. But in the front left-hand pocket of his pants he always leaves a handkerchief. Salsa has found over time dozens of handkerchiefs – white, monographed, linen, edge-stitched – but his are red-checkered working man's handkerchiefs, the kind she remembers her father carrying, which he would haul from his pocket crumpled and stuck together, a truly vernacular snot-rag. But this man's handkerchiefs, despite being the working variety, are perfectly clean, folded twice, as neat and comforting as birds' nests. And

Salsa imagines him tucking a handkerchief into that pocket as a talisman to hope, so that when it is needed, in case of tears or sticky hands or a dusty park bench, he produces – voila! – that handkerchief, not so white and dazzling that a woman would hesitate to wipe her eyes, but indisputably clean, marvellously comforting, smelling faintly of lemon grass.

These are the mysteries that Grit has read between the covers of books by Carol Shields, mysteries that unfold inside places like Glade's Dry Cleaners, where people drop more than soiled and crumpled clothes – the clothes, yes, but also the suspended particles of what they did wearing those clothes, happy or not, dancing or walking or flying, leaving them sad and marked, but picking them up again three days later, their sheen restored under those deadly plastic wraps, the laundry of life sanitized to erasure. Grit sighs with satisfaction over that completion and resolves to write a letter to Carol Shields, to tell her what reading she incites, and just as a sideline, to let Rita know that you wash those French scarves by hand, with Lux, a dip and a swish, no rubbing allowed, only the tenderest squeeze before the square of ardent cloth is spread carefully over a flat surface and left to dry itself toward an almost stiff page before, with the touch of a cool iron, it is restored to softness.

Such treasure, that fragrant word, dispersed between the pages of a Shieldsian story. Grit looks for its quintessential temptations, its inventive elegance, its deflection from the expected, characters over and over again stricken by minutiae, nothing important, but still blessed with miraculous and subtle knowing, joy or grief small but large. And always that gesture of protection, of succour and quick defence, a gentle averting of the face to spare the object of the gaze embarrassment, these women tender in their expectations, satisfied with a scarf or a good eye cream, the layer of foam at the top of an exquisitely balanced cup of coffee. Nothing outrageously *Sturm und Drang* here, extravagance laughably excessive, too hyperbolic a gesture to be ordained as worthy of the subtle grace inflected by the gesture of a wrist, the knot of tension visible in a throat playing a recorder. And Carol Shields, with the same outrageous courtesy and quiet, has died.

But Grit, grieving, will keep reading the words of Carol Shields because she no longer wishes to fall victim to an escalating fiction that promotes exaggeration, the wild surmise behind every character's glance certain to reveal a Dickensian childhood, an absconded parent, an abusive guardian, exorbitance in feeling and fondness, a spending frenzy of intemperance in motivation and its revenge. Grit is fed up with fiction that anatomizes the inordinate, the overpriced, the violently bloody.

Families are often fusty in their domestic ritual, generous and accommodating beneath the smell of mothballs. Families may be swamps of disfunction, rage, repressed abuse, a certain and inevitable horripilation needing to be revealed, wallpapered over with small moments of backyard contentment, a dash through the lawn sprinkler, an eruption of tulips along the wall of the white clapboard. Those happy gestures are surely tricks, deceptions, adamantly wrong. But as full of light as a glass of fresh orange juice.

Grit cherishes Shields's stories, where ill-mannered extremes are graciously ignored. Not avoided, oh no. The outrageous exists in moments hyperbolized by their very miniaturism, their intimacy. It is, of course, there that real revolutions occur. Grit shares with Shields the conviction that in the details of domesticity the extraordinary resides. True "lumber" is, yes, that little hallway between the bedroom and the bathroom, that rung of the kitchen chair where you tuck your feet while reading the paper and licking the foam from a cup of half-warm coffee, that blue light that filters through the window when, late at night, you stand drinking a glass of water at the sink, with time to wonder why the light is so translucent.

"It is not the rise and fall of empires, the birth and death of kings, or the marching of armies that move [the affections] most. When they answer from their depths, it is to the domestic joys and tragedies of life."[17] But these are writers forgotten, swept away by the textation of war and peace, and the trap of how we have been taught to read the sweeps of power and privilege as the truly heroic narrative. Damn all heroes with all their thousand faces, and let us now regard the extraordinary and continuously larger moment of a woman of indeterminate age, making her way from home to market and then onwards to a PTA meeting, with a quick stop at the dry cleaner's and a reminder to herself to rinse out her half-slip and to toss the wash in the dryer, to iron her newly washed silk scarf to softness.

NOTES

1 Shields, *The Orange Fish*, 130.
2 Bachelard, *Poetics of Space*, 182.
3 Shields, *The Orange Fish*, 169.
4 Barthes, "Death of the Author," 156–7.
5 Shields, *The Orange Fish*, 199.

6 Ibid, 2.
7 Shields, *Dressing Up for the Carnival*, 160.
8 Shields, *Swann*, 31.
9 Shields, *Various Miracles*, 87.
10 Shields, *The Orange Fish*, 35.
11 Ibid., 91–2.
12 Shields, *Dressing up for the Carnival*, 96.
13 Ibid., 54.
14 Ibid., 50.
15 See Shields, "Keys," in *Dressing up for the Carnival*.
16 Shields, *Various Miracles*, 89.
17 Barr, *Jan Vedder's Wife*.

WORKS CITED

Bachelard, Gaston. *The Poetics of Space.* Boston: Beacon, 1969.

Barr, Amelia E. *Jan Vedder's Wife.* New York: Dodd, Mead & Co., 1885.

Barthes, Roland. "The Death of the Author." In *Twentieth Century Literary Theory*, ed. K.M. Newton, 156–7. London: Macmillan, 1988.

Dickinson, Emily. *The Poems of Emily Dickinson.* Ed. R.W. Franklin. Cambridge, MA: Belknap, 1999.

Mink, Louis O. "Historical Understanding." In *History and Theory: Contemporary Readings*, ed. Brian Fay, Philip Pomper, and Richard T. Vann. Malden, MA: Blackwell, 1998.

Shields, Carol. *Dressing Up for the Carnival.* Toronto: Random House Canada, 2000.

– *The Orange Fish.* Toronto: Random House Canada, 1989.

– *Swann: A Mystery.* Don Mills: Stoddart, 1987.

– *Unless.* Toronto: Random House Canada, 2002.

– *Various Miracles.* Don Mills: Stoddart, 1985.

Index

Adair, Gilbert, 235n2
Adams, James, 239
Adorno, T.W., 62
Alcibiades, 215–16, 219n15
Alger, Horatio, 20
The Ambassadors, 210
Amiel, Barbara, 4
Amos and Andy, 21
Andersen, Hans Christian, 107
Anderson, Marjorie, 60, 69–70, 250, 251
Anne of Green Gables, 20–1
Arasse, Daniel, 158
Archer, Bert, 76n22
Aristotle, 210
Atwood, Margaret: *The Blind Assassin*, 131; and celebrity, 243–4, 245, 248–9; as essayist in N*egotiating with the Dead*, 67; *The Handmaid's Tale*, 112–13, 225; and modernism, 224; myth of Isis and Osiris in "Isis in Darkness," 205; and theoretical fiction, 234; as woman writer, 27
Austen, Jane: the quotidian in the works of, 112; romance

in the works of, 99, 100, 103, 109, 110; Shields's biography of, 59, 71–3, 74; as woman writer, 22
Autobiography of Red, 205

Bachelard, Gaston, 128, 160, 165, 257
Backscheider, Paula, 116, 118
Bacon, Sir Francis, 62–4, 66, 68–9, 70–1, 75
Bakhtin, Mikhail, 5, 11, 154–5n12, 174, 176
Barthes, Roland, 146–7, 159, 186n19, 209–10, 257
Bataille, Georges, 10, 157
Baudelaire, Charles, 217, 219n21
Beautiful Joe, 20, 21
Beauvoir, Simone de, 27
Benjamin, Walter, 177
Benvéniste, Émile, 211
Berton, Pierre, 25
Between Friends, 47, 180, 186–7n21
Birdsell, Sandra, 252
Blanchot, Maurice, 160
The Blind Assassin, 131

Bombeck, Erma, 175–6
Borges, Jorge Luis, 10, 155n24, 160, 170n22
The Bostonians, 188n45
Boston Marriage, 188n45
Bourdieu, Pierre, 241, 250–1
Bradley, Katherine, 188n48
Brand, Dionne, 67, 68
Brandt, Di, 28, 67
Brossard, Nicole, 67, 234
Buckler, Ernest, 232
Burke, Seán, 178
Burnard, Bonnie, 28, 68
Burney, Fanny, 47, 186–7n21
The Bush Garden, 158
Buss, Helen, 28, 240, 243, 245–6, 248–9
Butler, Judith, 117
Butrym, Alexander J., 65, 70

Caillois, Roger, 225
Calisher, Hortense, 18–19
Callaghan, Morley, 24, 25
Calvino, Italo, 224
Canada Council, 25–6
Capitalisme et schizophrénie, 219n17
Carr, Emily, 67

Carson, Anne, 205
Carter, Billy, 242
Carver, Raymond, 100, 103
Cather, Willa, 22
Cavell, Stanley, 80
Celtic Design Maze Patterns, 116
Certeau, Michel de, 5, 9–10, 148, 149
Chadbourne, Richard, 94n6
Cheever, John, 242
"The Children Stay," 205
Cixous, Hélène, 62
Clément, Catherine, 114n9
Cohen, Leonard, 26
Conrad, Joseph, 22
Cooper, Edith, 188n48
Cronan Rose, Ellen, 179
Crozier, Lorna, 60, 67, 68
Curtis, Andrea, 4

Dällenbach, Lucien, 224
Danica, Elly, 67
Danto, Arthur, 5
David Copperfield, 25
Davies, Robertson, 18, 26
"The Death of the Author," 257
De la Roche, Mazo, 243
Deleuze, Gilles, 159, 211, 216, 218n10, 219n13, 219n17
Derrida, Jacques, 257
Desire in Seven Voices, 60, 68
Dickens, Charles, 20, 25, 268
Dickinson, Emily, 21, 103, 256–7
"Discourse in the Novel," 154–5n12
La Disparition, 12–13, 224
"The Dog at His Master's Grave," 21
Drew, Nancy, 90, 91
Droit, Roger-Pol, 5
Durand, Gilbert, 164
Dvořák, Marta, 235n24
Dyer, Richard, 244–5

Eagleton, Terry, 203n1
Eco, Umberto, 164, 169n15, 197, 203n14
Écrits, 219n19, 219n20

Edemariam, Aida, 251–2
Einstein, Carl, 217
Eliot, George, 22, 199
Emerson, Caryl, 5, 174
Emerson, Ralph Waldo, 232
Engel, Marian, 26
Epstein, William, 245
Escher, Maurits C., 165, 198, 200
Essais (Montaigne), 61
Essays (Bacon), 62–3
Evelina: or, A Young Lady's Entrance into the World: in a Series of Letters, 47, 186–7n21
Exercises de style, 224
L'expérience intérieure, 157

"The Faithful Dog," 21
Farm Report, 25
Faulkner, William, 232, 242
Le féminin et le sacré, 112, 114n9
Findley, Timothy, 26, 224
Fitzgerald, F. Scott, 103
Five Stories, 205
Flaubert, Gustave, 102
Flesh and Paper, 187n40
The Forger's Shadow, 203n1
"The Form of the Sword," 155n24
Foucault, Michel, 158–9
Fraser, Kennedy, 28
Frege, Gottlob, 13, 223, 230
French, William, 28
Freud, Sigmund, 127
Friedan, Betty, 27
Frye, Northrop, 24, 158

Gabler, Neal, 240, 243
Gallant, Mavis, 18, 27
Gamble, Sarah, 128
Garbo, Greta, 244
"The Garden," 212
"The Garden of Forking Paths," 10, 160, 170n22
Genette, Gérard, 151, 155n24
"A Ghost Narrative: A Haunting," 234
Giardini, Anne, 44–5, 71, 242
Giltrow, Janet, 173
Girl of the Limberlost, 20

Godard, Barbara, 235n24
Gödel, Escher, Bach: An Eternal Golden Braid, 165
Goertz, Dee, 119
Good, Graham, 60, 61, 65, 75n2
The Great Gatsby, 103
Groom, Nick, 203n1
Grosz, Elizabeth, 179–80
Grove, Frederick Philip, 24
Guattari, Félix, 159, 219n17
Guest, Edward A., 20

Hammill, Faye, 100
The Handmaid's Tale, 112–13, 225
Hanscombe, Gillian, 47, 180, 186–7n21, 187n40
The Happy Gang, 25
Hawthorne, Nathaniel, 105, 113–14n3
A Heap o' Livin', 20
Heidegger, Martin, 3, 6
Helen's Babies, 20
Hemingway, Ernest, 20, 22, 38, 249–50, 251
Hesse, Douglas, 94n4, 94n7
Hoffmann, E.T.A., 216
Hofstadter, Douglas, 165
Holbein, Hans, the Younger, 210
The Honeyman Festival, 26
Honoré, Carl, 238, 247, 248
hooks, bell, 108
Houpt, Simon, 240
Howard, Blanche: *A Celibate Season*, 10–11, 46–8, 172–90, 191; correspondence with Shields, 47–8; and food in *Larry's Party*, 45; *Penelope's Way*, 250
Huckleberry Finn, 25
Hughes, Lesley, 77n26, 239–40, 246–7
Huizinga, Johan, 225
Hutcheon, Linda, 163, 182, 227
Hutcheon, Michael, 182
Huxley, Aldous, 82

In Visible Ink, 169n11
Irigaray, Luce, 62

"Isis in Darkness," 205

Jackson, Jennifer, 77n26
Jakobson, Roman, 226
James, Henry, 188n45
Jane Eyre, 126
Jankélévitch, Vladimir, 165
Joeres, Ruth-Ellen Boetcher, 65, 66
Johnson, Brian, 186n19
Johnson, Pauline, 243
Johnston, Ann Dowsett, 76–7n26, 154n6
Journeys through Bookland, 20
Joyce, James, 124, 232
Juliette (singer), 25

Kamboureli, Smaro, 67
Kaplan, Carey, 179
Karrell, Linda K., 184
Keahey, Deborah, 109
Kesey, Ken, 109
"Kew Gardens," 230
Kirklighter, Cristina, 63, 65
Koestenbaum, Wayne, 173, 179, 180
Kristeva, Julia, 112, 114n9
Kroetsch, Robert, 168, 205

Lacan, Jacques, 209, 216, 218n7, 219n19, 219n20
"The Lady of the Lake," 21
Lady Oracle, 248
Laird, Holly, 181
Landers, Ann, 74
Lanser, Susan, 139, 143
Lau, Evelyn, 68
Laurence, Margaret, 25, 26, 27, 67
Layton, Irving, 26
Leacock, Stephen, 25, 243
Lee, Hermione, 131
Lee, John, 235n2
Lefebvre, Henri: as a philosopher of ordinary life, 5; and the production of space, 9, 116, 120, 122–3, 127–30
Leonardi, Susan J., 179
"Let's murder Clytemnestra according to the principles of Marshall McLuhan," 205
Liberation, 169n19

The Life and Opinions of Tristram Shandy, Gentleman, 121, 140
The Little Mermaid, 107
Lives of the Saints, 252
Loitering with Intent, 29
Lopez, Jennifer, 13, 240
The Love of a Good Woman, 205, 259
Luck and Pluck, 20

McCarthy, John A., 64
McClung, Nellie, 21, 67
McCullough, Kate, 181–2
MacLennan, Hugh, 24
Madame Bovary, 102
Mamet, David, 188n45
Man, Paul de, 117
Mansfield, Katherine, 232
Maracle, Lee, 67
Marin, Louis, 211, 219n11, 219n12
"The Mark on the Wall," 230–1
Marlatt, Daphne, 67, 234
Marret, Sophie, 209, 218n6
Marshall, P. David, 245
Martin, Sandra, 141, 239
Martin, Violet, 188n48
Martin, Wallace, 142
Marvell, Andrew, 212, 219n14
Masten, Jeffrey, 179
Mathews, Harry, 224
May, Charles, 81–2, 94n5
Meehan, Aidan, 116
Mehta, Deepa, 108, 251
Melchior-Bonnet, Sabine, 197, 203n15
Michaels, Anne, 224
Miller, Henry, 27
Millett, Kate, 27
Milton, John, 126, 199
Minazzoli, Agnès, 206, 218n3, 218n4
Mink, Louis, 257
Mistry, Rohinton, 23
Mittman, Elizabeth, 65, 66
"Modern Novels," 230
Moir, Jan, 247, 248
Monaco, James, 242
Monk, Ian, 235n2

Montaigne, Michel de, 61–4, 66, 68–71, 75
Montgomery, Lucy Maud, 20–1, 243
Moodie, Susanna, 24, 26, 52, 57n34, 58n42
Mootoo, Shani, 68
Morson, Gary Saul, 5, 172, 174
Munro, Alice: and celebrity, 244; *The Love of a Good Woman*, 259; and myth in "The Children Stay," 205; *Open Secrets*, 131; as woman writer, 18, 27, 28; on writing, 249
Musgrave, Susan, 68
Musset, Alfred de, 110

Nabakov, Vladimir, 224
Naipaul, V.S., 18
Namjoshi, Suniti, 187n40
Negotiating with the Dead: A Writer on Writing, 67
Nodelman, Perry, 149, 150, 151

The Observing Self, 75n2
Oeuvres complètes (Baudelaire), 219n21
O'Keeffe, Georgia, 112
Ondaatje, Michael, 26, 243–4
One Flew over the Cuckoo's Nest, 109
101 Experiments in the Philosophy of Everyday Life, 5
"One Need Not Be a Chamber," 257
On ne badine pas avec l'amour, 110
The Origin of the Work of Art, 3, 6

Palleau, Françoise, 94n2
Paradise Lost, 126, 199
Penelope's Way, 250
Perec, Georges, 12, 223–6, 232–3, 235n3
Le Petit Prince, 103
Philip, Nourbese, 67
Plato, 215–16, 217, 218, 219n15

Poetics, 210

Pope, Rebecca A., 179

*A Portrait of the Artist as a
Young Man*, 124

Postman, Neil, 243

Potter, Christopher, 39, 49–51

"Preface to Lyrical Ballads,"
80

"Prelude" (Mansfield), 232

"Princess Brambilla," 115

Proulx, E. Annie, 242

Queneau, Raymond, 223, 224

Ragged Dick, 20

Rajan, Balachandra, 176

Ray, Nina M., 249

Reptiles, 169n19

The Republic of Love (film),
108, 251

Les Revenentes, 235n3

Ricci, Nino, 252

Richard, Jean-Pierre, 165

Richardson, Bill, 46–7

Ricoeur, Paul, 82, 232

Riley, James Whitcomb, 20

Roy, Gabrielle, 24

Roy, Wendy, 154n3

Rule, Jane, 67

Rushdie, Salman, 5

Russell, Bertrand, 13, 223,
230

Saint-Exupéry, Antoine de,
103

Sami-Ali, 5, 84, 86

Saunders, Marshall, 20–1

Saussure, Ferdinand de, 152

Schopenhauer, Arthur, 232,
233

Scott, F.R., 184

Scott, Gail, 67

Scott, Sir Walter, 20

The Seasons, 21

Shakespeare, William, 20

Shearer, Karis, 188n45

Shelley, Percy Bysshe, 233

Shields, Carol

– "Biography" (loose note),
54–5

– *The Box Garden*, 52, 191–3,
197

– *A Celibate Season*, 10–11,
46–8, 52, 172–90, 191

– *Dressing Up for the Carnival:*
"Absence," 12, 153, 197,
201, 223–37; "Death of an
Artist," 53; "Edith-Esther,"
38, 39, 41, 55; "Eros," 60,
67–9, 72; "Invention,"
227, 228, 229; "Mirrors,"
12, 131, 196–7, 205–20;
"A Scarf," 225, 260, 262;
"Soup du Jour," 4, 201–2,
231; "Windows," 15n17,
198, 200

– *Dropped Threads: What We
Aren't Told*: and essay form,
60, 67, 69–70, 71; promo-
tion of, 250–1; sales of, 73;
Shields as anthologist, 8

– *A Fairly Conventional
Woman*, 38, 186n6 (see also
Happenstance)

– *Happenstance*: art and craft
in, 126, 201; narration in,
173, 191, 193–4; publica-
tion of, 186n6; table scene
in, 195

– *Jane Austen*, 7, 59, 60, 67,
71–3

– *Larry's Party*: archival documents for, 39, 42–3, 45–6,
48–9; characterization
through geography of the
body in, 9, 139–56; docu-
mentation in, 52; images of
manuscript for, 34, 40, 46;
and masculine perspective,
173; musical version of,
239; personal transforma-
tion in, 203n5;
spatialization of biography
in, 9, 115–35; spatialized
construction of identity in,
10, 157–71; table scene in,
195

– "Narrative Hunger and the
Overflowing Cupboard,"
60, 67, 73–4, 77n31, 126

– *The Orange Fish*, 260–1;
"Collision," 150–1

– *The Republic of Love*: archival documents for, 39–41;

"Bodies of Water," 39–40,
98; film options for, 242;
film version of, 108, 251;
geographies of the body in,
9–10, 139–56; and narra-
tive form, 8–9, 191; rhetoric of romantic love in,
97–114, 218; table scene in,
195

– "Sense of Place" (film
script), 37–8, 56n3

– *Small Ceremonies*: archival
documents for, 39; craft in,
126, 199; documentation
and biography in, 51–2, 53;
double structure of, 191–3;
narrative hunger in, 126;
table scene in, 194–5

– "Speech on Being a Writer,"
37–8, 58n42

– *The Stone Diaries*: archival
documents for, 39, 43, 45,
48, 49–51, 52, 53, 56n18;
autobiography in, 151;
biography in, 116–17; critical reception of, 247; double structure of, 191;
images used in, 50; and
Larry's Party, 126–7; as literary breakthrough, 4, 239,
240, 242; narrative perspective in, 140, 143, 153–4;
personal transformation in,
203n5; publication history
of, 242; spaces in, 200–1;
table scene in, 195

– "The Subjunctive Self," 35

– *Swann*: archival documents
for, 39; biography in, 52–3,
54–5, 116–17, 245; celeb-
rity in, 13, 245, 250; film
options for, 242; image of
manuscript, 54; literary
authority in, 186n19;
women's writing in, 260

– *Thirteen Hands*, 43–5

– "Three Canadian Women,"
57n37, 58n42

– *Unless*: act of writing in,
199–200; archival docu-
ment for, 77n31; cancer in,
76–7n26; metatextuality in,

224–5; table scene in, 195;
theme of goodness in, 112
– *Various Miracles:* context for
writing, 38; "Dolls, Dolls,
Dolls, Dolls," 8, 80–96;
"Hinterland," 195–6; "Mrs.
Turner Cutting the Grass,"
39; ordinary vs. extraordi-
nary in, 80, 81, 119; "Oth-
ers," 183; "Scenes," 197;
"Times of Sickness and
Health," 200; "Various
Miracles," 52, 140, 142,
154n5
– 'The Vortex" (unpublished
novel), 36–7
– "Woe," 39
Shields, Donald Hugh, 50–1
Silas Marner, 22
Slopen, Beverly, 246
Solnit, Rebecca, 10, 148–9,
150
Somerville, Edith, 188n48
Spark, Muriel, 29
Stainsby, Meg, 173
Stanzel, F.K., 150
Sterne, Laurence, 121, 140
Stone, Marjorie, 182
The Stone Angel, 25, 26
The Studhorse Man, 205
The Sun Also Rises, 20

Taskans, Andris, 239
Tefs, Wayne, 109

A Theory of Narrative, 150
"They Say Miracles Are Past,"
154n5
This Is Me … Then, 240
Thompson, Judith, 182
Thomson, James, 21
Todorov, Tzvetan, 94–5n7
Tolstoy, Leo, 174
Tom Sawyer, 21
Tostevin, Lola Lemire, 67
Tristram Shandy, 121, 140
Trozzi, Adriana, 15n9
Trump, Ivana, 242
Turbide, Diane, 242
Try and Trust, 20
Twain, Mark, 21, 25

Ulysses, 111, 120
Updike, John, 242
Urquhart, Jane, 224

Vanderhaeghe, Guy, 26
van Herk, Aritha, 67, 169n11,
234
Vanish'd! 235n2
A Vanishing, 235n2
Vauthier, Simone, 140, 154n5
Verduyn, Christl, 235n24
Vernant, Jean-Pierre, 205–6,
216, 218n1, 219n24
A Void, 235n2

Wachtel, Eleanor, 4
Waddington, Miriam, 67

Wallace, Bronwen, 67
Wallace, Martin, 142
Warner, Inez, 42–3, 56n14
Watson, Sheila, 205
Watson, Wilfred, 205
Webb, Phyllis, 67
Welsh-Vickar, Gillian, 240–1,
242, 246
Werner, Mindy, 40–1
*What We Talk about When We
Talk about Love,* 100, 103
White, Patrick, 18
"Why Do Men Stupefy
Themselves?" 174
Wilderness Tips, 205
Wilson, Sharon, 235n24
Wiseman, Adele, 67
Wittgenstein, Ludwig, 13,
223, 230
Women of Influence, 28
Woolf, Virginia: as essayist,
66; as experimental writer,
12; as modernist writer,
224, 230–1; as woman
writer, 22, 27, 28
Wordsworth, William, 80
World Book Encyclopaedia, 20
Wyatt, Louise, 56n18

York, Lorraine, 173–4, 177,
180, 181, 187n43